American National Parks, Road Trips and Americana: a complete guide for the independent traveller

John Lea

MAPLE
PUBLISHERS

National Parks, Road Trips and Americana

Author: John Lea

Copyright © John Lea (2023)

The right of John Lea to be identified as author of this work has been asserted by the author in accordance with section 77 and 78 of the Copyright, Designs and Patents Act 1988.

Front cover photo: Leaving Death Valley National Park, California, towards Las Vegas, Nevada.

First Published in 2023

ISBN 978-1-915996-16-9 (Paperback)
　　　978-1-915996-17-6 (eBook)

Book cover design and Book layout by:
　　　White Magic Studios
　　　www.whitemagicstudios.co.uk

Published by:
　　　Maple Publishers
　　　Fairbourne Drive, Atterbury,
　　　Milton Keynes,
　　　MK10 9RG, UK
　　　www.maplepublishers.com

A CIP catalogue record for this title is available from the British Library.

All rights reserved. No part of this book may be reproduced or translated by any form or by any means, electronic or mechanical, including photocopying, recording or by any information storage and retrieval system without written permission from the author.

This book is a memoir. It reflects the author's recollections of experiences over time. Some names and characteristics have been changed, some events have been compressed, and some dialogues have been recreated, and the Publisher hereby disclaims any responsibility for them.

For my whippets,

Always living in the moment

Contents

Preface 6

Acknowledgements 8

1   **Introduction: Road Tripping in the USA** 11
    Slices of Americana Pie 29

2   **The Idea of a National Park** 31
    A Slice of Americana Pie – Woody Guthrie 38
    A Slice Of Americana Pie – VW Camper Vans 52
    List of the current American National Parks 55

3   **The Sierra Nevada Mountains of California** 59
    A Slice of Americana Pie – John Muir 70
    A Slice of Americana Pie – Steve McQueen 76

4   **Across the Lone Star State** 81
    A Slice of Americana Pie – Pick-Up Trucks 88
    A Slice of Americana Pie – The Texas White House ... 96

5   **West Coast to East Coast via Yellowstone** 101
    A Slice of Americana Pie – Harley Davidson Motorcycles 114
    A Slice of Americana Pie – The Lincoln Highway 122

6   **Rocky Mountain Way and the Wild West** 125
    A Slice of Americana Pie – On the Road 132
    A Slice of Americana Pie – Burma Shave Signs 138

7   **Up the Country to Acadia and Upstate New York** ... 147
    A Slice of Americana Pie – McDonald's Restaurants ... 154
    A Slice of Americana Pie – Woodstock 166
    Six Things to do in New York City 170

8	The Oregon Coast Highway and the Fire Mountains	173
	A Slice of Americana Pie – Hitchcock Movies	182
	A Slice of Americana Pie – Zen and the Art of Motorcycle Maintenance	194
	Six Things to do in San Francisco	198
9	The Blue Ridge Mountains of Virginia and on Top of Old Smoky	201
	A Slice of Americana Pie – Airstream Trailers	212
	A Slice of Americana Pie – Dolly Parton	218
	Six Things to do in Washington DC	227
10	The American South West and The Grand Canyon	229
	A Slice of Americana Pie – Laurel Canyon	236
	A Slice of Americana Pie – Route 66	246
	Six Things to do in Los Angeles	255
11	The Delta Blues and The Sunshine State	257
	A Slice of Americana Pie – Highway 61	262
	A Slice of Americana Pie – Chuck Berry	268
12	Conclusion: Re-creating in the American Great Outdoors	285
	Afterword	288
	Road Trips Juke Box and Song Credits	291
	References	292
	Index	305
	About The Author	314

Preface

The first American national park I visited was Yosemite, in Northern California, in 1980. Before then I had more knowledge of the cartoon character Yosemite Sam than I did of the park he was named after. I had a similar introduction to Yellowstone National Park, via Yogi Bear's exploits in the cartoon version called Jellystone. I didn't get to visit Yellowstone, in Wyoming, until 2005, after which I started to think more seriously about the whole idea of national parks.

Writing as a Brit who has spent a lot of time in the United States, it's enabled me to catalogue a long list of love-hates about the country. This book is very much about what I love. I particularly love the American national parks. While accepting that many things might compete with the judgement that they are 'America's best idea', the national parks could certainly be considered one of the better ones. I also love being on the road, and the United States is a great country for doing that. And given how hard it is to visit the parks without a car, it seemed natural to connect the two. But I also love memorabilia associated with the American great outdoors, including the nostalgia that many people now have for what is often called 'Americana'. This book offers a critical appreciation of these three aspects of American culture, along with an exhortation to readers to experience the American great outdoors for themselves.

I begin the book by outlining some practical steps for non-Americans to help facilitate a successful American road trip. The book does not assume for one minute that it would be feasible for most people to undertake one glorious road trip around the whole of the USA, perhaps visiting every national park. Rather, it assumes that readers will have – like me – perhaps a couple of weeks available each year in which they might contemplate a road-based adventure. It also assumes that readers will be – like me again – of limited resources and not able to afford 5-star luxury. One of the challenges I set myself for this book was to relay to readers that it is possible to have a great time without breaking the bank, and that the best experiences are often the ones that are free/relatively cheap and/or simple.

The book combines elements of information, entertainment and education, and has a straightforward structure. The introduction provides mainly information, on the feasibility of road tripping in the USA (large parts of which could be skim-read by those who have already made several trips to the USA). Chapter two provides a critical assessment of the central ideas behind the establishment of the national parks, including their history and role in American culture. I also include there an introduction to the notion of Americana and its role as a thread running throughout the book. The rest of the chapters describe some of the road trips I have undertaken, and the national parks (and other places of interest) I visited on each trip. Each chapter includes two examples of road-related Americana and offers a critical appreciation of them. Small vignettes of wider critical cultural comment also appear at relevant points. My hope is that these chapters will inspire readers to plan and undertake their own unique road trips, and to dig deeper into the role and significance of wider aspects of American culture and its great outdoors.

Most of the featured road trips took me around ten days to complete but could easily be extended with more time and money. They are not in the order I undertook them because I thought the narrative structure of the book would be enhanced by an even geographical spread across the chapters, while accepting that there are more national parks in the west than the east.

One of the great joys of being on the road in the United States is the chance to listen to a wide range of local radio stations. A further underlying theme running throughout the book is my celebration of what popular music is able to evoke when on the road. I have supplemented this by references to the places where some of this music was written and/or recorded. In this regard the book can also be read as a musical journey.

I conclude the book by discussing the extent to which time spent in the American great outdoors is able to open up some significant opportunities, not just for recreation, but also for re-creation – of the mind and spirit.

John Lea

Acknowledgements

I would like to thank all the people I have met on my travels, the vast majority of whom have been warm and generous. In lots of places around the world Americans have a reputation for being loud and brash. With the odd exception, this has not been my experience of them on their home soil, particularly in the national parks. I have also learnt a lot from the park rangers and others who work for the National Park Service, and I would like to acknowledge their consistently calm professionalism (which must surely be tested from time to time by some park visitors).

I would like to thank all those who read the earlier drafts of the manuscript and made suggestions, corrected errors and highlighted typos. Naturally, any that are left are entirely my responsibility. Thank you in particular, Maria, Peter and Caroline, whose suggestions were invaluable. I would also like to thank my friend and web designer Tris Arris, who did a wonderful job of turning my Americana Pie and Jukebox sketches into the professional images which feature in the book.

I have included detailed references to all the books, articles, films and songs which are mentioned throughout. I have also tried to ensure that the information in the book is accurate. I keep diaries of my road trips, which include details of the places I have stayed and the roads I have driven. If anyone notices errors or omissions, I would be glad to hear about these for future editions. If any copyright holders notice any errors or require more detailed acknowledgements, I would very happy to include these in later editions.

All the photographs included in the book are my own. They are 'snaps', taken with ordinary cameras and phones.

John Lea

Note about Covid 19

I finished writing the first draft of this book just after the world-wide pandemic took hold. I delayed publication because of it. However, I chose not to revisit the bulk of the text because I was unsure of the pandemic's long-term implications and any future travel restrictions. My expectation was that people would continue to want to visit the United States and take long-haul flights. Naturally though, people's attitudes may have changed or been modified by their experiences of the pandemic. That said, I hope the book's invocation to experience the American great outdoors can still be read in the spirit I originally intended it.

Note about spelling

This book is aimed at the non-American reader, and given that I am English, I have used Oxford dictionary spellings throughout the book, except where it seemed appropriate to use American spellings (for example, in naming locations and buildings). I hope I have been consistent.

Chapter 1

Introduction: Road Tripping in the USA

Arrival and Orientation

Before international travellers can even begin to experience the American great outdoors, they need to get there. Unless you are planning to make a week-long crossing of the Atlantic or Pacific Oceans by boat, or live elsewhere in the Americas, it is inevitable that you will have to take a long-haul flight. I start each of the road trip chapters in this book from a large US city because these are the places where long-haul flights will arrive. Pretty much every large US city is part of an established long-haul route, but on occasion it might be necessary to make a transfer. Where this was necessary for me, I have mentioned it in the relevant chapters. These transfers have been rare but when unavoidable, the major carriers, like Virgin Atlantic or British Airways, will provide a 'thru' ticket' so you will not need to check in again at the transfer airport and the stopover would normally be less than two hours.

I have no loyalty when it comes to booking flights. I just look for the cheapest company around the dates I intend to fly. It's always worth checking a few days either side of a preferred date because there can be a noticeable difference in price, and – naturally – it pays to avoid school holiday dates if you can. With some carriers, you tend to get more thrown in – like free alcoholic drinks – so it's worth checking. For a while, I preferred Virgin Atlantic, because of their comprehensive in-flight media package, which was particularly welcome on the longer flights to the West Coast of the US. On a seven hour flight from London to the East Coast I know I can cope with minimal service. That said, I think that all carriers do now have lots of ways to keep you entertained. If you can afford it, it's worth investing in some good noise-cancelling headphones. Just turning them on can help cancel out the drone of the airplane's engines.

If you ever feel you have been let down in any way by an airline, it's worth letting the company know, because you might receive some vouchers, by way of apology, which can be redeemed against items from their in-flight magazine.

Once in the USA, it is possible to get to some of the parks by public transport (for example, the Grand Canyon can be easily reached on a Greyhound bus, then local bus) but many parks are not located on obvious train or bus routes, and many parks have no realistic means to get around them other than by car. Some of them have free shuttle buses running around the central areas, but not all of them. And don't think for one minute that you might be able to walk around a typical national park. Most are absolutely huge, and although the majority contain some fantastic walking trails, you may still need a car to get to the trail-head in the first place. There isn't really any obvious way around this; yet. For the time being, the only practical way to get around a lot of the United States, even its wilderness, is by car. So, if you don't drive, your best bet is to go with someone who can, or plan very, very, carefully. This book assumes that you will be in a car for a lot of your time in the USA. I, for one, look forward to the day when other modes of transport, and/or more environmentally friendly cars will become cheaper and more widely available, and I discuss this at various points in the book.

On the road

Most of the road trips in this book are in the order of 2,000 miles. This is because that seems manageable within 10-14 days and wouldn't normally require any more than 300 miles of driving on any particular day. If, like me, you live in Britain, the prospect of driving such long distances might seem daunting, given the state of British roads, the road works, and the congestion. But put all of that out of your head. The United States was built for the motor car, and it is possible to drive for hours on perfect roads and only come across a few other cars. You might on occasion even feel that you are in a car advertisement, where the road ahead is always empty. There will also be lots of places to pull over to rest, eat, and use a clean toilet (well, most of the time). Toilets are usually signposted as 'rest rooms'.

Road signs are generally very clear, and usually repeated before you arrive at an exit or crossroads. The roads are mostly wide, with clear lane markings when turning left or right. Major crossroads will always have traffic lights (stop lights), and it's very rare to come across a roundabout (a rotary). You can also, legally, turn right at a solid – not arrowed – red stop light, so long as you stop first to check the road is clear, and not if pedestrians are crossing. If in doubt, I would advise stopping until you hear the car horn behind you telling you, politely, to move off. You should also stop if a school bus has its red lights flashing.

The vast majority of cars in the USA have automatic gearboxes – certainly all hire cars – and power steering, which means your right hand will only be required to find good driving music on the radio, leaving your left foot to tap out the beat.

Road signage on Historic Route 66, Flagstaff, Arizona

Renting a car is a very straightforward business and can be done in advance – at the time of booking a flight. There really isn't much to choose between the various companies and they all have outlets at major airports, which are always clearly signposted from the moment you leave customs. It's worth remembering that if you are travelling by public transport into a town first, it will always work out cheaper to hire the car from that town. There's a premium for hiring a car from an airport, but you have to balance that against the convenience for most travellers.

I always go for the cheapest hire car, which is usually an 'economy' or 'compact' car. Don't be fooled by the word 'compact'; it won't be a

Smart Car or Fiat 500. I usually travel alone, but a compact car would also be fine for two adults. The only thing to be careful about is the level of insurance cover you will be getting. Reasonable legal cover will normally be included in the price, but this is certainly where it pays to read the small print, and to familiarise yourself with terms like Collision Damage Waiver (CDW) – which exempts you from any liability (but will cost extra). Also, personal injury would not normally be covered (so check your own travel insurance cover) and drivers below the age of 25 are normally required to pay extra. Always asked if an additional charge might be waived. I have heard stories of companies charging extra for fictitious damage to vehicles when a car is returned, but this has never happened to me. To be on the safe side, I always take photos of the front and rear of the car before I return the keys.

A fully comprehensive insurance policy can sometimes double the price of car hire, and even if you've paid up front for the car and insurance (when booking your flight, for example) this may not stop the person at the rental desk in the USA bamboozling you about essential extras, which are usually far from essential. These will include paying extra so you can bring the car back empty of fuel; lost key cover, etc., etc. I just say no to everything, but you might want to consider a sat nav and/or toll payment sensor. Personally, I'm happy with a map, and I always ask whether I am actually likely to encounter any toll roads.

There's a lot to be said for booking and paying for everything you need before you leave home. That way you can check everything carefully from the comfort of your armchair, including what level of insurance and extras you really want or need. It also makes it much easier to just say no to the person at the rental desk if he or she starts the hard-sell. Whatever you decide, you will still need to leave your credit card details at the car rental desk and show your driving licence. All European style driving licences are fully recognised in the USA. But it's worth checking that the name on your license corresponds with your name as it appears on your credit card.

At the beginning of a road trip, you should be presented with a local driving map at the car rental desk. Quite often you will also be handed some instructions to enable you to get out of the airport environs. It's a good idea at this point to know the first highway/freeway or town you will be heading for, because the person on the front desk may be able to give you more specific instructions, or just use the sat nav if you've paid for one. You may be handed some car keys because you have been allocated a specific car which will be in a marked bay, usually just a short walk from the desk. More likely, you will be directed to a small fleet of cars all within your class of vehicle, from which you can choose the one you like the look of. In these cases, the keys will normally be in the ignition.

It's a good idea to familiarise yourself with all the main switches before you drive off in a hire car. You don't want to be looking for the headlight switch or the windscreen wipers while you are driving. It's not a bad idea to locate the petrol (gas) cap and how to remove it, so you don't get caught out at your first fill-up. Pretty much every hire car will take the lowest grade petrol. Don't worry if you think you may have chosen the wrong vehicle because there will always be someone at the final exit gate to check everything with you. He or she will also show you how something works if you are unsure. After that, it's time to head on down that road, imagining that you are any number of characters – from Sailor and Lula in the road movie *Wild at Heart* (1990), to Thelma and Louise in their road adventure of the same name (1991).

At the end of a road trip – if you pre-paid for your rental car from home, and you managed to get away scot-free from any hard sell at the car rental front desk, and you remembered to fill up with gas before you returned the car – you should then be presented with a receipt with a big fat zero on it. It's worth checking at the time because you don't want to get home to find a credit card bill with additional car rental charges on it. If you are happy with your receipt you will not need to go back to the front-desk because the person in the rental car parking lot will produce your receipt from a hand-held machine after he or she has checked the car over. I usually check the car myself well in advance of arriving at the drop-off, because it's very easy to leave sunglasses and other personal items in the glove box or around the dashboard, particularly when you've got your flight home on your mind. If you drop off your car at the airport there should be a courtesy bus waiting to take you to your terminal, so don't forget to check it from your flight information. Remember, large airports can have many terminals. If you can't find your terminal information, just tell the bus driver the name of your airline company; most companies will only use one terminal for their international flights.

Petrol is still ridiculously cheap in the US, particularly when compared with Europe, but remember that an American hire car, even a small one, will not do many more than twenty five miles per gallon (and an American gallon is slightly smaller than an imperial one). Don't forget that Americans don't do litres or metres as a rule. All road distance signs on the road will be in miles, and yards. And they always measure temperature in Fahrenheit, not Centigrade or Celsius. The rough and ready conversion is to subtract thirty from the Fahrenheit figure and then divide that number in half. Throughout this book I have used American measurements.

When I undertook the road trips in this book, renting a petrol-powered car was the only realistic option. In the last few years it has become possible to rent an electric car, and most of the big car rental companies now have electric cars for hire. At the time of writing, we are very much in a transitional phase, and you will need to plan more carefully if you want to try an electric road trip. Personally, the fear of running out of petrol in a desolate part of the USA often plays on my mind, and 'range anxiety' is often reported as a major issue for drivers of electric cars. You may also find it frustrating to have to wait to recharge your vehicle. That said, I am looking forward to my first long-distance road trip in an electric car. We are in a fast moving world here, so it's certainly worth weighing up the pros and cons and keeping an eye on developments. By the time this book is published, no doubt, things will have moved on apace, and it may not be long before an electric car will be the natural choice for a long-distance road trip. As it stands, it will be more expensive to hire an electric car, compared with a 'traditional' one, but that should be weighed against the possible savings on re-charging compared with petrol fill-ups.

It's worth remembering that the west coast of the USA is three hours behind the east coast. There are actually six time zones if you include all the territories which make up the country. For the majority of the road trips in this book you will find yourself staying in the same time zone, but on occasion you will cross into another. This will most likely happen when you move in and out of the Mountain Time zone, which covers the area surrounding the Rocky Mountains, to the west of the country. It can be a little frustrating if you forget, particularly if you've made plans to arrive in places at certain times. But, given that the majority of road trips will involve an obvious loop back to where you started, whatever time lost (or gained) will even out in the end.

There was a time when there was a fixed national speed limit of 55mph, brought on by the oil crisis in the early 1970s, but this has been slowly relaxed, and it is not uncommon these days to see speed limits of 70, 75 or even 80, particularly on some of the major interstate freeways. These roads are normally clearly signposted in blue, but can be quite boring to drive on, so I try to mix it up as much as I can, using the freeway when I want to get somewhere quickly. Police Highway Patrol cars are everywhere and often seem to lie in wait to catch speeding motorists. But you are unlikely to be stopped if you are just a few miles over the limit. Most hire cars will have a cruise control function, so you will be able set it to the speed limit on long straight roads (of which there are many).

I have been stopped by the police on a few occasions. When this happens, I think it helps if you make a big thing of being an international traveller and that you are eager to learn. That said, it didn't help me when I was clocked doing 89mph while travelling through the Badlands of South Dakota (see chapter six). I also remember driving through Arizona at 7.00am in the morning, with nobody else on the road except a police car, which overtook me and then proceeded to slow down in front of me. After a few minutes I was then pulled over and cautioned about driving too close to a police car (see chapter ten).

Some roads have tolls (called turnpikes in the east) and these are always clearly signposted and wouldn't normally cost more than a few dollars, but, actually paying the toll can be a problem if there is no attendant in a booth and no opportunity to throw money into an automatic machine. This is because there is an increasing assumption, particularly in areas where there are many toll roads (like the Chicago area), that your car will be fitted with an automatic payment sensor which registers as you pass into the toll zone. As I said above, I always check with the person who hands me the car hire keys whether I am likely to encounter any tolls and what would be the best way to pay for them (including hiring a car with a sensor, if necessary). At the time of writing, the vast majority of roads in this book did not have any tolls.

It probably goes without saying that most of the USA is very hot in the summer months and very cold in the winter months, particularly when compared with most of Europe. In which case, undertaking road trips in the Spring and the Autumn (Fall) is a good idea. But it's worth checking the National Park Services websites for average climatic conditions for individual parks because the USA is huge, and the length of seasons can vary enormously. I made this mistake when visiting Yellowstone in May (see chapter six). I also remember staying in a cabin in Yosemite in April and never having felt so cold. Because of this it's worth paying attention to the fact that day-time temperatures are often no guide to night-time temperatures. I distinctly remember going hiking in the canyons in-land from Los Angeles, thinking that my lightweight sleeping bag (bought from a supermarket the previous day) would be more than adequate for the night. I hadn't fully appreciated that I was actually entering the desert, and after enjoying a fantastic evening laying on my back and looking up at the stars, I woke up just a few hours later absolutely freezing, and staring at my plastic container of water, which had frozen. I also remember running towards the sun the following morning in order to warm up. The moral of this tale is an obvious one: bring a range of clothing, particularly layers, which could be added to or removed, as required.

Sleeping

Most of the places I've ever stayed overnight were just convenient places to pull off the road. It's not unusual to be confronted with a number of motel choices, particularly around major interstate junctions and on the roads leading into large towns, and your budget will dictate what you can afford. I always haggle on the price of a room, even if I know I will only be able to knock a few dollars off. These dollars can mount up over a couple weeks, though. There is always the risk that you will cause offence, but motels are used to this, and being from abroad can help, because you can just apologise and say that you're not from round here. But remember, the price you negotiate will always have sales tax added to it when you check out, which for some motel rooms can be in the order of 10% above your quoted price. The actual tax rate varies from state to state and sometimes town to town. Good news though is that you always pay per room, not per person. The other thing to remember is that it is okay to ask to look at a room first, and even to ask if they could recommend other places nearby which are more in your price bracket. There have been occasions where the person on the desk has made a phone call for me to tell another motel to expect me.

Classic American diner in the Chicago suburbs, Illinois

My general rule with motels and hotels (in effect there is little difference between the two) is to consider them offering me – literally – a bed-room; so long as the room is clean (which it normally is) and the bed is comfortable (which it normally is) then I'm happy. I never expect to spend much time in the room. If there is somewhere to eat close by (which there normally is) and the shower is good (which it normally is) then these are added bonuses. Year-on-year I have got used to paying more for a room, because of creeping inflation, but also because my back prefers a comfier bed these days, so I am willing to pay a little more for this luxury. As a general rule, any breakfast on offer at a cheap motel will be very basic, but some motels (not always the expensive ones) will offer a free cooked breakfast. You might also be lucky and find an old-fashioned diner right next door to your motel, and I always look out for these.

The Motel 6 chain of motels got its name because it charged $6 per night. You obviously won't get that price today (more like $60, at least) but they remain one of the cheapest places to stay, but the rooms are usually very basic. Super 8 got its name for the same reason and was one step up in terms of luxury, although still quite basic, but for around $80 (possibly more) you will get a very comfortable room.

My personal guide for many years was to consider $75-$95 as my going rate. Sometimes I have had to pay more and have been happy to do that if the room, or hotel, or view is special, or there simply aren't many options, or it's late and I'm tired. You will soon get used to the chain of motels that you feel comfortable with, and don't be afraid to stop off at more up-market places, like the Hilton chain – sometimes their price is below $100 and that will include a very nice breakfast the next morning. One thing you can be sure of throughout this book is that any place I stayed in will not have been expensive (between $50-$100 normally). That said. I haven't mentioned the names of the motels or the actual prices in this book, for fear this could be misleading. Motels change ownership and names quite regularly, and prices creep up every year, of course. In the majority of cases I will have stayed at a major chain motel (which I refer to as 'chain-motel' throughout), but sometimes I like to opt for somewhere which looks quirky, just for a change, or because it seems to be offering something unique or attractive – like a wooden cabin by a stream.

There have been occasions where I have managed to secure a room for less than $50, but I've usually regretted it. These rooms are mostly very tired looking to say the least and the objects and furniture in the room look like they would break if you touched them with any pressure. A notable case was a room I took near the Mesa Verde National Park, in Colorado. I took the room because I saw a very nice Italian restaurant further down the street. After returning to my room from the restaurant, feeling pleased that I had eaten well and secured a cheap room ($40), I quickly fell asleep, but I was soon bolt upright on the bed when I heard the local police at work outside my door (see chapter five).

Some national parks have cabins and lodges, and most have camping facilities. I would have liked to have taken more advantage of these opportunities, because I love camping. But there are some obvious problems for the non-American traveller, chief amongst which is the need to bring a tent and everything which goes with that, or to buy it all on arrival. And the cabins are often not as cheap as you might think, and they are often booked up months in advance. Personally, I don't like to be tied to arriving and leaving on particular dates, and for that reason I don't normally book any accommodation in advance. People have asked me what I would do if a motel was fully booked; well, I'd just go down the road to the next one. In my experience motels are rarely fully booked, and they expect people to be dropping by, particularly as the sun sets.

In the parks

Most national parks are not free to enter. Expect to pay between $25-$35 (per car) to enter one of the bigger parks, like Yosemite or Yellowstone. Some of the smaller ones are cheaper. As you might expect, the more remote parks are free to enter. The exception is the Great Smoky Mountains National Park which, although very accessible and very popular, has always been free.

You can check the latest fee for a park on its website. I have included the current fee for each park in the full list of national parks at the end of the next chapter, but they can creep up year-on. Your ticket/ visitor pass will normally last for one week, so you will be able to come and go from the same park throughout that week. A simple paper sticker attached to your car windscreen is the evidence that you have paid. There is normally a formal entrance with a ticket booth on most of the main roads into a park. Where there isn't a booth, you are expected to stop at the nearest visitor centre in the park to obtain your pass. I've never seen a park ranger checking the stickers on cars, but once you are in a park it soon becomes clear that your entrance fee is money well spent. The parks always have excellent visitor centres, and many have well stocked book and gift shops, and some have full-service restaurants. Ecology is taken very seriously, and visitors are under strict instructions not to leave their mark anywhere in the park. The rangers often provide guided tours within the parks, and it is difficult not to be impressed with the way that everything is immaculately presented and preserved.

If you intend to visit three of more parks on one trip it is worth considering a yearly pass. A pass currently costs $80 (2023), and you just need to show it at the entrance booths or visitor centres in order to obtain your car sticker. You can buy a yearly pass at any booth or visitor centre, but it is worth checking whether it will be worth it on any particular road trip. For example, in the year I undertook the Texas road trip (see chapter four) a yearly pass was $60, but Big Bend National Park cost me $25 to enter, Guadalupe Mountains was only $7, and Carlsbad Caverns was only $10, so I didn't bother with a pass. On the same trip I also visited the home of President Lyndon B. Johnson, which is run by the National Park Service, but is free. Of course, you could be clever and make a trip back to the United States one month before your pass is due to expire and visit several parks on the second trip, effectively for free.

When I first had the idea of more systematically visiting the parks, rather than just the occasional visit, I naively assumed that I would be able visit every park in around a ten-year period. I based this on the educated guess that there were probably around 20 parks. It turned out that there was nothing educated about this guess. There are currently 63 full national parks (2022), and hundreds of other locations which are part of the National Parks Service (I will explain the difference in the next chapter). Then I looked at a map which included all the parks and realised that there was no way I would be able to visit every park. Because of that, please don't assume that this book includes trips to every single national park. The road trip chapters in this book follow routes which would enable you to visit the most famous and most accessible parks – 44 in total. Some careful planning would be required to get above this number. And don't forget that several more parks might be designated while you are visiting the existing ones.

If you do want to visit all of the current parks you would need to organise trips to Alaska (where there are 8) and Hawaii (where there are 2), as well as a visit to the US Virgin Islands and American Samoa. Ignoring these 12 parks, only 7 more are not mentioned in this book (see the full list of current national parks at the end of the next chapter). I have visited 30 national parks, which includes most of the famous ones. With some luck and some serious planning, I may be able to visit a few more, but I'm very happy with my running total. Most Americans

I have spoken to in the parks have lower running totals, so you may find that you could be on equal terms with many Americans after only a few road trips.

The next chapter looks at the whole idea of a national park. The more I visited the more I wanted to find out about their history, and who exactly decides that somewhere should be granted the status. It turns out the decisions can be quite complicated, and often political. But one thing is clear, that all of the parks are special places. Yellowstone was the first area to be granted park status in 1872, but you might be surprised to hear that many of the parks were only granted park status relatively recently. For example, Death Valley in California, famous for its intense heat and harsh environment, did not become a national park until 1994, and Joshua Tree National Park, also in California, was not a national park at the time that U2 recorded their album of the same name. These parks feature in chapter ten.

For me, the parks never disappoint and always keep giving. I say this because there have been occasions where I've found myself sitting at home planning a future trip and thinking that the next one will not be as good as the previous one. But this never happens. Every trip is always as good as the previous one; indeed, it is pointless to compare trips because they are always very different. Even on the odd occasion where I have returned to the same national park, I have enjoyed it just as much, if not more, and found new things to do.

People ask me which park is the best or which one is my personal favourite. There really is no answer to either of these questions, because the parks are all very different and special in their own way. There is no doubt that Yellowstone is very special indeed. It is huge, diverse, and quite simply other-worldly, but how do you compare that with riding a bike up Cadillac Mountain at sunrise in Acadia, in Maine; hiking 9,000 feet up Guadalupe Mountain, in Texas, on one day, and the very next day descending 1,000ft ft underground into Carlsbad Caverns, in New Mexico; or just staring at the rock formations in Arches, Utah. I did really like the Smoky Mountains, because it seemed to be somehow very American, or, perhaps better, Americana – where the people and the music in Tennessee all just seemed very special in a Dolly Parton kind of way. But what about that time I first saw the Yosemite Valley, in

California, and its waterfalls...or the time I first saw the magically blue water in Crater Lake, in Oregon...and so it goes on...

Naturally, if you prefer an urban environment and/or shopping or laying around a swimming pool, then you may well take some persuading about the joys of spending time in the American great outdoors. But if that's you I doubt you would have picked up this book. Personally, I do enjoy urban, even industrial, landscapes, and for that reason I have spent a little bit of time in each chapter saying something about the big cities where you are very likely to start or finish a road trip. I am working on the assumption that any trip to the United States will be somewhat special and you will want to make the most of your time. You can always skip the town talk if you only want to experience the American great outdoors each time. On that front there have been many occasions where I've found myself driving around a large city trying to find a parking space or a cheap motel and wishing that I'd just headed straight *outta* town.

A word about the natives

I have been visiting the United States all my adult life. I lived in California for a couple of years, and for a few months in New York. I have criss-crossed the country on many occasions, including driving on the Pacific Coast Highway, Route 66, and Highway 61. I have taught American Studies in a British university, taken British undergraduates to many American cities, and travelled to US colleges, recruiting American students to come and study in Britain. This has given me lots of time to develop my love-hate relationship with the United States. I love the vibrancy of its cities, the scale of its great outdoors, and (with the odd exception) I love its people. But I hate the guns, I hate the fact that it doesn't have a national health service, and I hate the obsession with money making (often, it seems, for its own sake). But I always manage to forget all of that when I'm on the road. I love nothing more than having breakfast in a diner, then listening to talk radio or a country radio station as I drive, and then pulling off the road to look around an automotive junk yard.

On the guns, I have learnt to respect the cultural differences, particularly in places like Texas, where hunting is a way of life, and many people still live with the view that security is a private matter.

'In Texas we don't call 911'; well, I suppose that makes sense if the nearest police station is 100 miles away. In reality, most travellers are unlikely to come across a gun while visiting the USA (unless stopped by the police, of course).

The health care issue is another matter. I remember being bitten by a poisonous spider while in the Everglades National Park in Florida (see chapter eleven). I had no idea why one of my legs had become twice the size of the other one, and I remember being quite angry as I dragged that leg into the local medical centre to be greeted by a receptionist who refused to offer any assistance until I showed her a major credit card. I needed antibiotics, which I bought in the US, and I was told I would need more of the same once back home. My doctor in the UK was shocked by how much I had paid for the medicine in the USA, because the same tablets were a fraction of the cost in the UK. Naturally, there's a whole load of politics here as well as economics, but the practical lesson is obvious: Don't travel to the US without adequate medical insurance. I buy an annual cover which costs me around £75 each year, after which I'm ready to do political battle with anyone who wants an argument with me about 'socialized medicine'.

Never was a truer word spoken when Britain and the United States were said to be two nations divided by one language. Wherever you are in the USA you may need to repeat yourself when asking for something, but you may also be complimented on what a lovely accent you have. I have often been mistaken for being Australian, even though I was born in London, and have an obvious London accent. When you pull off the road you also need to be on guard because a few simple things have 'gotten' lost in translation; for example, a biscuit has become a lump of bread, and chips have become crisps.

Never forget that American coffee on the road will be universally awful. It's probably best described as a warm brown liquid in a plastic cup. Lest you forget, treat those pyrex containers sitting under a coffee machine, or those big flasks from which you have to squirt the coffee, as your prompts to think twice. My advice is to bring a small cafetière over in your suitcase and buy some proper coffee from a supermarket. At least that way you will get one good cup each morning. You can still use the coffee machine in the room just to boil some hot water. Or, when on the road, look out for places like Starbucks and ask the barista to add an extra shot of espresso, or ask them not to fill up the cup with water. If you like tea, it's a good idea to put a box of tea bags in your luggage.

When you are out and about, remember that the collective noun for everything is 'bunch', as in: 'Watch out, there's a bunch of wild birds just around the corner', and it's very common for Americans to describe things as 'pretty', even the most spectacular view, which to my ears doesn't sound quite right. Perhaps it's marginally better though than having something described as 'awesome', when the something they are referring to is actually rather ordinary.

Carving a likeness of Crazy Horse in the Black Hills of South Dakota

Don't forget that the US is a very politically correct society particularly when it comes to naming social groups. There seems be some collective guilt being felt by the American white middle class, who have concluded – or someone else has concluded for them – that some of this guilt can be alleviated through a series of renaming exercises. In my experience so called African-Americans are quite happy being referred to as black. Once again, being a stranger can be very useful because you should be able to politely ask someone how they would like to be referred. And remember, the true natives are the Indians or Native Americans, or First Peoples. All these terms are actually quite problematic. For example, 'Indians' refers back to Christopher Columbus and his mistaken view as to where he had landed, and 'Native American' has little meaning if your people were there before the occupation and naming of the continent by foreign peoples. And it's not as if the indigenous population had not already named itself – as Lakoto, Sioux, Pueblo, etc.

It would be an understatement to say that mainstream American society has a troublesome relationship with its indigenous population. You only have to look at any, so-called, 'Cowboys and Indians' Hollywood films to see that, and their relationship with the national parks is also a chequered one, which is discussed in the following chapter. Even today, the carving of the image of legendary figure Crazy Horse in the Black Hills of South Dakota has been controversial (see chapter five).

Some practical advice

To finish, some very practical advice: Book a flight, book a car, and complete an on-line ESTA form (Electronic System for Travel Authorization), which means you can visit the US for up to 90 days without a visa. Use the official ESTA website, because there are other websites who will charge you for acting as a go-between. You only need to pay the ESTA authorities *their* fee – which is currently $21 (2023) and will last for two years. Once your completed form is submitted you should get a message soon after to say that you are 'good to go'. It can take up to 72 hours to get this message, so don't leave it to the last minute. You don't need to print this off, but you may want to be on the safe side.

Make sure you have a major credit card (it's really difficult to do anything without one), and don't forget your passport and driving licence (if you have one). Tell your credit card company your travel plans in case they suspect fraudulent use of your card and block it. There's nothing worse than trying to fill-up at a gas station only to find that your card has been frozen back home – which has happened to me. Check with your mobile phone company what the deal is when using your phone while in the United States, and make sure you have the phone number of your travel insurance company stored in your phone and/or in your purse or wallet.

When you first arrive at the airport, it's not uncommon for the customs officer to ask you where you will be staying in the United States. I find this a bizarre question, for a country which invites people to get out on the road and explore. In order not to be thrown by this question, before I leave the UK, I write down the address of a motel which is not too far from the US airport where I will be arriving. Normally, I will have no intention of staying there, but it gets me past this trick question and means I can maintain a confident air.

I travel a lot so I keep an international wallet, which will hold my passport, and all the things I will need when travelling abroad, including my driving licence (which I wouldn't normally need in the UK), the details of my ESTA status, and the details of my travel insurance. I also have a credit card which I only use when abroad, one which doesn't charge you every time you use it, but remember this is unlikely to include cash withdrawals from a bank machine (an ATM), so I only do this if I really need to.

Expect, pretty much, to have to pay for every service in the USA, and if it includes contact with people, you will be expected to tip them, and not just for good service, but simply for doing their job. In effect, tourists and travellers are supporting a low wage economy, by topping up American workers' wages. There's no practical way around this, particularly in restaurants. You might even see a couple of Brits being chased down the street by a waiter demanding his or her tip. This is probably an urban myth, but a waiter (or server) will be disgruntled if you don't leave at least 15% of the total bill. I leave 20% if the service was good, and 15% if it wasn't.

When a foreign currency is doing well against the dollar, the US can seem like a relatively cheap place to visit, but don't forget that once sales tax is added (which it always is, even on secondhand goods) and then a tip is added, it's not unusual for a good or a service to have cost a third more than its ticket price. And don't forget that the people who clean your motel room will also expect a tip to be left in your room as you leave. Lest you forget, there's always the daily reminder that your room has been cleaned, when you glance at the toilet roll holder and see that the first sheet of paper has been subject to some simple origami.

Slices of Americana Pie

Throughout the book (two in each chapter) you will find my examples of Americana, with cross-references to them in the main text. Each 'slice' offers a critical appreciation of the role it has played in American culture, and can be consumed as a break within each chapter, or as and when the mood takes. The *concept* of Americana is discussed in the following chapter.

The Contents page indicates which chapters include which slices.

The word 'pie' has a generic meaning in the United States. It applies equally to a range of sweet cakes and gateaux, as well as various savoury food items. On the east coast, some old Italian pizzerias still refer to their pizzas as tomato pies or pizza pies.

Chapter Two

The Idea of a National Park

"Thousands of tired, nerve-shaken, over-civilized people are beginning to find out that going to the mountains is going home; that wildness is a necessity; and that mountain parks and reservations are useful not only as fountains of timber and irrigating rivers, but as fountains of life"

John Muir *Our National Parks* (1901:1)

Half Dome, Yosemite National Park, California

This chapter was composed while singing:

This Land is My Land, as performed by Woody Guthrie (1940) and

Buffalo Soldier, as performed by Bob Marley and The Wailers (1983)

Consuming a national park

When I was planning my first trip to Yosemite, I remember my excitement about the prospect of visiting what a guidebook had described as a 'majestic wilderness', mixed with some trepidation about the prospect of coming across a bear. I also remember those feelings becoming doubly mixed when I found myself booking my camping ticket through the same agency I had bought my Bruce Springsteen concert ticket a few months earlier. Then I looked up the route to the park and I soon realised that I would be on a paved road all the way to my cabin in the woods. At the time, I remember thinking it was going to be a very interesting 'wilderness' experience. The German philosopher Karl Marx described capitalism as 'a vast accumulation of commodities', where a commodity is defined as a contradiction between something which has an intrinsic use (desirable) value, but also an extrinsic exchange (monetary) value (Marx, 1867). Given that the USA is, *par excellence*, a society where it is impossible to avoid being confronted by a huge number of such commodities on a daily basis, I was still surprised to find that places like Yosemite appeared to have submitted to this logic. Any leftover surprise then evaporated completely when I saw the gift shop located right in the heart of the Yosemite Valley.

When I started to read about the history of the national parks, I quickly realised that my mixed feelings were not the products of the late 20th Century but were actually at the heart of the debates about the very idea of national parks over one hundred years earlier. When John Muir, the great champion of the American wilderness [see John Muir Slice of Americana Pie], returned to the Yosemite Valley in 1889 – after a break of nearly fifteen years – he was disappointed to see how much the valley had succumbed to commercial interests during his absence. Not only was this the result of farming cultivation but also because of the various forms of entertainment being supplied for the growing number of visitors, many of whom, no doubt, were visiting because they had come under the spell of Muir's own exaltation to experience such a beautiful and undisturbed place. Muir's case for protecting Yosemite was made easier for him by the increasing disquiet being felt about one of the other spectacular places on the continent, Niagara Falls, which was slowly but steadily being exploited by a vast array of commercial interests and commodification.

Although Yellowstone was the first national park (established in 1872), the Yosemite Valley had been identified as worthy of such a status a decade earlier. After much debate Yosemite became an area which would be managed and protected by the State of California (in 1864), and didn't become a truly *national* park until 1890, after long running political disputes and arguments about its proposed geographical boundaries. In addition, both Yosemite and Yellowstone were also subjected to vociferous debates about what exactly these areas needed protection *from*. For some politicians they clearly needed protection from marauding Indians, whereas for others they were rich in natural resources and therefore needed protection from those who would hold back wealth creation. Even Muir's clear message about the need to conserve places like Yosemite met with opposition from people with different views on conservation. An alternative narrative, often proclaimed by Muir's contemporary, Gifford Pinchot, emphasised, not the need to preserve these areas in some crystallised state, but only to ensure that their eco-systems were sustainable, resulting in a harmonious interaction between Man and Nature. The Native Americans, who had occupied these areas for thousands of years, also seemed to have practiced this version of sustainability; no doubt aware, for example, that excessive hunting of an animal species would threaten their very way of life.

Conservation and its discontents

My knowledge and understanding of the national parks was greatly enhanced by reading *The National Parks: America's Best Idea*, by Dayton Duncan and Ken Burns (2009), and watching the accompanying TV series, which I hugely recommend. Duncan and Burns popularised the notion of the parks as 'America's best idea', but the parks might equally have been described as one of its worst ideas, because the original idea corresponded with the White man's decision to herd the Red man into the restricted spaces of the 'reservations', thereby simultaneously freeing up the resultant wilderness, but also helping to destroy another way of life. As it turned out, the Native American tribes continued to make excursions into the newly formed parks for many years afterwards, perhaps accepting that while the reservations were to be their new homes, the park land could not become someone's property – a direct philosophical challenge to a fundamental principle of a capitalist system.

There are many reasons why we need to place the word 'wilderness' in inverted commas. For example, are we to understand the 'wilderness' as something untouched by humankind, as Nature intended, or, rather, as a manufactured space – literally a 'man-made' environment? For Native Americans there would surely only ever be a merely rhetorical need to refer to a world where there was no interaction between Man and Nature, and, for the *new* Americans, calling a national park a 'wilderness', in reality, meant a calculated attempt to design and manage a contrast between Man as architect and Nature as architect.

The Hetch Hetchy Valley with 'man-made' reservoir, Yosemite National Park, California

Muir was clearly humbled by the notion of Nature as architect, but it does have limited use as a universal metaphor for all the national parks; for example, the Mesa Verde, in Colorado, is essentially a celebration of very real human architects (see chapter six). And what role do free roaming animals play in all this? For example, what are we to make of a '*managed*' return of the wolf into Yellowstone (see chapter five)?

Just as Christopher Columbus could only have 'discovered' America in the sense of making the land open to the possibilities of re-appropriation by its new visitors, the national parks might also be viewed in the same way. Not as an attempt to preserve a space, but as a re-purposing or re-creation of it. As one author put it: "... uninhabited wilderness had to be created before it could be preserved, and this type of landscape became reified in the first national parks." (Spence, 1999: 4).

The notion of recreating also has an important double meaning, because the parks very quickly became spaces of recreation, both in the sense of being places where one could relax and recharge, in retreat from (and in preparation for a reabsorption into) capitalist work practices, but also in a deeper John Muir sense of being places where one might literally re-create *oneself*, and possibly even uncover a truer self – a self that had been forced into retreat by the demands of these work practices. Of course, if that experience becomes transformational one might never return to one's previous life, or perhaps return with a very different outlook on the purpose and meaning of that life – as happened to Muir [see John Muir Slice of Americana Pie].

The people's parks

Another way in which the parks might be viewed as 'America's best idea' flows from them being *national*, that is, under federal or central government control. With such a status it would be much easier to present them as *people's* parks, created in the spirit of the Declaration of Independence – as parks created by, and for, the people. This was certainly the view of President {1901-1909} Theodore Roosevelt, without whose support the first national parks might well not have survived. After a visit to Yellowstone his invocation to see the parks as: 'for the benefit and enjoyment of the people' was subsequently etched into a newly constructed arch at the northern entrance to the park (see chapter five).

Putting something under federal control in the USA is never far from controversy, however, because people on the political Right are often quick to claim that government control of anything will, in the end, produce something less effective than if it had been left in private hands. There is a paradox here, because many of these people will be supporters of the Republican Party, but the original idea of a Republic had, at its core, the need to take *collective* responsibility for anything identified as being particularly edifying for its citizens. And we should not forget that although the parks are protected and preserved by federal legislation, people are still charged a fee to enter the majority of them, and it was often very wealthy benefactors who initially stumped up the money to buy the land on which the early parks sat. Chief amongst these was J.D. Rockefeller Jr., who spent millions of dollars of his family's wealth in helping to establish Grand Teton National Park, in Wyoming; Acadia National Park, in Maine; and the Great Smoky Mountains National Park, in Tennessee and North Carolina. This was in no small measure to prevent commercial interests from running roughshod over the land, and here we see an on-going battle between private wealth holders with opposing interests. In the history of the national parks it is never a simple case of the central government taking control of a nation's assets.

These controversies aside, I love the democratic appeal of the national parks, and I love its practical manifestation when I speak to people in the parks and discover, for example, that the two strangers walking alongside me up the slopes of Mt Rainer, in Washington State, have not only travelled all the way from New Jersey and Illinois respectively, but they also come from very different walks of life. Or, that a geographically scattered extended family have decided to meet up around a campfire in the Great Smoky Mountains of Tennessee. In this regard the parks come close to being what Woody Guthrie meant by the land belonging to everyone – not as private property but as a collective inheritance. But Guthrie was also acutely aware of how fragile this inheritance can be, to which the subversive element in the lyrics of his most famous song testify [see Woody Guthrie Slice of Americana Pie].

All that said, I have also often found myself in a park thinking that everyone around me looks very white and reasonably well-to-do. There seem to be a number of practical, and cultural, reasons for this. For example, the inaccessibility of many parks pretty much dictates that you will need a car, a budget for on-the-road accommodation, and a decent amount of spending money, in order to fully enjoy the experience. This combination may be just a little out of reach for many families. If we then combine those financial constraints with a cultural dynamic which puts the national parks on the radar of some families but not others, we can see that it would be easy to compile a profile of those most likely to visit a national park. This could partly explain why many black families do not, routinely, visit the national parks, but we should also remember that in the era of post-Second World War prosperity the United States still had many so-called 'sundown towns', which effectively banned black Americans from the streets after dark. In these circumstances, long distance travel cannot have been easy and it may well take generations to undo this discriminatory cultural dynamic.

Black Americans in the 'sundown town' era who were determined to travel would certainly have carried a copy of *The Green Book* while on the road – a travel guide which listed where black Americans would be welcome. This also became the title of the film (2018), which depicts the life of the black pianist Don Shirley, mainly through the eyes of his white chauffeur and minder, Tony Lip, as they toured the southern states in 1962.

There is also a much older historical irony here, because we should remember that when the first national parks were being established it was sometimes to the regiments of black soldiers that the authorities turned in order to ensure that the parks were made safe for their new visitors. This fact also helped to cement the view that there is a myth being created about the type of 'wilderness' a visitor could expect to experience – a sanitised one, free of the undesirable, including many animals and Native Americans. 'Buffalo Soldiers' was the nick-name given to the all-black American regiments. The story goes that the name came from the Native American tribes who thought their hair looked like the hair of the buffalo. They might also have been referring to their doggedness, because evidence suggests that the Buffalo Soldiers did a good job in the so-called 'Indian Wars'; helping to sanitise the early parks, so that a particular version of a 'wilderness' experience could be had. Perhaps, even, an artificial one?

The French philosopher Jean Baudrillard once commented that Disneyland had played a perfect post-modern trick on American society, because its artifice stands in contrast to the 'real' world outside of it,

A Slice of Americana Pie

A critical appreciation of: Woody Guthrie (1912-1967)

Woody Guthrie was the bard of the everyday working American. He spoke for the poor and the dispossessed in a time of economic depression. The social critic Studs Terkel, in his foreword to Ed Cray's (2004) exhaustive biography of Guthrie, called him 'a slip of leather': a perfect description for his small-framed figure. The description neatly captures the essence of the whole man; a rambling unpretentious balladeer, who travelled from state to state, writing and singing songs aimed at stirring the spirits of ordinary folk. His music was folk music in every sense – music about folk and for folk, which could be performed at any social gathering. Furthermore, the music belonged *to* the folk; he wasn't interested in owning it, only that it be performed and enjoyed.

Woody Guthrie was born in Oklahoma in the same year that Woodrow Wilson became President and was named after him: Woodrow Wilson Guthrie. Woody's formative years coincided with economic upheaval: The Wall Street Crash of 1929 followed by the Depression and Dust Bowl era of the 1930s, which dislocated thousands of Americans, including himself. His songs reflected what he saw: people on the move in search of better lives, but often confronting ruthless capitalists, only too aware of their power to exploit working people for their own gain.

His father was politically active, including contributing to debates about Socialism and Christianity, and many of Guthrie's later songs would have undercurrents of both in their lyrics. But his first musical influences came mainly from his mother's renditions of traditional folk tunes, and later, when he discovered the music shows on the radio. Through the radio he became obsessed with trying to imitate The Carter Family, the famous country act – which included a young June Carter, who later married country legend Johnny Cash.

His young life was dogged by trials and tribulations. His father was caught up in unsuccessful business adventures, forcing the family to downsize, and his mother was slowly sinking into mental illness, later diagnosed as Huntington's disease. His sister also died in an accident, caused by a fire in the family home. Then, along came the Great Depression, and the Dust Bowl storms – huge dark clouds of dust stretching for miles, caused by soil erosion from intensive farming. It was at this point that he decided to get on the road, leaving his first wife and first child at home.

His education reads like the narrative from an old blues song. He was self-taught in every way. He didn't excel at school, but copiously consumed books and distance learning courses, and mastered a wide range of skills, including sign painting and portrait painting. He also dabbled in fortune telling and faith healing, which he learnt from his father's second wife. His first musical instrument was the harmonica, which he apparently took up after being enamoured by the musicianship of a black shoeshine player outside a barbershop. He then picked up the guitar, then mandolin, and onto every musical instrument he could get his hands on, which, by all accounts, were never in particularly good condition.

He scraped a living from all his skills and played music wherever he was invited, which eventually included a short but regular radio slot in California, on the station KFYD (1937-1940). By this time he had begun writing his own songs, initially imitating the songs he had heard throughout his youth, but slowly introducing his own stories about what he was witnessing. He was also educating himself as he went. Significantly, he realised that he had adopted many of the racist attitudes he grew up around and began correcting this by increasingly singing about the *universal* human dignity to be found in meaningful, non-exploitative, work.

Guthrie's songs were witty, political and subversive. From the multiple contexts he worked in he began instinctively adjusting his lyrics to suit his audiences, whilst maintaining his critical social commentary. This was perfectly exemplified in his most famous song *This Land is Your Land* (1940) which, to this day, American children chant as a celebration of the American ideal, but in its full-length version we see that the song has an important moral imperative: that the land *should* belong to everyone.

There is also a beautiful anti-capitalist sentiment in the song *Pretty Boy Floyd* (1945) with its warning to ordinary folk to be as wary about being robbed by someone wielding a fountain pen as by someone wielding a gun. This was also part of his emerging idea of economic fascism, and the celebration of the outlaw who actively opposes the institutions which keep people oppressed. The final lines of *Pretty Boy Floyd* hammers home the point, where he observes that outlaws don't drive people out of their homes. The sentiment was immortalised in the slogan painted on his guitar: *This machine kills fascists*.

Guthrie spoke the truth because he wrote about what he experienced. A famous example is his song *Do Re Mi* (1940); a not-so-veiled reference to the money which was demanded of economic migrants by corrupt police officers as they tried to cross into California to escape the Dust Bowl in search of work. These migrants were often called Okies, a derogatory label and reference to Oklahoma, where Guthrie was born.

Guthrie's influence stretches far and wide, including on Bob Dylan – who sung in celebration of Guthrie on *Song to Woody* on his first album in 1962. Guthrie also had a big impact on the legendary folk singer Pete Seeger, and rock icon Bruce Springsteen. They performed a duet of the full version of *This Land is Your Land* at the presidential inauguration of Barack Obama in 2008, on the steps of the Lincoln Memorial in Washington DC. Guthrie's son, Arlo, also became a successful musician, singing protest songs in the same vein as his father. In a strange contemporary twist, even Woody Guthrie's Brooklyn apartment has become significant because when he complained to the landlord about why all the tenants were white, that complaint was aimed at the father of President Trump.

Guthrie's life was cut short by the early onset of Huntington's disease – inherited from his mother's side of the family – and he died at the age of 55, in 1967. He lives on because his songs set the mould for the American singer-songwriter and because he composed songs about authentic American experiences in the true folk tradition. Because of all that, he epitomises the idea of Americana but what this really does is disguise how much artifice there actually is in American society at large (Baudrillard, 1983). We might say that Disneyland is actually more real because it doesn't ever claim to be anything other than what it is. By contrast, many cultural experiences in the USA hide their manufactured and highly choreographed nature, which in turn dictate what the parameters of a cultural experience will be. This is very noticeable for me in places like the Cracker Barrel chain of restaurants, which specialise in creating an idealised and mythical old-style Country and Western experience, complete with nostalgic gift items. Personally, I like the experience, but I also recognise the post-modern artifice. It would be far too harsh to claim that a typical national park experience is highly choreographed, but I do sometimes find myself thinking this, particularly when signs keep warning me not to stray from the designated path, and when a path's terminus dutifully tips me out into a gift shop.

National park chronology

Although Yellowstone was the first designated National Park (in 1872) – not just in the United States but also in the world – a significant amount of attention – as already noted – had been given to areas of outstanding natural beauty in California. No doubt spurred on by the writings of John Muir, it was clear that not only was the Yosemite Valley such an area, including its high country, but also several surrounding collections of Giant Sequoia trees, particularly in the area known as the Mariposa Grove. When Yosemite finally became a fully-fledged national park in 1890, two other areas of Giant Sequoias located to the south of Yosemite were also granted separate park status. These became known as Sequoia National Park and General Grant National Park, but the latter was substantially extended and renamed Kings Canyon in 1940.

Discussions also began in the last decade of the 19th century about the need to protect other areas of outstanding natural beauty, which resulted in the establishment of Mount Rainier National Park in the State of Washington, Crater Lake in Northern Oregon, Wind Cave in the Black Hills of Dakota, and the Mesa Verde in Colorado. Crater Lake is the deepest lake in the US, and arguably the clearest, resulting from a volcanic explosion, which literally blew the top off the volcano, and thereby created the space for this pure water to accumulate. And The

Mesa Verde is an extraordinary collection of cliff-hanging dwellings, dating from the 12th Century. The latter also pointed to the need to protect some sites for their *historical* interest as much as for the beauty of their natural landscape.

The concerted efforts to preserve these extraordinary places resulted in eight designated national parks by 1906: Yellowstone (1872), Yosemite (1890), Sequoia and General Grant (1890), Mount Rainier (1899), Crater Lake (1902), Wind Cave (1903) and the Mesa Verde (1906).

It is the President of the day who commissions a park, but only after having received approval from the Congress of the day. But there is often a considerable time lag between a proposal, a vote, and the actual establishment of a park. Where approval could not be secured, the area under consideration might still become a State park – managed by a State's authorities, not the federal government. But there is a long history of State parks eventually becoming national parks (starting with Yosemite).

In 1916 The National Parks Service (NPS) was established; a body who would administer and manage all the national parks. Its first head, Stephen Mather, was a champion of the great outdoors and of the need for Americans to experience the healing qualities offered by what he considered to be a national park *movement*. The decision to create the NPS was important because the early parks remained under constant threat from commercial interests, no matter how many conservation laws were passed. The problem persisted, partly because of the difficulty of monitoring the parks from offices in Washington DC. But Stephen Mather, and his assistant Horace Albright, were definitely the right people for the job, because they had no intention of ensconcing themselves in offices. They conducted many trips to the parks, showing influential people what they had to offer.

The early parks were heavily dependent on pioneering individuals, like John Muir who had battled to promote the very idea of conservation. Others included George Bird Grinnell, who was instrumental in establishing Glacier National Park in northern Montana (1910), and Enos Mills, who was instrumental in establishing Rocky Mountain National Park in northern Colorado (1915). And with the establishment of the NPS at least there might now be the prospect of some wider coordination of these individual efforts. The photographer Ansel Adams (1902-1984), whose collections of vivid black and white images were shot around the national parks, also provided another significant boost to the national park movement, particularly given his conservation credentials. Many of his collections of photographs were taken in the Yosemite Valley and the Sierra Nevada Mountains of California.

Nature's Wild West, Colorado National Monument, Colorado

The NPS also began administering a wide range of other sites, deemed to be of historical interest, such as military forts and ex-presidents' homes. Amongst these sites were the national monuments. National monuments are a presidential prerogative begun with President Theodore (Teddy) Roosevelt, which gave sitting presidents the power to grant this status on a site without the need for wider political approval (under the Antiquities Act of 1906).

These monuments would not be parks as such, but smaller areas deemed to be worthy of special attention and preservation. One of the most famous of these is Monument Valley in Utah, which if it wasn't part of the Navajo Indian Nation Reservation might well have become a national park. Similarly, in different circumstances, the Colorado National Monument might well have been designated national park status.

The Grand Canyon was originally a national monument, which severely tested the idea that these should be small areas. This became a redundant issue when the Grand Canyon became a fully-fledged national park in 1919, but its original status certainly seems to have established a precedent for a wide range of places becoming national monuments. State parks, national monuments, memorials, and other protected places continue to this day to be re-designated as national parks, including the last four parks to be established – Gateway Arch in St Louis, Missouri (2018); Indiana Dunes National Park, Indiana (2019); White Sands National Park, New Mexico (2020), and New River Gorge National Park and Reserve, West Virginia (2020).

California currently has the most national parks (nine) one more than Alaska. Utah has five national parks, which is significant given its much smaller geographical area when compared with both California and Alaska. The next in line is Colorado with four. Colorado and Utah border each other, which means that nine parks are actually in close proximity to each other in this part of the country. Seven of the Alaskan national parks were established in 1980, although lobbying had been on-going for many years before. The legislation was finally passed by President {1977-1981} Jimmy Carter's administration, and was in no small measure due to the tireless efforts of the environmentalist Margaret Murie. California, Colorado, and Utah have steadily increased their number of parks throughout the 20th Century and now beyond. The net result of these developments is that it is feasible, although perhaps not advisable, to visit nearly half of the national parks in just three extended trips: to California, Colorado/Utah and Alaska.

A trip to Alaska should not be viewed like any other road trip in the contiguous United States. For a start, you are not going to find the usual spread of motels, and you would be very unwise to venture out into the Alaskan wilderness without a full range of hiking and camping equipment and prior experience of hiking in remote places. Battles over the Alaskan wilderness continued throughout the 20th Century, the net result of which means that the State's national parks probably come closest to what many environmentalists and conservationists would consider to be truly 'as nature intended'. They might also be the places where we could legitimately drop the inverted commas around the word wilderness.

Before you contemplate doing anything in Alaska it wouldn't be a bad idea to start by reading *Into the Wild* (Krakauer, 1996) and/or watch the film of the same name (2007). Both the book and the film chart the journey of Christopher McCandless who eventually set up a makeshift camp in an abandoned bus, close to Denali National Park. Denali National Park and Preserve (to give it its full title) was one of the first national parks, established in 1917. Previously known as Mount McKinley National Park, it received its new name in 1980 at the same time that all the other Alaskan parks were established. It also had its acreage increased to cover over 6 million acres – nearly three times larger than Yellowstone, but still over half the size of the newly formed Wrangell-St. Elias National Park & Preserve, also in Alaska.

The rate of establishment of national parks has not slowed. There have now been as many established after 1950 as before. Indeed, the last four national parks (mentioned above), have been added to the list since I started writing this book. You might be tempted to conclude from this that some of the newer parks clearly cannot be as outstanding as the earlier ones, but I'm not sure I would want to make this argument very forcibly. Given that many of the newer parks have simply been re-designated from State parks and national monuments, it could be argued that, had different political circumstances ensued, many would probably have become national parks much earlier. A stronger case might be made by arguing that many of the early parks had more to prove, that is, they were established in a period when it wasn't clear what a national park actually was, and when notions of conservation were much more in dispute.

When Gateway Arch in St Louis, Missouri became a national park in 2018, it was the first urban-based park, which may be the start of a new turn in park designation. Cities like Washington DC, San Francisco, and New York City (which feature throughout the book) have many existing protected spaces and structures, any number of which could become urban-based national parks in the future. Formerly known as Jefferson National Expansion Memorial, Gateway Arch National Park features the famous steel arch, which symbolises the gateway to the west. And although the park may not be part of the American great outdoors, it certainly points towards it. Somewhat paradoxically, I cannot remember being more claustrophobic than when I went on the tiny tram that takes you to the viewing deck at the top of that arch.

A full list of the National Parks can be found at the end of this chapter.

Nation building

There are many symbolic reasons why the national parks are important. Arguably, they play an important role in nation building. Essentially, they are things a nation can be proud of: Greece has the Acropolis; Rome has the colosseum; England has Stonehenge; but the United States has the Grand Canyon. As we have already seen, they also play a role in reminding everyone of the dangers of unfettered capitalism and commercial exploitation – highlighting the need for balance and a more profound understanding of value. For some they might even be used as a proof for the existence of God – for how could there not be a deistic architect behind all this beauty? For all these reasons the parks occupy a very special symbolic place in American society, perhaps even for those who've never visited one.

National parks are not unique to the United States; for example, there are around forty in Canada, and fifteen in the UK, all of them recognised as places of outstanding natural beauty and in need of some protection from commercial interests. This consideration seems to carry more weight in the US, because the country has always had a very aggressive attitude to the exploitation of natural resources. Deep frustration from some entrepreneurs alongside deep appreciation from many conservationists seems to be a contradiction at the heart of American nation building, particularly in relation to its national parks.

Although I have mixed feelings about how and why the first American parks were established, I soon forget all of that when I start hiking or cycling in one of them. It is at this point that my thoughts start becoming bigger and deeper, as if to reflect the scale and grandeur of my new surroundings. The parks might not be able to help you discover the meaning of life, but I'm sure they will provide some serious food for thought. In this regard the parks also seem to offer some significant character-building opportunities.

Consuming Americana

I really enjoy travelling to and from the parks, and I've always considered the road trip as very much part of the experience. Many Americans may take the journey for granted, but I really like the way that the wide vistas of the landscapes, and the sense of freedom which comes from driving on unclogged roads, are able to invoke in me a calm reflective disposition. I hope this book is able to convey some of these feelings and is read not just as an invitation to visit some astonishing places, but also to enjoy being 'on the road'. To my mind, this aspect is likely to be enjoyed much more if you share an interest in all aspects of Americana.

What is 'Americana'? For me it has always meant a nostalgic attraction to those objects and activities which are associated with everyday American culture – such as drive-in movie theatres, old pick-up trucks, and those portable aluminium cooler boxes advertising Pepsi or Coca-Cola. I chose those particular examples because they specifically relate to road travel, but then so much of what has come to be associated with American cultural life is road related. Having spent a lot of time on the road in the USA, I almost naturally fell under the Americana spell, and now routinely stop off and look for artefacts which strike me as uniquely American – as opposed to European. I also love taking photographs of scenes which strike me as quintessentially American, such as the petrol filling station at the crossroads in the middle of nowhere; a downtown area which has horse hitching rails; or a landscape in which a John Wayne character or someone resembling Crazy Horse might appear at any moment.

As mentioned in the introduction, you will find my own examples of Americana scattered throughout this book, including discussions of why I included them. I wouldn't consider them to be the essence of Americana, and they only relate to the themes of the book, but I hope, nonetheless, that they will resonate, and I hope you will agree that sharing an interest in Americana is likely to enhance any long-distance road trip in the United States.

There is, though, a deeper dimension to Americana, referring to the pride in uniquely American achievements, and to periods in American history deemed to have been great times to live. The period around the start of the 20th century appears to top that list. This nostalgia is a moving target, and the mid-twentieth century is now also often considered by many Americans to have been a better period to live in than the present day. Of course, nostalgia always comes with a free pair of rose-tinted spectacles, enabling the wearer to focus on a largely manufactured ideal, while pushing any undesirable elements out of view. Reflecting on my own collection of Americana artefacts I would date my nostalgic love for the American past in the period from 1955 to 1975.

Pure on the road Americana, New England

I'm what Americans would call a 'real sucker' when it comes to collecting items of Americana. I love car license plates, particularly the old ones (which are becoming expensive these days); anything advertising anything from the past; and any small serviceable electrical items, like toasters. Many of these things can be found at flea markets – which are often just off main highways – or in any number of roadside places that have a collection of rusting items outside their front door. I did once have to get straight back in the car when I realised, after stopping, that the rusty items I spotted from the road were actually the occupants' garden (yard) furniture.

The national park visitor centres often have replicas of old posters for sale, along with baseball caps, and old-style sew-on patches for jackets and hoodies. I love being confronted by this vast accumulation of commodities and see it as part of the road trip and park experience. On the subject of posters, I was surprised to find out that many of the old poster designs are actually no such thing, but are new designs made to look like many of the original posters which advertised the first parks. Perhaps this is further evidence of a desire to manufacture a form of nostalgia, speaking to a better or simpler past. Regardless, I still love them and buy them. Many of them are contained in the wonderful collection published by the company which designs and prints them. The collection was published to commemorate 100 years of the National Park Service in 2016 (Anderson and Anderson, 2016).

Road tripping and its discontents

Is there anywhere else in the world where cars, and associated modes of transport, are so key to the way that many aspects of a nation's culture are experienced? Like those occasions when I have asked someone on the motel desk to direct me to a local restaurant, to be told that there's one just around the corner. Then, when I then ask how long it would take to walk, the reply indicates that only some kind of fool would attempt such a venture. Indeed, I have often felt very foolish after only a few minutes into a walk, when I find that there isn't even a pavement (sidewalk) beyond the motel confines.

So ubiquitous is driving in everyday life in the US that drive-in movie theatres soon became drive-in banks and drive-in fast food and coffee shops. After a couple of months of living in California I distinctly remember dreaming that I was driving up the aisles in the local supermarket and asking my friends to wind down the windows to pick the food off the shelves. For all these reasons, even if you are not actually a driver, you will probably experience a lot of American culture through aspects of road-based culture, and, as I have already said, it would be very difficult to experience many of the national parks without a car.

The cultivation of the notion of 'wilderness' and its subsequent protection and invocation to experience it, corresponded almost directly with the development of the internal combustion engine and the laying of paved highways. Because of this, it was perhaps inevitable that the American great outdoors would become almost synonymous with being – literally – on the road. Indeed, it wasn't long before the internal combustion engine became firmly associated with wider notions of freedom and the pioneering spirit; which was already deeply embedded in the American psyche. Hardly surprising therefore that the appeal of the pick-up truck to Americans appears to have a root in this pioneering spirit [see the Pick-Up Trucks Slice of Americana Pie]; that trailers like the iconic Airstream often appeal to a rootless wanderlust [see Airstream Trailers Slice of Americana Pie]; that the Harley Davidson motorbike became associated with anti-authority feelings of freedom [see Harley Davidson Motorcycles Slice of Americana Pie]; and that the VW camper vans in the USA became a symbol of anti-establishment sentiment in the 1960s [see VW Camper Vans Slice of Americana Pie].

There is a strong case, though, for taking a more serious green/environmental stand on the unsustainable and wasteful use of natural resources in order to keep the internal combustion engine on the road. That said, I would advise not being too principled about this when you are actually on the road yourself because it is likely to make any visit to a remote part of the US extremely tortuous and frustrating. One can only wonder what John Muir might have made of the fact that all the parks have paved highways running through and around them, and that internal combustion engines have been constantly stop-started over the years as people pull over to admire the views. Again, best to keep these musings confined to your armchair rather than your driving seat for fear of totally ruining your 'wilderness' experience. If you are not careful, you will find yourself wracked with guilt every evening, particularly when you should be enjoying your camp fire; the wood for which you will have to hope has come from a sustainable source. You will also have to hope that at least some of the entrance fee you've paid to get into a park really does go on serious conservation work. I'm pretty sure it does, and it would be very harsh to blame park rangers for some of these wider aspects of American culture over which they will have little control.

If, like me, you carry guilt about taking long-haul flights and hiring gas guzzling cars, it's worth spending some time calculating your own yearly carbon footprint and then asking how it could be reduced and/or how your carbon emitting travel could be offset. There are schemes you can join, which usually involve you giving some money to green causes, but you could just choose your own green cause and either directly give money to it or contribute by actually getting involved. You could also spend as much time as possible between flights on your bike, train, or green bus. The policy I have stuck to (pretty well) for the last 20 years is only to use my car at weekends and then only for journeys which are more than ten miles, making sure I at least double up on places I need to get to. During the week, while moving between work locations, I only ever use a combination of bike and train. Virtue-signalling? In my case, I very much hope not.

If you are concerned about maintaining your green credentials while in the US, but still feel the need for a car, you could always ensure you hire the most economical car for your road trip and always ask the car rental companies about their green policies, including their electric car plans. While on the road you could also ensure that you don't use the hire car to make those small trips you could easily undertake by foot, and always look to hire a bike whenever you get the chance. I have hired a bike in many national parks, most enjoyably in the Grand Canyon, the Great Smoky Mountains, and Acadia. If you have limited personal mobility you will pleased to hear that many parks are investing in accessibility, but you could also ask about their future plans.

All that said, it is easy to see how the automobile became so central to modern American life. One could argue that it is actually pivotal, and not just to the American economy but also to American culture and the American psyche. So much so, that getting a driving licence is like having a birth certificate, and a driving licence also acts as an important form of personal ID throughout the US. I wonder what a police officer would say to someone if they chose not to have one?

Of course, there is no need to dismantle the whole road infrastructure to bring about positive change. Cars don't have to be powered by internal combustion engines, and certainly not petroleum-based gas-guzzling ones. Although the road network is largely there to facilitate cars and trucks, there is no reason why more environmentally friendly buses could not use that existing network. Several new bus companies have sprung up in the last ten years, and we might therefore look forward to some of those buses not just ferrying people around national parks but also getting them there as well. As it stands it can be quite tortuous getting to many national parks by bus. We also shouldn't forget that when some of the first national parks were being established – before the road network existed – it was to trains that people looked in order to visit them. There is surely no reason why some of those lines could not be reinstated, or at least made more affordable. I've often been dismayed by the cost of many train tickets in the US, which probably explains – partly at least – why so many people still use their car, even when they live close to a train station.

It should also be noted that the automobile perhaps did not always win the transport game by fair means. Yes, the personal freedom it afforded individuals and families was important, as was the advertising that went with that. But some accounts paint a more conspiratorial picture. I remember when I lived in southern California being more than a little surprised – particularly given the smog alerts – that cities like Los Angeles didn't have a thriving public transport network. The grid system of roads alone surely lent itself to this. But the more I asked about this, the more I found people pointing the guilty finger at large corporations who had vested interests in keeping people in cars. Some of these companies actually did have a stake in public transport, but – and so the conspiracy goes – perhaps they did this in order to ensure that it didn't thrive? There were court cases, and these cases have been analysed by academics and commentators, making for a complicated story (e.g. Goddard, 1996; Post, 2006). The controversy also featured in the mystery novel *Who Censored Roger Rabbit?* (Wolf, 1981) and the film spin-off *Who Framed Roger Rabbit?* (1988).

What's the solution? Perhaps more government legislation or more federal funds for public transport? But that doesn't sound like the American way of doing things. We may just have to wait for American capitalism to find ways to make green thinking more profitable.

A Slice of Americana Pie

A critical appreciation of: VW Camper Vans

A small German built bus originally designed to transport light goods might sound like an unlikely choice for a slice of Americana, but like no other vehicle it has come to symbolise that sense of freedom which comes from being on the road throughout the United States. Popular all round the world, Americans became affectionately attached to the VW camper van in the 1960s, particularly in hippy counter-culture, where it also became associated with anti-war feelings of peace and love.

The little bus is ubiquitous throughout American popular culture; it can be seen behind Bob Dylan on the cover of his album *The Freewheelin' Bob Dylan*, as he walks towards his apartment in Greenwich Village, New York; it can be seen at the hippy commune in the film *Easy Rider* (1969), as Dennis Hopper and Peter Fonda ride east from California; and it was surely an obvious choice of vehicle for the family in the poignant comedy film *Little Miss Sunshine* (2006), as they rush across the southern states of the US towards California.

The story of the VW camper van is a fascinating one, including in its cast an Austrian dictator, a Czechoslovakian engineer, a British Army captain, and a Dutch businessman. The dictator was Adolph Hitler, who in the 1930s harboured the desire to produce a car for the people – literally a volk's wagen – which workers would be able to purchase through a government savings scheme. The engineer was Ferdinand Porsche, who designed the rear-mounted, totally air-cooled, engine, which remained pretty much untouched in all VWs (and Porsches) until the 1980s. The army captain was Major Ivan Hirst who was given the job of dismantling the VW car plant in Wolfsburg, Germany, as part of the post second world war reparations programme, but decided instead that it could become a going concern. The Dutch businessman was Ben Pon, who famously sketched the design for the little bus in his note book. Until that point the only mass-produced VW was a car, affectionately now known as the Beetle or Bug. In the newly relaunched factory the Beetle was simply known as the Type 1, and the little bus as the Type 2. The VW factory referred to the bus as the Type 2 right up to 1979, when it launched a redesigned version, the Type 25 (VW had already named another model the Type 3 by that point).

The little bus has been modified constantly throughout its lifetime, but its basic design has remained pretty much intact. August 1967 saw the first major design changes, when the original split windscreen and large V shape on the front were replaced by a large single bay windscreen and a more uncluttered body shape. The double side doors were also phased out and replaced by a single sliding door. The new bus was also slightly larger and benefitted from uprated engine and brake modifications. Although the new bus was still called a Type 2 by the VW factory, owners affectionately referred to the early version as a 'splitty' and the later version as a 'bay window', or sometimes as a 'bread loaf' because of its overall shape. In 1979 that Type 25 was launched, with a boxier shape, which became affectionately known as a 'wedge'. The early versions of this new design retained an air-cooled engine, but these were phased out in 1982, when all engines became water cooled. Here was the end of an era, but VW have continued to produce a bus – in type 4, 5, 6, and now, 7, versions.

Right from its early days as a goods transporter, VW had recognised its potential as a people carrier and had designed a version with rear seats instead of a flat-bed for goods. But others had also seen its potential as a camping vehicle. The very early camping conversions were just a camping box – literally a box – which could be installed at the weekend and removed again at the beginning of the working week. This is one of the reasons that the vehicle is still often referred to as a bus, because this is what the factory actually produced. Increasingly, more substantial conversions were undertaken by a growing number of companies, some of them authorised by VW, but there were also numerous other small converters, and some conversions were custom made by enthusiastic owners. For this reason it is possible to find a dozen buses all manufactured at the same time by the factory, but each with its own unique interior. Surprisingly, the VW company itself did not actually produce its own camping conversion until the 1990s.

VW camper vans are now part of road folklore, and even those who have never owned one can still buy into what they invoke. 'Buy in' could be taken literally here because there is a huge industry associated with the VW camper van – including tee-shirts, mugs and posters. The VW company is highly protective of its VW logo and the vast majority of this merchandise is not authorised by the company, so it is not uncommon to see the official VW logo replaced by the, so called, 'ban the bomb' peace logo on a lot of this merchandise. The logos are similar, and because the VW camper van has become synonymous with the peace movement, this substitution of logos is easily missed.

I own a 1967 VW Splitty, imported into the UK from California in 2005. It was originally registered in Torrance, Los Angeles, in November 1966. Like many similar vans it began life as a seven-seater bus, but it has undergone many transformations and modifications since then, including the addition of a very rare elevated roof. These roofs were manufactured by a small conversion company based in the San Fernando Valley in Los Angeles County. One of the fun things about owning such an iconic vehicle is trying to find out as much as possible about its history. I also like thinking about what would have been playing on its first dashboard fitted radio – particularly in the summer of 1967 – including, most likely, *California Dreamin'* by The Mamas and Papas (1965), and *San Francisco (wear some flowers in your hair)*, by Scott Mackenzie (1967).

Peace and love, man!

Road trip itineraries

The following chapters describe road trips I have taken in and around many of the national parks in the US, in the hope they might inspire you to follow the same or similar routes. In all cases I have driven the exact routes, but on occasion I have added some achievable detours to reach parks which were not on my itinerary. The detours would certainly be achievable if more days were added to a road trip, but I have not tried to shoehorn in some of the more remote and isolated parks.

The road trips include information on some of the major cities which are either on the main route or within easy reach of a route. Each chapter also includes some guidance on what to expect while on the road, some things not to miss, national park highlights, information about other notable sights, and some cultural and historical commentary. Detailed park information is not included because this information is readily available from the relevant National Park Service web pages for each and every park, and it seemed pointless to reproduce that information. While in the parks themselves you may find that you don't have good internet access, but once you've paid your entrance fee you will always be provided with a very well-presented brochure, which will give you all the information you will need to orientate you around the park in question, including maps and trail information. I treat these brochures as souvenirs of a park visit, and I religiously collect them.

To finish, I have heard it said that record companies will often test out a song by listening to it in a car, knowing that this is how many Americans will access music. At the end of the book you will find a jukebox list of songs that came into my mind when I was either driving the routes or writing the chapters in this book. My guess is that most of the songs could only have been written by American performers, and many reflect exuberant feelings about being on the road. A full list of all the songs mentioned throughout the book are contained in the references at the end of the book.

The American National Parks

Park Name	State	Established	Road trip*	Vehicle fee**
Channel Islands	California	1980	Mentioned chapter 3	Free (not boats across)
Death Valley	California	1994	Featured chapter 10	$30
Joshua Tree	California	1994	Featured chapter 10	$30
Kings Canyon	California	1940	Featured chapter 3	$35 (with Sequoia)
Lassen Volcanic	California	1916	Mentioned chapter 8	$30
Pinnacles	California	2013	Featured chapter 3	$30
Redwood	California	1968	Featured chapter 8	Free
Sequoia	California	1890	Featured chapter 3	$35 (with Kings Canyon)
Yosemite	California	1890	Featured chapter 3	$35
Denali	Alaska	1917	Not included	$15 (per person)
Gates of the Arctic	Alaska	1980	Not included	Free
Glacier Bay	Alaska	1980	Not included	Free
Katmai	Alaska	1980	Not included	Free
Kenai Fjords	Alaska	1980	Not included	Free
Kobuk Valley	Alaska	1980	Not included	Free
Lake Clark	Alaska	1980	Not included	Free
Wrangell-St. Elias	Alaska	1980	Not included	Free
Arches	Utah	1971	Featured chapter 5	$30
Bryce Canyon	Utah	1928	Featured chapter 10	$35
Canyonlands	Utah	1964	Featured chapter 5	$30
Capitol Reef	Utah	1971	Featured chapter 10	$20
Zion	Utah	1919	Featured chapter 10	$35
Black Canyon of the Gunnison	Colorado	1999	Featured chapter 5	$30
Great Sand Dunes	Colorado	2004	Mentioned chapter 5	$25
Mesa Verde	Colorado	1906	Featured chapter 5	$30
Rocky Mountain	Colorado	1915	Featured chapter 5	$35
Grand Canyon	Arizona	1928	Featured chapter 10	$35
Petrified Forest	Arizona	1962	Mentioned chapter 10	$25
Saguaro	Arizona	1994	Not included	$25
Biscayne	Florida	1980	Mentioned chapter 11	Free

Park Name	State	Established	Road trip*	Vehicle fee**
Dry Tortugas	Florida	1992	Mentioned chapter 11	$15 (per person)
Everglades	Florida	1934	Featured chapter 11	$30
Mount Rainier	Washington	1899	Featured chapter 8	$30
North Cascades	Washington	1968	Mentioned chapter 8	Free
Olympic	Washington	1938	Mentioned chapter 8	$30
Haleakalā	Hawaii	1916	Not included	$30
Hawai'i Volcanoes	Hawaii	1916	Not included	$30
Big Bend	Texas	1944	Featured chapter 4	$30
Guadalupe Mountains	Texas	1966	Featured chapter 4	$10 (per person)
Grand Teton	Wyoming	1929	Mentioned chapter 6	$35
Yellowstone	Wyoming	1872	Featured chapter 6	$35
Badlands	South Dakota	1978	Featured chapter 6	$30
Wind Cave	South Dakota	1903	Mentioned chapter 6	Free ($12 cave tour)
Carlsbad Caverns	New Mexico	1930	Featured chapter 4	$15 (per person)
White Sands	New Mexico	2019	Mentioned chapter 4	$25
Congaree	South Carolina	2003	Not included	Free
Acadia	Maine	1919	Featured chapter 7	$30
American Samoa	American Samoa	1988	Not included	Free
Glacier	Montana	1910	Mentioned chapter 6	$35
Crater Lake	Oregon	1902	Featured chapter 8	$30
Indiana Dunes	Indiana	2019	Not included	$25
Cuyahoga Valley	Ohio	2000	Not included	Free
Gateway Arch	Missouri	2018	Mentioned chapter 6	$3 (per person)
Great Basin	Nevada	1986	Mentioned chapter 10	Free
Great Smoky Mountains	Tennessee-North Carolina	1934	Featured chapter 9	Free
Hot Springs	Arkansas	1921	Mentioned chapter 11	Free
Isle Royale	Michigan	1940	Not included	$7 (per person)
Mammoth Cave	Kentucky	1941	Mentioned chapter 9	Free
Shenandoah	Virginia	1935	Featured chapter 9	$30
Theodore Roosevelt	North Dakota	1978	Not included	$30
Virgin Islands	Virgin Islands	1956	Not included	Free

Park Name	State	Established	Road trip*	Vehicle fee**
Voyageurs	Minnesota	1971	Not included	Free
New River Gorge	West Virginia	2020	Mentioned chapter 9	Free

* 'Featured' means I visited the park in the relevant road trip chapter. 'Mentioned' means I didn't visit the park, but it could be added to the road trip. 'Not included' means I considered the park too difficult to access from any of the road trip chapter itineraries.

** Fees creep up year on. The vehicle fee usually lasts for one week. Individuals without cars normally pay around half the vehicle fee. Motorbikes pay slightly less than the car fee.

Chapter 3

The Sierra Nevada Mountains of California

National Parks: Sequoia, Kings Canyon, Yosemite, Pinnacles, Channel Islands

Other notable sites: Highway 1 (The Pacific Coast Highway)

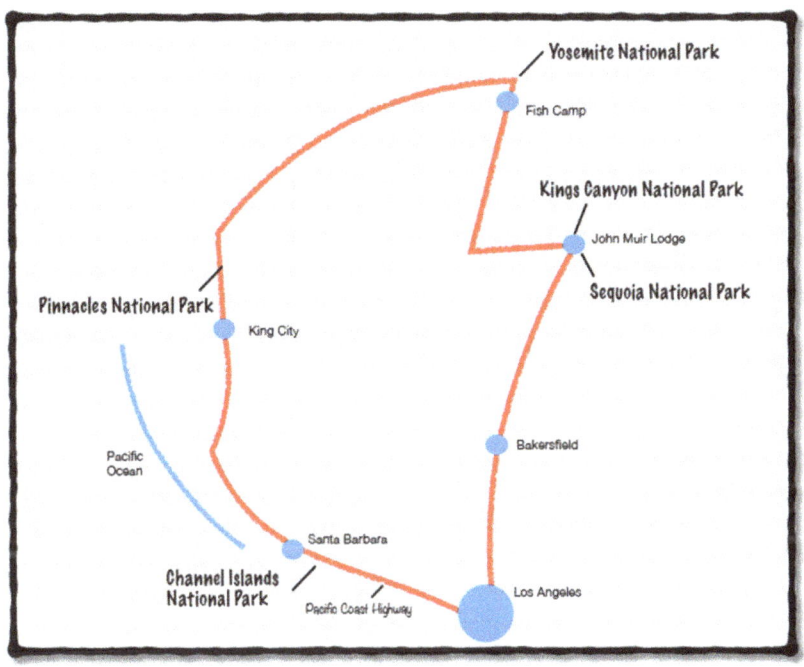

This chapter was composed while singing:

Promised Land, as performed by Johnnie Allan (1983), and

Ventura Highway, as performed by America (1972)

Introduction

I undertook this road trip in May 2017. The idea was to complete a loop around central California, by heading inland into the Sierra Nevada Mountains and then returning via the coast. My route would incorporate Kings Canyon, Sequoia, Yosemite, Pinnacles, and the Channel Islands national parks, as well as sections of the Pacific Coast Highway. It took ten days to complete.

Arrival in Los Angeles

For this trip you might consider flying into San Francisco and starting from there, but I chose Los Angeles (LA) as my starting point. If you want to spend some time in LA either at the beginning or the end of the trip it is worth doing some motel and road planning ahead of time. Cheap places to stay in LA are not readily available and driving can be slow and sometimes nightmarish, particularly when the freeway grinds to a halt – which you can pretty much guarantee will happen at some point. The interstate freeway I-405 which cuts right through LA from north to south is particularly prone to slow traffic, and the rush hour begins around 3pm. This is worth remembering when booking a flight to LA. If you want to get out of LA as quickly as you can then it's worth trying to book a flight set to arrive at the airport – LAX – before or around midday. If you do plan to stay in LA a list of some cheap or free things to do are included in 'Six Things to do in Los Angeles' at the end of chapter ten.

I was held up at the car rental place at LAX. Many flights had been delayed that day and a good many of the rental staff were at lunch. This meant that I didn't get on the I-405 until 3.30pm and it was already beginning to grind to a halt. It's a relatively simple couple of turns from the airport before you hit the I-405 and the car rental people will direct you. I was heading north to Bakersfield, not because I planned to spend any time there, just that it was a convenient place to stop. It did once have a thriving country music scene and some of this can still be seen in the downtown area, but I was just looking for a chain-motel close to the freeway. The giant neon signs clearly located a number of them, and I pulled into the most convenient one. It was more expensive than I was hoping for, but it did include a full cooked breakfast, and there was a very nice place for dinner right next door.

It's just over 100 miles from LAX to Bakersfield, and it will take 2-3 hours depending on the traffic out of LA. Once free from that LA traffic you should be able to cruise along, and if you tune into a soft rock station on the radio, you will soon be in a southern Californian state of mind. I-5 is the fastest and most direct route north and is well signposted from the I-405 heading north out of LA.

Sequoia and Kings Canyon

The other reason I chose Bakersfield for a stop-over was so I could include a little excursion up to Isabella Lake the next morning. This served as a nice introduction to what was to come. The weather was typically Californian – warm air and vivid blue sky – and the lake was beautiful. There's a very interesting Native American cultural centre by the lake (closed Monday and Tuesday) and I also enjoyed an hour in the quaint little town of Kernville, before making my way back towards the road that would take me up into the Sierra Nevada mountains. I decided to take some of the quiet roads north, and I'm glad I did. The roads were pretty much empty, and the countryside was rolling. Whatever you decide to do, you will eventually need to be on Highway 65 (heading north from Bakersfield) which will take you right to Highway 198 – if heading for Sequoia National Park – or Highway 245 – if heading for Kings Canyon National Park. I arrived at the South Entrance to Kings Canyon around 4pm, but you could easily arrive by midday from Bakersfield if you take a direct route.

For this trip I wanted to stay in the park itself, so I went on-line before I left home and booked a cabin close to John Muir Lodge. When I arrived it turned out that they were not fully booked, but I didn't want to take that risk. The cabin was more expensive than I would have liked – they're never cheap – but it was a fantastic place to stay. It had two double beds, heating, and a wood burning stove outside on a patio. The toilets and showers were in a separate building close by, and breakfast and dinner could be had at the lodge which was within walking distance. There was also a well-stocked store within walking distance which sold pretty much everything you might need, including firewood. I could also see that a new restaurant was being built on the site, and it looked pretty much close to completion.

I was sure that wood and supplies would be cheaper at the roadside place I saw before I entered the park, so I made my way back there to stock up. Unfortunately, they were awaiting more wood but two guys at the bar overheard my conversation and said they had plenty of wood I could have for free. One of them was English but he had lived up in the Sierra Nevada mountains for fourteen years. He was born in the same part of London as me, and after sharing some comparisons between Britain and California, I followed the two of them back to one of their houses a few miles down the road. As we pulled away, I started thinking about the film *Deliverance* (1972), but soon dismissed these thoughts as I looked up at a beautiful azure blue sky and then admired the back of their home-made flat-bed on their pick-up truck. I had one more scary moment as I stepped out of the car when I saw loads of spent gun cartridges strewn around the place. But we were soon stacking wood in the boot of my hire car, after which I had a quick tour of the place before waving them goodbye.

Kings Canyon and Sequoia are two separate, but adjoining parks. They are both as old as Yosemite – their more famous cousin – having been given park status at the same time, in 1890. Originally, Kings Canyon was known as General Grant – established to protect the Giant Sequoia tree groves – but this was eventually extended to include the whole canyon area (in 1940), when it adopted its new name. The road which connects the two parks is the General's Highway, which, like most roads in the area is open subject to snow restrictions. For a lot of the time, in both parks, you will be well above 5,000 feet, and it will not be uncommon to be above the snow line even in May. That said, the General's Highway drops very quickly as you travel south through Sequoia National Park, and then again as you drop down into Kings Canyon to the north. This change in elevation means that the weather and temperature can vary enormously within one hour of driving in either direction.

I booked my cabin for five nights because I wanted to fully explore the whole area, but 2-3 nights would still give enough time to visit some of the main sites in both parks. My cabin was in the small built-up area known as Grant Grove which includes a visitor centre, gift shop, and post office, as well as the John Muir Lodge. The General Grant Tree, along with the accompanying grove of Giant Sequoias, is just a mile or so away, and I would recommend taking an early morning walk there. From there, you will also have easy access onto the road that takes you down to the Kings Canyon. The journey is an absolute delight and it's difficult not to keep stopping to take photographs and enjoy the views. Eventually, the canyon itself will come into view, and from there you will begin to see road signs telling you that you are approaching road's end.

The Senate of Giant Sequoia trees on the Congress Trail, Sequoia National Park, California

This is literally what it means, because at that point you will have to turn round and follow the same road back up the canyon. That journey back is likely to be much quicker though, depending on how often you stopped on the way down. Before you begin the journey back you should certainly consider taking at least one hike down in the canyon. Most of the longer trails begin at the road's end and are clearly marked. I followed the short and undemanding trail through Zumwelt Meadow, which took me on a circular route around the most beautiful meadow, with views of the rock faces all around.

The next day I drove east all the way along the General's Highway, which began within a mile of my cabin, in the opposite direction to the route I took the previous day. After about ten miles you will see the signs leading to the Sequoia grove which includes the largest (by volume) of the big trees – The General Sherman. The Congress Trail, which winds around this grove, is a must do, and can be extended by taking any number of paths which break away from the shorter circular route. Considering that some of these trees are estimated to be well over three thousand years old, this place certainly helps to put human history in perspective.

Driving further down the highway you will see signs to Sequoia Park Museum and a road on the left that leads up to Moro Rock (right fork further up the road) and Crescent Meadow (left fork). Both are really worth exploring. At the top of Moro Rock you will have a 360-degree view of the whole area, and Crescent Meadow is magical in its beauty. If you have the legs it's worth hiking to the far end of the meadow where you will find a log cabin – literally, a log cabin, because it is made from a fallen Sequoia tree, and one which appears to have been visited by John Muir himself [see John Muir Slice of Americana Pie]. You will also find access to the High Sierra Trail in this area, with a sign telling you that you are 60 miles from Mt Whitney, the tallest mountain in the country.

At this point along the General's Highway you will need to decide if you wish to venture to the end of the highway. That journey will see you descend rapidly along a winding road, the route of which you can see from the top of Moro Rock. Towards the end of the road you will come across Hospital Rock, where you can see evidence of a previously thriving Native American community, and a beautiful trail which takes you along Buckeye Creek. To get back to the Grant Grove Village you will need to go back along the General's Highway. Just before the top end of the road you will see a sign to Redwoods Canyon. This is definitely worth the detour and will involve you having an off-road experience for two miles or so (but any car should be able to cope with this). At that point you will see a parking area, which is the start of two circular trails, both of which will take you on a fantastic journey around many fire-scarred Sequoias. It's remarkable how these trees manage to survive intense forest fires. I would recommend taking one of these routes in the early morning. Both trails can also be joined together to make one much larger circular route. Back up on the General's Highway, just as you rejoin it, you will see a sign opposite directing you to Lake Hume. This is also a pleasant detour, which led me to a large recreation area, run by a Christian community. There is also a gas station here where you can fill up with extortionately priced petrol. I continued to the end of the road, where I found myself back on the Kings Canyon road.

The General's Highway, from Moro Rock, Sequoia National Park, California

Yosemite

On the morning I was due to leave Kings Canyon I awoke to find two inches of snow had fallen overnight and a small family of deer were playing just outside my cabin. It was early May and I was told that these conditions were not unusual and that it was wise to be prepared for any conditions at any time of the year. My suitcase did include two Hawaiian shirts, a beanie hat, a hoodie, shorts, and a pair of gloves, so I considered myself pretty well prepared. After being reassured that the weather was set to improve, I started my drive out of the park and up towards Yosemite. The road out of the park took me along Highway 180 towards Fresno. Fresno and Bakersfield are the two large cities that sit in the Central Valley of California. They are very similar – both boiling hot most of the time and sprawling. I don't think many tourists spend much time in either city, but they are fascinating, nonetheless. It was a Sunday morning, so I stopped at a local flea market and then turned right just before the city proper begins, in order to undertake my first detour of the day, up to Shaver Lake. As I drove up to the lake the fog and clouds thickened by the minute, but I was lucky to witness a cloud clearing as I sat eating a banana on the shore of the lake. To be honest, the detour was hardly worth making, and I was pleased to be on the road up to Yosemite shortly afterwards.

Whatever detours you decide to undertake you will eventually need to position yourself on Highway 41 heading north, which will lead you directly to the south entrance of Yosemite National Park. I stopped for lunch at Oakhurst, where I was told by a waitress that there was a rodeo just a few miles away. I drove up there, and for an hour or so I witnessed a huge slice of Americana, which included the audience as well as the performers. Back on the road I stopped one mile short of the official entrance to the park in a tiny hamlet called Fish Camp, where I booked into a grand-sounding lodge. It was actually a very nice, reasonably cheap, motel, laid out rather like the infamous Bates Motel from the film *Psycho* (1960), except this one was set against a lovely wooded area which led down to the river. The owner was friendly and extremely kind, and I really enjoyed staying there. The only problem was that he had recently lost his chef, so breakfast and dinner were not on offer. That said, there were plenty of places to eat close by and although Fish Camp was tiny it did have a well-stocked general store in walking distance from the motel. My room had a microwave oven, so I wasn't too concerned about the food situation, and I had a great Mexican meal at a restaurant just north of Oakhurst. I'd had a busy and enjoyable day on the road between the national parks, but the distance between my cabin in Grant Grove and my new motel room in Fish Camp was only just over 100 miles.

As discussed in the previous chapter, Yosemite National Park was designated in 1890, at the same time as Sequoia and General Grant, but it had been recognised as an area of outstanding natural beauty for many years before then, and was already a State park. The push to protect as much of the area as possible was in no small measure down to John Muir, who first came into the valley in 1868 [see John Muir Slice of Americana Pie].

As you drive into the park, you will eventually find yourself at a junction where all the south and west roads meet. This then becomes one circular route around the main valley floor. Nothing really prepares you for what you are about to experience. Even to say that it is sublime sounds like an understatement. You will get your first glimpse of what is to come by stopping at what is known as Tunnel View. This is before you are on the valley floor and immediately after exiting a short tunnel, so it is worth slowing down as you approach the end of that tunnel. What you then see is probably one of the most photographed views on the planet, as the whole Yosemite Valley is suddenly laid out before you. On the left you will see El Capitan, the striking sheer rock face, and on the right, the Bridalveil Fall which, if in full flow (springtime), is spectacular. In the far distance you should be able to see the Half Dome, literally a giant half domed rock. From this viewing position you can also begin to see how all of this has been crafted, by the action of an enormous glacier, which sliced away at the rock faces and then left hanging valleys from which the many waterfalls now tumble into the resultant U-shaped valley.

As you drive further down into the valley you will come across the exit on the right which will enable you to witness the Bridalveil Fall close up. If it is in full flow the spray will soak you, and the ground may well be covered with small streams of water. As you drive further into the valley you will begin to get views of Yosemite Falls on the left. The closer you get the more you will be able to see the split which divides the upper fall from the lower fall. Both are accessible from separate walking paths. The walk to the lower falls is gentle but impressive as you approach the spray area. The walk to the upper falls is much more of a hiking trek.

I hired a bike from the Yosemite Lodge (bike hire located just by the swimming pool) and I then spent a very happy couple of hours cycling around the whole valley floor (around thirteen miles in total). There are numerous walking paths in the valley, and some will take you beyond the valley. One of the most notable trails will take you past the Nevada Falls and Vernal Falls. This one begins at the far eastern end of the Valley (the Half Dome end) and starts just by the Happy Isles area, where you will also find access to the John Muir Trail – the same trail you may have come across in Sequoia National Park. Another very pleasant walk is the two mile round-trip up to Mirror Lake, which starts a little further round. The good news about all these paths is that their starting points are accessible via free shuttle buses which circle the valley floor every 20 minutes or so. Free maps will provide you with information on the bus stop numbers for the various paths.

The next morning I drove north from the main valley heading towards the Hetch Hetchy Valley. To get there you need to first head west out of the park on Highway 140 then north on Highway 120. The 120 is a splendid road which will provide you with glorious vistas. It also takes you past two groves of Giant Sequoia trees. If you have just been to the Kings Canyon and Sequoia Parks you may feel that you have had your fill of large trees, but if not, the Yosemite area has three famous groves. The Mariposa Grove is back near the southern entrance to the park. The Tuolumne and Merced Groves can be accessed directly from Highway 120. I spent a very happy hour or so descending into the Tuolumne Grove, which is also located on the old high road to Yosemite. This road was used by some of the first non-Native American visitors to the area, many of whom would have made the journey by horse and cart from the San Francisco Bay area.

I saw a black bear here, which crossed my path just a few feet away. I remain scared of these beautiful creatures but having now come across several in my travels – only the black kind – I am becoming just a little more relaxed about them. That said, my fear did shoot up a notch again when I read chapter two of Bill Bryson's book *A Walk in the Woods* (Bryson, 1998). Problem encounters with bears are usually sparked by adult bear perceptions of your potential threat to their cubs, so it's definitely a good idea not to find yourself between a mother and her young cubs.

As you travel north you leave the park only to re-enter it again as you approach Hetch Hetchy. The road to Hetch Hetchy is well sign-posted and involves a right turn onto the appropriately named Evergreen Road. Hetch Hetchy is sometimes referred to as the second Yosemite Valley. When you first catch a glimpse of the valley from the left-hand side of the road you soon see why. It looks remarkably like Yosemite's younger cousin, but for one 'man-made' difference. In 1913 it was deliberately flooded in order to produce a reservoir to service the growing population of San Francisco. This development infuriated John Muir who loved this valley [see John Muir Slice of Americana Pie].

On his behalf I was expecting to be annoyed too, but on seeing the crystal-clear water I was quickly seduced by its current beauty. Dams, particularly close up, are impressive structures, so even if you share John Muir's concerns about disrupting the natural environment, it is difficult nonetheless not to be impressed by the engineering project. The reservoir has not destroyed the effect of the hanging valleys, and the waterfalls still pour into it. There's a wonderful walk around the edge of the reservoir towards the Wapama Falls, which I thoroughly recommend. On that walk, I found myself reflecting on whether the valley might ever be returned to its natural state, but also just how difficult it is in the modern world to balance the needs of urbanisation with rural preservation.

The Yosemite Valley, from the Tunnel View turn-off, Yosemite National Park, California.

Pinnacles

The following morning I began heading west towards one of the newest national parks, Pinnacles. Including a few little detours, the route there involved me travelling west on Highway 140, eventually arriving in the town of Hollister, just south of the San Francisco Bay Area.

A Slice of Americana Pie

A critical appreciation of: John Muir (1838-1914)

John Muir is sometimes referred to as the Father of the National Parks. He didn't directly help to establish the first national park – Yellowstone in 1872 – but his influence was growing by that time. A few years earlier, his pioneering work had begun in the Yosemite Valley and the Sierra Nevada mountain range in California, where he started formulating his case for wilderness protection and the need to save areas of outstanding natural beauty from the rampant commercial interests of the time. In the process he also began to shape the very idea of the American great outdoors.

Muir's story is a fascinating one. He was not an American, having been born in Dunbar, Scotland, but was moved to the United States when his father took the family's farming expertise across the Atlantic in 1849, when he was just ten years old. The family settled in Wisconsin. His upbringing was strict and austere, directed by his father's Christian fundamentalism. His father could probably have taught Thomas Calvin a thing or two about the need to earn a place in heaven through a life of hard labour, abstinence and strict adherence to biblical doctrine. The young Muir quickly realised that this was not the life he wished to emulate, but many of its associated attributes did serve him well, particularly his growing sense of unease about conspicuous consumption, unbridled commercialisation, and the merits of a stoical dedication to causes.

Even at an early age Muir proved himself to be a creative and productive free spirit. While on the family farm, he designed and manufactured a number of tools and machines, without formal technical knowledge or training, and might easily have had a highly productive and lucrative career as an engineer had he not experienced the call of the wild. An industrial accident, which rendered him temporarily blind, seems to have been an important trigger in this regard. The accident coincided with his growing concern that the industrial revolution seemed to be pulling people away from a much deeper, more ingrained, relationship with Nature, and it wasn't long before the young Muir began to recognise the full significance of his own calling in this regard.

His father's exclusive commitment to the knowledge of the bible left the young Muir hungry for wider forms of knowledge, and he enrolled at the University of Minnesota at the first opportunity. While there, he soon came under the spell of the growing evolutionist movement and its scientific challenge to faith-based creationist arguments. He was also now hungry to fully experience the wild and undertook walking treks in Canada and Florida, before finally making his way to California and the Sierra Nevada Mountains where he discovered the Yosemite Valley in 1868. This valley had a transformative effect on Muir, and although he made several other extensive trips, notably to Alaska, Yosemite was his spiritual home. It also became his physical home when he lived in a small cabin in the Yosemite Valley itself, working for a sawmill owner, but later on he lived with his new wife and children a little further north, where he cultivated fruit for a living.

Muir was remarkable in many ways. Alongside his deeply held belief in the healing qualities of the natural world, particularly for those suffering from the alienating effects of capitalism, he was able to combine this with a growing scientific awareness of how places like Yosemite had been formed. His detailed exploration of the area revealed to him the work of glaciers. Today, this is readily accepted knowledge but at the time it pitted Muir against the prevailing wisdom of his time. Had Muir not also been such a gifted writer – using eloquent and evocative prose with ease – perhaps some scientists would have been quicker to latch on to his ideas. Instead, they were put off by language they felt was inappropriate for detached observation and experimentation. His writing however did catch the attention of those who wished to experience first-hand what Muir was describing, including politicians – most notably President Theodore Roosevelt, who was persuaded of the need to protect large areas of the American wilderness. In the main because of its blindness to what would be lost if it was not checked. Not only would Nature be irreparably damaged but so would the human soul.

A large part of his later life was dedicated to fighting on various political fronts. He was particularly determined to see the whole of the Yosemite area come under the full protection of the federal government in the form of a national park (in the same way that Yellowstone had become). To this end he was largely successful, but the battles were hard fought, including with people who had alternative conservation ideas, like Gifford Pinchot, who advocated a form of 'wise use' of Nature. On that front Muir lost a battle very dear to his heart, when the Hetch Hetchy Valley – an area very similar to the Yosemite Valley and just to the north – was deliberately flooded to form a reservoir. On a happier note, though, he founded the Sierra Club, which is the longest standing conservation group in the United States.

I first became aware of John Muir when I took a walk in what is now Muir Woods – a small protected park of Giant Redwood trees just north of San Francisco, across the Golden Gate Bridge. A similar walk inspired the writer Mary Colwell to write a biography of Muir, which I thoroughly recommend (Colwell 2014). I greatly admire Muir's dedication to his causes, but I also love his evocation to take pleasure in the simplest of things – like a small blooming flower – while at the same time standing in awe and appreciation of the sheer beauty of the wider natural landscape, including the clusters of Giant Redwood and Giant Sequoia trees. These trees are native to the West coast of the USA – with Redwoods mainly hugging the coast of Northern California, and Sequoias mainly found in groves on the western slopes of the Sierra Nevada mountains. I lived in California for a couple of years and was able to spend many an enchanted hour in the company of the Giant Redwood and Giant Sequoia trees he helped to preserve.

Muir's legacy lives on. Almost immediately after his death in 1914, his influence on the naturalist Enos Mills helped establish the Rocky Mountain National Park in Colorado, in 1915. As the key national park pioneer, Muir stands as a form of pure Americana – in helping to define what it means to experience the American great outdoors.

If you want to make a slightly more serious detour at this point, it is really worth travelling a little further north from here, to visit the San Juan Bautista Mission, one of many Catholic Missions, originally intended for those dedicated to the cause. Not only is this a fascinating Mission in its own right, but it was also the location for some of the key action in the film *Vertigo* (1958), directed by Alfred Hitchcock [see Hitchcock Movies Slice of Americana Pie]. Hitchcock knew this area very well because he owned a house in nearby Scotts Valley, close to Santa Cruz. If you have seen the film, you will most likely be pleasantly surprised by how little the Mission has changed. Apart from one key feature, the Bell Tower, which is no longer there and that's because it never was. Those scenes were shot on the film lot back at the studios in LA. The tower you see in the long shots was just a matte painting. The film also features another Mission in the early shots. This was Mission Dolores, 320 Dolores Street (at Sixteenth Street) in south San Francisco, and is certainly worth a visit if ever plan to visit San Francisco (see chapter eight).

To get to Pinnacles you need to head due south from Hollister on Highway 25. This is a great road to drive, with lovely bends and rolling hills on either side. Within about thirty minutes you will see the signpost on the right leading to the east entrance of Pinnacles. Excluding the detours, it's around 170 miles from Yosemite to Pinnacles. This area previously had national monument status, but became a fully-fledged national park in 2013. It is possible to access the park from the west side, but unfortunately both roads do not meet up, so you have to choose from which side you wish to access it, or just decide to circle round to gain access to the other side. I decided not to do this, but didn't feel that I had missed out. Once in the park, if you walk for long enough, you will meet people who have accessed from the opposite side. The park is called Pinnacles because of its craggy rock formations, the result of volcanic action, and subsequent movement along the famous San Andreas fault line, which dissects California from north to south. The San Andreas fault line is also what makes California such an earthquake-prone area.

A few miles past the official entrance to the park you will see the visitor centre. You will need to stop here to pay the park fee (which is half the price of the bigger parks). The centre has a good supply of camping and food basics, and a good collection of park souvenirs. The rangers will orientate you around the park, giving advice on which paths to take depending on how much time you have. I arrived just after midday, intending to leave around 7pm, which the rangers assured me was plenty of time to undertake some interesting hikes. They were right, of course, and after parking up at the popular Bear Gulch, I set off up the path towards Bear Gulch Cave. When I arrived at the foot of some of the rocks from which the park takes its name, I was glad to have caught up with a small party of other walkers because the next part of the journey involved clambering through a cave formation, which was pitch black in parts. My fellow walkers were well prepared, with bright torches, so I just followed in their footsteps until I emerged into the sunshine a few hundred feet further up. After a few more twists and a bit more clambering about you eventually arrive at a very nice reservoir, where you can take stock, and decide how much more walking you wish to do.

It was a very pleasant temperature the day I visited, and I decided to take several paths, which give me views of the rocks and some larger vistas across the Central Valley of California. All the paths are clearly signposted and well-trodden, but they are quite steep in places. You could decide from the start to undertake the loop trail which will enable you to take in most of what the park has to offer, but this will probably involve you walking for around 4-6 hours

I eventually arrived back at my car just after 7pm, and then spent a fantastic hour driving further down Highway 25 towards King City where I decided I would stay for the night. To my mind, that road pretty much defined what a driving experience should be – winding road, empty of other cars, and accompanied by beautiful evening sunshine. I chose King City because it would place me on Highway 101 the next morning. Once I had located the 101, I looked for the motels which always hug these thoroughfares, and I decided on one which was close to a Denny's Restaurant. This meant I could be eating dinner within a few minutes. The motel turned out to be very nice, with a hot breakfast, and wasn't too expensive. It also had a bunch of road construction workers staying over night, who told me that a lot of work was currently being undertaken to repair Highway 101 and Highway 1 after a very wet California winter.

The Pacific Coast Highway – south

The quickest way to travel north-south in California particularly if you are heading for San Francisco (north) or Los Angeles (south) is to take Interstate 5, but this can be quite boring for obvious reasons, particularly because it takes you away from the coast. That said, some of its route follows the historic route 99, which was the original highway. But if you want to enjoy the coast then you will need to follow the 101, and particularly Highway 1, which hugs the coast. Both roads intersect at several points, the 101 being slightly faster, but Highway 1 will give you the closest access to the coast and the beaches. Having spent much of the previous week above 5,000ft I was looking forward to seeing the coast again. I also had another reason because I wanted to pass by the place I had lived for a couple of years, just outside Santa Barbara. I mention this because if you will be flying back to Europe from Los Angeles, there's a great opportunity here to spend a day or two hugging the coast before dropping off your car at LAX. It's only 100 miles from Santa Barbara to LA, so you could be back at the airport (LAX) within a couple of hours from there, if necessary (always traffic permitting).

Heading south from King City on Highway 101 will soon have you approaching the coastal town of San Luis Obispo. This town is worth a stop, but if you want something a bit quieter and more spectacular you might consider heading slightly further north, towards Morro Bay. This area has a wonderful cove beach and will probably find you making plans to move there as soon as you can. Alternatively, if you would prefer to keep heading south, then you could easily stop for coffee and a walk at Pismo Beach. From this point you then need to decide how much time you have on your hands. The more time you have the more you might want to stay on Highway 1, the less time, the more you might want to stay on the 101. Either way, if you're anything like me, you will probably find any number of songs about California entering your head as you cruise along. I had a mix-tape playing in my head which included lines from the songs: *California Soul* (1968); *California, Here I Come*, (1992); and *Big Sur* (2003). The area of Big Sur is on the coast, back up Highway 1, and too far out of my reach for this trip, but would certainly be a great stopover if you are contemplating taking a trip up the coast from LA to San Francisco (or vice versa). It's about two-thirds of the way up and has a glorious unspoilt mixture of forest and coast, and you could rent a log cabin to complete the experience.

I was heading south towards the thriving student community next to the University of California at Santa Barbara (UCSB), where I had been a student. Even if you have little interest in student affairs it's certainly worth a visit, and may well turn out to be a cheaper place to stay than Santa Barbara, which although beautiful, can be very expensive. The area around Santa Barbara has been the home to many celebrities over the years, including President Reagan and Michael Jackson.

I booked myself into one of the many motels just by Santa Barbara airport, in the little town of Goleta, between Santa Barbara and Isla Vista, where I had lived. Looking across at the airport it reminded me of some late sixties student radicalism, this being the place where the students at UCSB once laid on the runway to prevent Ronald Reagan, then Governor of California, from landing. Students also burnt down the Bank of America in Isla Vista in 1970, as a symbolic gesture of anti-establishment defiance. Little of that history is in evidence today; my guess is that most students at the time and since have been much more focused on chilling-out in the warm sunshine. When I was a student there, UCSB was affectionately known as UC Surf Board, and being – literally – on the beach it's easy to see why. It's an idyllic setting, with a large lagoon, impressive University buildings, and direct access to a south-facing beach. The student community of Isla Vista is directly adjoining. Despite its laidback appearance, the academic reputation of the University is high, so it's difficult to work out what not to like about this place.

The following morning I headed south towards LA. My flight back to London was not due to leave until 9.35 that evening, so I had a whole day ahead. I checked in for my flight on line from my motel room and spent a little bit of time packing my suitcase in order to save time later on. I was on the road at 8am, listening to KTYD on the radio. I thoroughly recommend this station while on the road in this area (FM 99.9). It will help complete the southern Californian driving experience, as it plays one soft rock track after another. If you're lucky you might even hear *Ventura Highway* (1972) by the band America, as you make your way down past the town of Ventura. You will also, most certainly, see some very cool Californians cruising along in brand new open-

A Slice of Americana Pie

A critical appreciation of: Steve McQueen (1930-1980)

Like Marilyn Monroe, Steve McQueen is such an iconic Hollywood star it's easy to confuse the image with the person. But McQueen was very aware of the person he was, and treated Hollywood like a well-paid day job. The money enabled him to do the things he really wanted to do, which was mainly to be around cars and motorbikes. Records indicate that he owned well over one hundred bikes and cars during his lifetime. Not that his films didn't include these things; indeed, cars and motorbikes were central to three of the films he starred in – *The Great Escape* (1963), *Bullitt* (1968) *and Le Mans* (1971).

The last two of these films were not set in the United States (how could they be) but their themes lie at the core of defining much of what has come to be associated with the American psyche – restlessness, seeking resolution in forms of personal freedom, escape, and adventure. These themes are normally associated with male characters but also surfaced strongly in the film *Thelma and Louise* (1991), starring Geena Davis and Susan Sarandon; the final scene of which appears to be at the Grand Canyon, but the film's actual outdoor locations were in and around Arches and Canyonlands national parks. Key moments in all of these films involved the car or motorbike as the means to experience freedom, escape, and adventure.

In the film *Bullitt* (1968) – named after the character that Steve McQueen played – we see one of the most famous car chases in film history, up and down and through the streets of San Francisco [see Six things to do in San Francisco]. The film is also remembered for how cool McQueen's character was. So cool, that a dictionary definition of the word could just say: see Steve McQueen in the film *Bullitt*. By all accounts Steve McQueen, the person, was also very cool, and used the hipster counter-culture language of the day. In a famous recollection, when asked to play a character in a particular way, he is said to have responded with: "You're twisting my melon, man". This phrase seems to neatly encapsulate the so-called 'generation gap' between old and young Americans in the 1960s. This phrase was later used by Shaun Ryder of the Happy Mondays at the beginning of *Step On* (1991); their remake of the John Kongos hit from 1971.

McQueen's character, Frank Bullitt, was a restless police lieutenant, displaying an individual doggedness, which also seems to be ingrained in the American pysche, and often seen in Clint Eastwood's roles. But there is a good reason for choosing Steve McQueen over Clint Eastwood for this slice of Americana, because both the icon and the person were much more allied to a central theme of this book – the idea of being on the road. So much so that McQueen would often be found on a big screen road from Monday to Friday, but would then quickly transfer onto a real road at the weekend, to indulge in some motorsport. Some of that indulgence was captured in the cult classic movie *On Any Sunday* (1971) where McQueen is shown as a regular guy, along with hundreds of other like-minded people, all enjoying their love of motorbike racing. For McQueen, though, this was not just a hobby, because he was fiercely competitive and became an accomplished rider and driver. In another life it is highly likely that he would have become a full-time professional motorbike or car racer, and probably a very successful one.

All that said, Steve McQueen had been an irregular teenager, having been sent to a – so called – school for troubled adolescent boys, brought on by family troubles and breakup. His largely positive experience of the school appears to have helped him stay grounded, particularly after his steady rise to superstardom in the film industry. That superstardom resulted in McQueen's screen characters becoming idolised, but McQueen himself idolised his very-grounded motorcycle heroes, including Mert Lawill, Malcolm Smith and Bud Ekins. Ekins was a stuntman who ran a motorbike shop in the district of Hollywood, Los Angeles, and McQueen would often be found there, either just hanging out or learning about bikes from his mentor. It is Ekins who actually executes the leap over the barbed wire fencing in that famous scene in *The Great Escape*, because the film producers weren't prepared to take the risk with one of their stars. But insiders have subsequently claimed that McQueen did make the leap, away from the cameras, to prove he could do it. Ekins also did some of the stunt driving in the car chase scenes in *Bullitt*.

In the film *Le Mans*, which McQueen co-financed, he wanted to capture the very essence of the mixture of danger and excitement associated with motorsport, but soon found himself embroiled in arguments with co-producers. The film was completed and released, but it is clear from watching it that it ends up as strange compromise – with a human-interest angle almost at odds with the exploration of what is compelling about motorsport. It appears to have been something of a final straw and confirmed what McQueen had probably believed for some time, that he would never be fulfilled within mainstream Hollywood. He only made a few more film appearances, slowly becoming more and more reclusive, but maintaining his love of motorsport. He died in 1980, at the age of 50, of cancer.

Many of the artefacts of Americana associated with Steve McQueen live on. Indeed, he was instrumental in establishing some of it as Americana. A very interesting example can be found in the decision of Matisse – the British motorbike company – to market a replica of the bike that Steve McQueen ordered from them in the 1960s. Even the modifications and extras that McQueen ordered for the bike are now offered as standard on the McQueen Desert Racer. The bike is hardly likely to appeal to a modern youngster looking for his or her first motorbike, but for anyone knowing anything about the McQueen legacy it is surely irresistible. The bike *is* British, but also strangely all-American because of Steve McQueen. The Ford Mustang fastback that McQueen's character Frank Bullitt drove around the streets of San Francisco has also become iconic and has helped cement the Mustang brand as one of the classic cars to own, particularly the early ones from the mid-sixties and early seventies.

top Porsches, or classic Ford Mustangs from the 1960s [see Steve McQueen Slice of Americana Pie]. Also, if you've ever wondered where all those camper vans and RVs (Recreational Vehicles) park up at night, it's worth coming off the highway at this point and following the route of Highway 1, because you will see hundreds of them parked (legally) by the side of the road, overlooking the Pacific Ocean. Having spoken to several of these people over the years, it's clear that a good number of them have no fixed home anymore, having sold up and headed out onto the road in their brand new – and usually huge – RV.

Ventura is the town you need to head for to catch a boat across to the Channel Islands National Park. There are five islands which comprise this national park: Santa Cruz, Anacapa, Santa Rosa, San Miguel and Santa Barbara. There is a well signposted visitor centre if you want to get orientated. It also shows a very informative film about the diverse nature of each island, including the history of the inhabitants – both human and animal. You have to choose which island(s) you want to visit, and you will need to leave early, so it's worth checking out the boat timetables on-line in advance – and possibly buy a ticket on-line, particularly if you are visiting at a busy time of year. You might also consider booking into a motel close to Ventura harbour. You will see several motels on the road through the town, as you follow the signs to the park.

The Channel Islands National Park is free, but you still have to pay for a boat return – which takes 1- 4 hours each way depending on which island you visit. The two larger islands are only one hour away. You can take a flight if you have the money, and you can camp on the islands with a bit of forward planning. I had visited the islands before so I gave it a miss this time, but it's certainly worth spending a day on one of the islands. On the boat over you might also be lucky to see a passing whale. And, given your proximity to LA, it's difficult not to start reflecting on the fact that although the trip to the islands is a very short one in terms of miles, it's worlds apart in every other respect.

If you continue down Highway 1, often signposted as Pacific Coast Highway or PCH, you will eventually find yourself entering the Los Angeles area via the exclusive beach community of Malibu. Although this area is home to the rich and famous, with private roads everywhere, there are several places where you can stop by the ocean. You will also pass the famous surfing area around Zuma Beach. If you have the time and inclination you might want to call in at the John Paul Getty Museum, which is off to the left, but still on the coast road, just before you enter Santa Monica. It is signposted but easy to miss. You have to pay to park inside the gates, but parking elsewhere could be difficult so it's well worth it, particularly given that there is no further entrance fee to the museum itself. The museum was the late oil tycoon's home, where he kept his huge art collection. As that collection grew, he wanted to be more imaginative about the way they were displayed, so he commissioned architects to reproduce a Roman villa (the home of Julius Caesar's father in law was the template). The whole place is a sea of tranquility and probably as close as you will get to experiencing the splendour of an ancient Roman villa – given that the ones in the Bay of Naples are all in ruins.

Just at the point where Malibu finishes and Santa Monica begins you need to decide whether you want to continue along the coast, past Santa Monica Pier and on to Venice Beach (which does have a small canal network), and where you will find the famous outdoor Gold's Gym, or, instead, venture inland by turning left just before you enter Santa Monica, onto Palisades Drive, which quickly becomes Sunset Boulevard. In chapter ten you will find more details about some of my recommendations for exploring these areas [and see 'Six Things to do in Los Angeles'] On this particular trip I decided to head further south towards Manhattan Beach. This is a huge stretch of beach where you will find the QE2 ocean liner permanently housed. For me, it served as a good place to chill-out for an hour or so before I made my way up to the airport, which is only 20 minutes or so from this beach. It was also a good place to check the car over before returning it. As ever, the signs directing you to the 'car returns' area of the airport were clear, and I was soon on the free shuttle bus to my terminal. I try to get a rental car returned around two and a half hours before my flight. This is normally plenty of time, if you have checked-in for your flight on-line beforehand.

Conclusion

When I lived in California, I remember being told that 80% of Californians live within twenty five miles of the coast. As a statistical fact I always took that with a pinch of salt, but the general point is clear: the Californian coast – which stretches 800 miles – is a magnet for both visitors and would-be inhabitants. But California is a huge and varied state and a trip inland is guaranteed to bring huge rewards to any traveller. A trip into the Sierra Nevada mountains could even be magical if you are in the right frame of mind. 'The mountains are calling, and I must go' is a phrase associated with the father of the national parks, John Muir [see John Muir Slice of Americana Pie], and one trip to Yosemite, Sequoia and/or Kings Canyon is very likely to have you hankering for more. If you have the opportunity to combine coast and mountains on a road trip you should get the best of both worlds, and also get a clear sense of why California has been called 'The Promised Land' by countless migrants seeking fame and fortune, or just honest work [see Woody Guthrie Slice of Americana Pie].

Note: The Pacific Coast Highway and the national parks north of San Francisco, into Oregon and Washington State, feature in chapter eight. The deserts and national parks of Southern California feature in chapter ten.

Chapter 4

Across the Lone Star State

National Parks: Big Bend, Guadalupe Mountains, Carlsbad Caverns, White Sands

Other notable sites: The Alamo Mission National Historical Landmark, Fort Davis National Historic Site, The Lyndon B Johnson National Historical Park

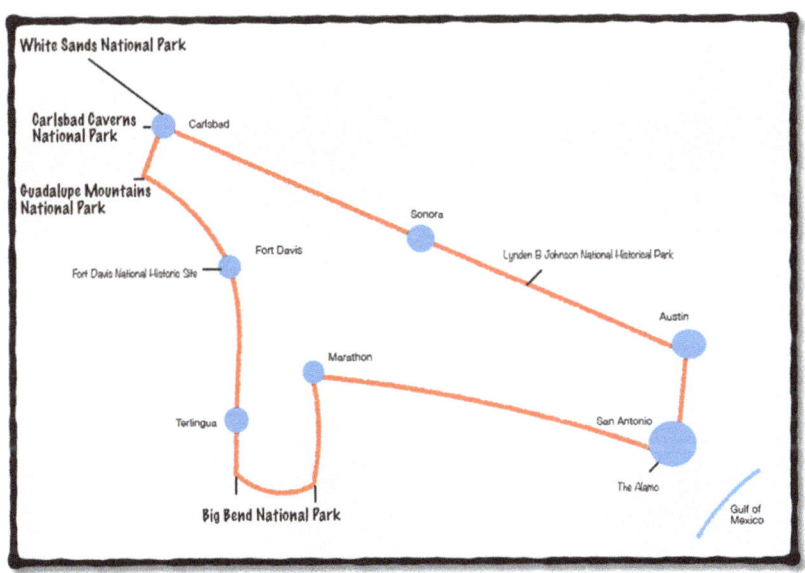

This chapter was composed while singing:

Born to be Wild, as performed by Steppenwolf (1968) and

Running on Empty, as performed by Jackson Browne (1977)

Introduction

The idea behind this road trip was to travel across Texas from east to west and back again, by creating a loop which would incorporate Big Bend National Park in the south west, and Guadalupe Mountains National Park in the north west. A short hop across the border into New Mexico would also enable me to visit Carlsbad Caverns. I made this journey in October 2016, and allocated ten days to complete the loop. I chose October to avoid the blistering summer heat of the southwestern USA, but the temperature was still in the 90s for some of the time. At one point in Big Bend National Park the thermometer in my car measured the outside temperature at 100F.

Arrival in San Antonio

I started the trip in San Antonio. This required a flight transfer from a London-Atlanta flight, which was very smooth and only involved a two hour stop over. My luggage went straight through to my transfer flight so all I needed to do was walk to my new gate, giving me enough time for some lunch and coffee. I arrived in San Antonio late afternoon and after securing my hire car I headed off in the direction of downtown. This was my first time in San Antonio, and I was a little disoriented, so I made a snap decision to stop at the junction which took you out west – in the direction I would be heading for most of the next week. There were a number of motels hugging this junction and I chose the most convenient.

It was a Saturday, and after a little bit of haggling I got a good weekend rate for a room for two nights, which included breakfast and some dinner vouchers, including a free alcoholic drink. All this hospitality was very nice, as was the room. I explained at reception that I would be heading downtown the next morning and asked whether I could take a bus. The receptionist told me that there was free street parking on a Sunday and that it would be fine to drive, so this is what I did. It didn't take long to find somewhere to park, and I was soon wandering around the downtown streets heading in the general direction of The Alamo. I was surprised to see that this historic site was actually in the town; I had imagined it to be a somewhat desolate place, but it soon became clear that San Antonio had grown considerably since 1836, when the famous 13-day siege took place. This growth had also produced an optical dwarfing effect, because The Alamo appeared tiny amongst its more modern surroundings.

The Alamo is one of four Spanish Missions in the area. As with the Missions commonly found up and down California, they were originally homes for missionaries, dedicated to promoting Catholic culture and practices. The Alamo Mission's real name was Mission San Antonio de Valero, but its adopted name has now become synonymous with the cause of independence (even though its literal meaning is 'cottonwood tree'). Inside the grounds, sitting in the sun, I was able to get a great history lesson by listening to an animated retelling of the story of The Alamo by a local guide. The grounds were lovely, and the buildings contained many artefacts, maps and images, which told the story of Texas' historical relationship with both Mexico and the USA. This turned out to be a great introduction to the whole road trip and helped to explain why the state's motto is: 'Don't mess with Texas'. It also helped to explain some of the deeper resonances behind that other slogan associated with the state: 'In Texas, we don't call 911'.

After leaving the Alamo I made my way towards the river front, which winds through the city. The banks of the San Antonio River were a hive of activity, with many people having lunch at the numerous restaurants, while others milled around tacky souvenir shops. There was also a great selection of live entertainment, which you could tune in and out of as you wandered along. I enjoyed it all enormously.

Big Bend

The next morning it was time to get my motor running, travelling out west on the highway across the Lone Star State. I was up early because I was hoping to make it across to Big Bend National Park in one hit. I chose Highway 90, and not the freeway, because I took it for granted that the former would be more interesting. I stopped roughly halfway, at the town of Del Rio, near the Mexican border, for lunch. This was a journey of around 150 miles. It was a pleasant enough town, but I was glad to be back on the road. The second half of the journey was pretty much everything you'd expect from long distance driving: nice clear road, lovely sunshine, with bends and rolling hills, which gradually got bigger as I went on. Here was a stretch of road where it was possible to believe you could just keep running on empty, both literally and metaphorically. This road certainly helped me make the transition from what was on my mind to what I wanted to be on my mind. I was heading for the small town of Marathon, a further 150 miles west, at the junction for the Big Bend turn off. It turned out to be very small indeed, but perfectly formed, with a selection of shops and railway paraphernalia. There weren't many accommodation options, but the little hotel I chose turned out be an excellent.

The people on the hotel reception were great, as was the room – all kitted out in vintage style. The grounds of the hotel were also lovely and there was a swimming pool. It was a little more expensive than I would have liked, but I had no complaints, given what I got for the money. The only disadvantage was that my room didn't have its own bathroom, but the excellent shower room down the hall was hardly an inconvenience. There was also a great restaurant right next door, where I had dinner. After dinner I strolled to the edge of town – which didn't take long – in order to lose the small amount of light pollution, and then looked up at the night sky, at which point I started singing lines from Michelle Shocked's song *Anchorage* (1988), because here I was, standing in the middle of the largest state in the USA, bar Alaska.

The next morning, I was up before dawn to make the most of the day in Big Bend. I was told by the people on reception that there was a small diner just a few doors down which would be open early. The breakfast there was great, and I was soon on my way towards the park on Highway 385, just as the sun was coming up.

Big Bend National Park was established in 1944. It covers a huge area of south Texas and is desert-like in appearance, except for the striking Chisos Mountains. It lies on the US side of the Rio Grande, with the river acting as a natural boundary between the USA and Mexico. Whenever I heard 'Rio Grande' as a kid I imagined a mighty river, with huge rock formations, and warring Cowboys and Indians, so I was pleasantly surprised when I was able to dip my toes into a very shallow part of the river, knowing that I could be on the Mexican side within a few minutes of further wadding.

I spent the bulk of the day hiking around the Chisos Mountains Basin Loop. The weather was beautiful, the hiking wasn't too strenuous, and it was nice to meet the odd fellow hiker from time to time. There were several bear warning signs on the trails, and an alarming sign warning me about a lion. I was also alarmed by the accompanying advice, should I come across the lion, which suggested that I throw stones or sticks. Wouldn't that just antagonise it? Perhaps here was a case for carrying a hand-gun? And I've always wondered about that other piece of advice you often see: 'Bang pots and pans together'. Isn't it only in films you see people walking along with aluminium dinner accoutrements dangling from their back packs? In my case, I don't think a plastic water container and a packet of trail mix would register on any decibel measuring device.

After dinner that evening I sat by the hotel's fire-pit with a beer. I was soon joined by some other hotel guests. What ensued gave me a fantastic insight into American politics. We were just a few weeks away from the 2016 American presidential election, with media coverage reaching fever pitch, particularly concerning Donald Trump's call for a wall to divide Mexico from the USA, and his other call to 'lock her up' – referring to his rival, Hillary Clinton. The first to join me that evening were a couple from Texas, who ran a small business. Just as they were explaining to me how Trump would support the kind of free enterprise they wished to see more of, a well-to-do New Yorker overheard the conversation, sat down, and quickly launched into how Trump was just a dodgy property developer who didn't know the first thing about politics or economics. A few minutes later we were joined by a Texan businessman, who told us that he had little respect for Trump, but had even less for Hillary Clinton – who was just a career politician. The arguments between my camp-fire mates started to ratchet up, and although I was keen to get involved, I decided that I was getting privileged access here and I should just listen. The only point I got a little concerned was when the New Yorker turned her wrath on the National Rifle Association, which resulted in the female Texan reaching for her handbag to show us that she carried a gun at all times. In the end it calmed down when all of them became interested in my British take on all things American.

After breakfast the next morning I checked-out of the hotel and then admired two beautiful Indian motorcycles which were sitting directly outside the hotel. As I drove away, I had two thoughts on my mind: first, maybe Donald Trump could just become the President of the United States, and second, that it would be great to try to get across the Rio Grande into Mexico. I drove back into the national park, and after enquiring about legally crossing the Rio Grande, I was soon on my way back down to the river looking for the Rio Grande Village, and then on to the small border crossing – signposted as The Boquillas Crossing Port of Entry. Before making the crossing, I parked up and spent a great couple of hours exploring the winding, hilly paths, which gave me great views of the river and surrounding landscape.

The Rio Grande and the Chisos Mountains, Big Bend National Park, Texas

I also kept coming across small handmade wire-framed models of road runners and cacti, which were sitting on small rocks by the side of the paths. I guessed these were made by local Mexicans, and that you just took the ones you wanted and left the money in the small boxes which were close by. I dutifully did this, and by the time I got back to my car I was armed with a small collection, which now sit proudly on my mantle-piece back home. Unfortunately, for the rest of the day I kept saying 'beep, beep' in my head, and singing lines from the song *Road Runner*, by Bo Diddley (1960).

At the border crossing I had my passport stamped and was directed towards a small boat which would take me across to Mexico for a small fee. I enjoyed the smiles of the border guard when I mentioned Trump's wall, because it was impossible to imagine how it could sit in the middle of the river at this point. On the other side of the river I walked the mile or so into the border town of Boquillas del Carmen. The southern part of the national park borders the two huge Mexican States of Coahuila and Chihuahua and I was very pleased to be greeted by a number of namesake dogs as I walked into town. I say greeted; what I should have said was confronted, because they are natural guard dogs and fiercely territorial. I own one, so I was not concerned by this; only by the fact that mine was clearly obese when compared with these skinny cousins.

You have to have your documents looked at again when you arrive in the town, but this was straightforward and only took a couple of minutes. The small town was exactly as you might imagine, with dusty roads, blistering heat, and small houses and tavernas which looked to be straight out of a Hollywood set for a film featuring Sancho Panza or Che Guevara. At one point a Mexican border guard patrol drove menacingly through town as I was enjoying an authentic Mexican lunch (which was very cheap, and I paid in US dollars). I remarked to the owner of the restaurant how menacing it looked, but he replied that they meant no harm and were just doing their job. Before returning to the US I bought a large Mexican rug for my nomad tent back home in the UK.

I drove west out of Big Bend and into the town of Study Butte, where I filled up with petrol. Places to stay overnight looked few and far between but here was a town which did have a few motels. I turned into the first one I came across. The rooms varied in price, and I took a cheap one, which was perfectly adequate, if a little dated. If you were being kind you would call it 'authentic retro'. If not, you might wonder why no one had thought to do anything with the rooms since 1957. I liked it, and after buying some beer to consume on the porch outside the room, I then headed up the road to the, so-called, ghost town of Terlingua, which the person on reception had recommended for dinner. I'm glad I went there. Ter-lingua implies that Spanish, English and Native American tongues would originally have been heard here, and it is called a ghost town because it was quickly evacuated when mining ceased in the area. It was far from a ghost town now, with a small range of busy shops and a great bar/restaurant. On the way back down, it was fascinating to look at the array of houses, many of

A Slice of Americana Pie

A critical appreciation of: Pick-Up Trucks

Is there anything which typifies American road culture more than the pick-up truck? It is so ubiquitous that you almost forget it's there. But take a good look around any supermarket parking lot, anywhere in the United States, and you might even see a whole row of them. Indeed, up to one in five vehicles at any moment in a parking lot could well be a pick-up truck. Hardly surprising, if you are in one of the more rural parts of the United States, but you will still see a fair number even in the most urban of environments.

To European eyes this certainly needs some explaining, particularly knowing that the average US car customer is confronted daily with any number of comfortable car choices, all complete with large trunks and ample room for a large family. So why would someone choose to drive around in a vehicle with a large open flat-bed on the back – which is unlikely ever to be full up – and often with only one long bench seat in the passenger area? On top of that, how could it ever be as comfortable, and handle as well, as even the most basic of American cars? To even ask these questions clearly misses the point, big time. But what exactly is that point?

For a start, most pick-up trucks, even the old ones from the early post-Second World War era, are more comfortable than they look. As soon as the big manufacturers – Ford, General Motors, Chrysler – realised the potential that the truck had in appealing to a wider market than just the farmer, they made sure that their trucks did have comfortable seats, along with a range of creature comforts, including power steering and air conditioning, even if they were just options on some of the earlier models. But perhaps far more important in the marketing of the post-war truck was an appeal to ruggedness, a deep-seated pioneering spirit, and most fundamental of all, a message about how a truck was an essential part of what it means to be truly American (as opposed to European). All of this could also be said about the truck's close cousin, the sports utility vehicle (SUV), typified by the Chrysler Jeep, which still contains design features from its original Second World War incarnation.

In this regard there is perhaps much more to Fredrick Turner's American Frontier Thesis than he originally articulated (Turner, 1893). He saw the true American as an enterprising free spirit, necessitated by the need to venture westward across the continent. In the process, carving out – literally in many cases – a livelihood and identity. This would have required a degree of pragmatism and stoicism, but equally, a large dose of doggedness. The pick-up truck is just a logical extension of this mentality – a vehicle perfectly in tune with American character. A vehicle which, if required, will go anywhere, do anything, and accommodate all the tools necessary to get the job done – even if, in a modern context, that's just a trip to the local DIY store.

Maybe this is why advertisers never had to work that hard on promoting the pick-up truck, because it is so ingrained in the American psyche, that it's intuitively obvious that it will appeal to the spirit of free enterprise. Not for nothing do Americans still talk of going 'out west', but returning 'back east', as if to imply that there is still something to be forged out there in the American great outdoors. This is wonderfully exemplified by Johnny Depp's character, in the Jim Jarmusch film, *Dead Man* (1995).

Pick-up trucks are everywhere in American popular culture. So much so that you would only need to catch a glimpse of a pick-up truck in a film or TV show to know what is being signified. Could Clint Eastwood's character (Robert Kincaid) have been seen driving anything else in *The Bridges of Madison County* (1995)? Even though the film *Grand Torino* (2008) centres its plot around a car, we see the owner – Walt Kowalski (played by Eastwood) – only ever driving his 1972 Ford F-100 pick-up. And in the film *Twister* (1996) isn't it obvious what is being signified by the male character, played by Bill Paxton, driving his new truck, compared with the female character, played by Helen Hunt, driving her beat up truck?

To the uninitiated it may look as if one pick-up truck is much the same as any other, after all the design is pretty basic. But many Americans will be able to tell you precisely what year a truck was made and what model it is just by looking at some of its outward design features. There is also huge brand loyalty, with some people only ever buying a Ford, while others would only ever be seen in a Chevy. Owners – particularly those with classic trucks – will speak eloquently about the distinctive style features of the Chevy vs the classic smooth lines of the Ford. Others again, will say that the Dodge is the only true choice. Some of the more modern versions of these trucks may have less to wax lyrical on, but there is no doubting that a new pick-up truck is still an essential purchase for many families. So much so, that the large auto-manufacturers are currently cutting down on their car models in favour of more trucks.

I own a 1971 Ford F-100 pick-up truck, one of the last of the classic trucks, from Ford's 1967-1972 range. It has all those features typical of that era, including the long bench seat and huge rear flat bed. It also has a nice patina, courtesy of the original golden-brown paint job, now mixed with surface rust. It was imported to the UK from Santa Cruz, California, where it appears to have spent the majority of its life. It has two of the most popular modifications: it's been slightly lowered at the front and now sports alloy wheels, but apart from that it remains totally original. Do I really need it? Probably not, but I enjoy driving it, looking at it, and knowing that I can transport pretty much anything in it and on it. I also know I can throw my tent and camping equipment over the side onto the flat bed, along with some wood, and then drive off into the forest, my arm firmly resting on the rusted paintwork patch around the opened window. That patch also provides me with the evidence that all its previous owners will have done the same.

which looked self-built, along with all the objects strewn around them. This certainly seemed to be the sort of place where you could escape a previous life and be left pretty much to your own devices. I loved it.

Guadalupe Mountains

The next morning, I started heading north on Highway 118 in the general direction of Guadalupe Mountains National Park, close to the border with the State of New Mexico. The road was lovely and relatively empty and before long (around 100 miles) I was in the town of Marfa, which I was keen to spend some time in. I had to come off the 118 at the town of Alpine to join Highway 67 going west, but this was hardly a detour. The town has two claims to fame: first, in and around the town there have been many sightings of UFOs, and second, it is where some scenes for James Dean's last film *Giant* (1956) were filmed. I had also read that the town had a thriving Arts culture. Perhaps because of all this hype I found the place rather disappointing. It didn't seem to be very buzzing. Perhaps I just came on the wrong day. It was certainly a great place to take some photographs because the town appeared to be authentically 1950s, with a nice selection of old pick-up trucks parked up around town [see Pick-up Trucks Slice of Americana Pie]. I intended to stay overnight, but the two motels I checked out had room prices which were higher than some places I'd stayed in New York. I probably didn't help my cause by mentioning this to one of the receptionists, but I also saw this as sign that I should move on.

I looked at the map and decided to head further north to the town of Fort Davis, which was only another 20 miles or so further north on Highway 17, which turned out to be an almost dead straight road. Further along, I found myself rejoining Highway 118 going north right in town. Time was getting on, so I was very pleased to find a nice place to stop, right on the main road. The rooms were very reasonably priced, and it was a short walk to some restaurants. After dinner I sat outside my room drinking beer with a couple of bikers, who were touring around the West. In the morning, I had an interesting chat with a guy over breakfast, who recommended that I buy the Ken Burns DVDs on the history of the American national parks, which I dutifully ordered the next time I had an internet connection.

Having travelled further north than I had intended the previous day it gave me the hour or so I needed the next morning to visit the actual Fort Davis, now run by the National Park Service. The fort is just a couple miles north of the town. The place was immaculately preserved and full of information about the role of these forts in American history. This particular fort played a significant role in the defence of the US western frontier, and it was also fascinating to read about the life of the first black graduate of the military academy at West Point. He was stationed at Fort Davis in 1880, around the same time as a unit of the so called 'Buffalo Soldiers' – one of four units composed entirely of black soldiers.

El Capitan, from the road heading north into Guadalupe National Park, Texas

I continued my journey north west on Highway 118, and when I realised that it was less than 20 miles to the McDonald Observatory I decided to call in. I was up at the crack of dawn that day, and even though I had stopped for a cooked breakfast and visited the fort it was still only 10.30 in the morning. I took an official tour and the guide was knowledgeable and witty. I was intrigued by the Star Parties, which were guided tours of the night sky, and if I had more time, I would have loved to have booked a place.

After a quick early lunch, I was soon on my way up to the Guadalupe Mountain range, via Highway 118, then west on I-10 for a short distance, before turning north again on Highway 54, then Highway 62, which was all very straightforward. It was about 150 miles from the Observatory to the Pine Springs Visitor Center in the national park. I stopped briefly in Van Horn where I spoke with a lovely couple who, on retiring, had sold their house, and now spent their lives on the road with their articulated pick-up truck and RV home on the back. It all sounded very exciting. I also stopped just as I approached the Guadalupe Mountain Range to take some photos of El Capitan, the second highest peak in Texas, which could be seen for miles. I found myself singing lines from *The WASP (Texas Radio and the Big Beat)* (1971) by The Doors, which seemed to fit the mood nicely.

The Guadalupe Mountain Range became a national park in 1972 when the privately-owned land was donated to the National Parks Service. After a quick orientation from one of the rangers on reception at the visitor centre, it became clear to me that I would be hiking up to the highest point in the park. I had enough time and couldn't resist the prospect of reaching the highest point in Texas – Guadalupe Peak, at nearly 9,000ft. The Guadalupe Peak trail was clearly signposted, with car parking spaces at the foot. It was steep in places, but nothing to bother a reasonably fit person, and no special equipment was required, other than decent shoes, some water, and snacks – which were available at the visitor centre. There weren't many people on the trail, but sufficient numbers so you didn't ever feel completely isolated. I did at one point think that perhaps I should turn back, but someone told me that I was only another twenty minutes from the top at that point, so I ploughed on. I was a little worried that I would be the only idiot at the top in the late afternoon, but I was pleasantly surprised by how many people were milling around the peak. The views from the top were stunning. After the obligatory photo of myself at the official summit, I started off at a brisk pace in order to get to the bottom before dusk. I was also conscious that I needed a room for the night, but not too concerned because I knew that I would be close to two small towns once back at my car. The trail was listed as 8.4 miles round trip, and it took me around four and a half hours, although I was moving at quite a pace coming down.

With more time on my hands I would certainly have walked the trail to McKittrick Canyon, the entrance to which I saw on the road as I headed north out of the park towards Carlsbad Caverns National Park, which I planned to visit the next day. McKittrick Canyon was the location for the opening grisly scenes in Nevada Barr's first novel, *Track of the Cat* (Barr, 1993). She went on to write a string of mystery novels featuring intrepid park ranger Anna Pigeon, whose plots feature many national parks, including Big Bend and Carlsbad Caverns.

Descending into Carlsbad Caverns, New Mexico

Guadalupe and Carlsbad Caverns are less than forty miles apart, but in different states, and worlds apart in nature. I stopped at the town closest to Carlsbad Caverns, Whites City, but – perhaps because of its proximity to the park – I found the rooms a little pricey. The receptionist at one motel told me that the next town had a much bigger and cheaper choice of places to stay. That town was Carlsbad itself, only another ten miles up the road. It was much more of a city than Whites City, which was clearly punching above its weight on the city front. Time was getting on, so I was pleased to see the highway strewn with places to stay on either side of the road as I approached the town. I plumped for one of the cheaper looking places because I knew I'd only be in the room for a few hours. It was also close enough to some restaurants so I wouldn't need to drive anymore. The motel was classic-retro, and probably had hardly changed since it first opened – most likely in the late fifties/early sixties. My room was absolutely huge, with two king-size beds and kitchen facilities. It would have been great value for a family. I had dinner in a huge all-you-can eat style Chinese restaurant just down the road, which was cheap and cheerful.

Carlsbad Caverns

The next morning, I ate breakfast at a diner close to the motel and was soon on my way back down the road to Carlsbad Caverns National Park, just as it was opening. The caverns became a national park in 1930, and can be reasonably explored in 2-3 hours, either self-guided or by joining a ranger guided tour.

Anyone who has been in a cave structure will know what to expect, except the scale is spectacular. Realising at one point that I was 1,000ft below ground made the contrast with the previous afternoon – when I was 9,000ft above ground – rather stark. I also found it difficult to comprehend that the largest 'room' in the caverns – called The Big Room – had been measured at 8.2 acres. For these reasons I was not surprised to learn that Carlsbad Caverns are also a World Heritage Site.

The oddest feature in the caverns seemed to be the huge toilet block buried deep underground. Naturally, this was very convenient, but it also struck me as a little bonkers, particularly knowing how the parks pride themselves on not disturbing the natural environment. That said, the presence of an elevator, underground lunch space, and smooth paved routes throughout the caverns, ensures that the caverns are widely accessible. I spent the whole morning exploring the caverns, after which I had a good wander around the gift shop and had lunch at the restaurant. Over lunch I read about the daily ritual which takes place at dusk, as thousands of bats fly out of the main entrance to the caverns in search of food.

If you are feeling intrepid and have the time (an extra day at least) you could visit one the latest additions to the national park list – White Sands National Park, New Mexico. To do this you would need to head north from Carlsbad on Highway 285, then turn left (west) at Artesia, to join Highway 82. It would be a big detour, but doable. It's a 400 mile round trip. White Sands National Park is a huge area of white gypsum sand dunes, in the northern Chihuahuan Desert, and was re-designated from a national monument in 2019. I undertook this road trip before its re-designation, and it would have been too big a detour for me, given the days I had allocated for this trip.

After finishing my coffee in the visitor centre, it was now time to start making my way back across East Texas. While I was checking my road map, I saw that there was a 10-mile off road loop close by and I decided to head there first. The Walnut Canyon Desert Drive was well signposted, and great fun. Although all the other vehicles were huge American 4x4s, my little hire car had no problem with the ups and downs and twists in the road. After rejoining the paved road, I started my journey east towards Austin. I was keen to get at least halfway that afternoon, so I took what seemed to be the fastest route, by heading back up to Carlsbad town, then south on Highway 285, in order to join the interstate I-10, at Fort Stockton, heading east. I made it as far as Sonora (which also has caves close by), where I stayed overnight at a very pleasant and reasonably priced chain-motel, just off the interstate. I had driven 300 miles since leaving the caverns, so I was very pleased to find a nice diner next door, where I had dinner and then breakfast the next morning.

East Texas Hill Country

Early next morning I was back on I-10. I came off at Highway 290 heading east towards Johnson City because I wanted to visit the home of President Lyndon B. Johnson, which is now owned by the National Park Service. On my way I stopped off at the very German inspired town of Fredericksburg, and from there made an impulsive short detour to the irresistibly sounding Enchanted Mountain State Park. This turned out to be a large pink granite dome, littered with people making the 425ft climb to the top. I couldn't justify the time it would take to do the same, so I made my way back to Highway 290. I was now entering east Texas, locally known as Hill Country. The drive was lovely, and I could understand why so many people are drawn to the area, both to visit and live. I could also see why local boy Lyndon Baines Johnson preferred to conduct presidential business at his home in this Hill Country rather at the White House, his official residency from late 1963 until December 1968. The Lyndon B Johnson National Historical Park is signposted directly off Highway 290, around 15 miles west of

A Slice of Americana Pie

A critical appreciation of: The Texas White House

Lyndon Baines Johnson (LBJ) became the 36th president of the United States in the aftermath of the assassination of President John Fitzgerald Kennedy (JFK) in Dallas on the 22nd November 1963. As Vice-President, LBJ and his wife were in the presidential motorcade that drove through Dallas on that day, just a couple of cars back from the President's car. The Texan location was poignant for the Johnsons because they were due to have the Kennedys stay at their Texas ranch that very evening. The story goes that Lady Bird Johnson had even planned to present Jackie Kennedy with a pecan pie, at her request.

This slice of Americana could had referred to either of the Johnsons, but I have chosen their ranch to encompass both of them and to say something about the 1960s in general in American cultural life. This slice of Americana is therefore much bigger than cars and parks, but LBJ did love his cars and Lady Bird certainly loved the national parks. Indeed, in terms of legislation at least, LBJ arguably begun the modern environmental movement in the USA.

It was the Press who referred to their ranch as The Texas White House because President Johnson preferred to conduct presidential business there whenever he could, rather than at the true White House on Pennsylvania Avenue, Washington, DC. The land surrounding the Johnson's house was so big that it could accommodate a runway and hanger for a presidential jet, which was regularly used by LBJ to shuttle him and his guests to and from Washington, DC. One of LBJ's favourite pastimes was to transfer his guests as soon as he could to one of his convertible Lincoln Continental cars, and take them on a tour of the ranch. Or better still, to transfer them to his amphibious car, which he would deliberately drive into the lake, and then watch as his startled guests slowly realised that they were floating and not sinking. He would also regularly drive around the ranch swigging from a whiskey flask!

The ranch lies just outside Johnson City, in the East Texas Hill Country. The town was not named after him, but does refer to a relative from the past. Although the ranch is now a tourist attraction, it does still have a working side, where LBJ branded cattle can still be seen. Although LBJ dedicated most of his adult life to political affairs you couldn't label him a career politician, because he remained firmly tied to his Texan roots and its outdoor rural pursuits. With this in mind it would have been difficult to argue that LBJ was out of touch with ordinary folk; if anything it was the other way round, with LBJ being out of touch with the Washington elite. He certainly enjoyed giving them a piece of his Texan mind. The evidence for which can be found on the numerous taped telephone conversations he had with them, including the heads of the three TV companies at the time of his presidency. Extracts from some of these phone calls can be listened to when visiting the house, including a conversation with civil rights leader, Martin Luther King Jr.

LBJ's presidency came at a time of enormous cultural change in American society, the legacy of which is still being felt today. He was behind the escalation of the Vietnam

War, which resulted in American troops remaining there until the mid-seventies, and thereby, unintentionally, he helped establish the anti-War movement, which spilled over into broader anti-establishment feelings and other counter-culture movements. He was also instrumental in orchestrating the domestic War on Poverty, including affirmative action policies, the establishment of the Medicaid health-care program, and policies which significantly advanced the civil rights movement – after some pushing by Martin Luther King Jr. and significant peaceful protests. He even helped (indirectly) to establish the rationale behind the long running TV series *Sesame Street*, which was originally part of the Head Start program, begun under his administration, and aimed at raising the aspirations and achievements of disadvantaged social groups.

LBJ also oversaw the race to the moon, initiated by JFK, which culminated in the three Apollo 11 astronauts successfully returning from the moon in July 1969, and before the decade was out, just as JFK had predicted. In the area just outside his house you will find the hand prints of several of the Apollo program's astronauts, cast in concrete slabs, or 'friendship stones'. These stones also include the hand prints of dignitaries from around the world who visited The Texas White House during his presidency.

In and around The Texas White House you can also find beautiful examples of Americana, including paraphernalia associated with hi-tech communication for the period. You can also see TV sets arranged in banks of three in rooms around the house, so he could keep an eye on what each channel was broadcasting. There is also a small CIA monitoring facility in the back yard.

All the living rooms have been restored to how they would have looked in the 1960s. The one exception to the nostalgia is Lady Bird's bedroom, which has the furniture and wallpaper from how she left it before she died. Whereas LBJ died shortly after the end of his presidency, Lady Bird outlived him by more than 30 years, and regularly stayed in the house throughout that period. In her bedroom there is also the evidence of her interests, including bird watching and wildlife preservation. Lady Bird was particularly interested in the national parks and initiated a 'beautification' movement in the USA. She is commemorated in the Redwood National Park in California through the establishment of the Lady Bird Johnson Grove, and in Washington D.C., through the renaming of a small island on the Potomac River, now known as Lady Bird Johnson Park.

Although LBJ won the presidential campaign of 1964 with a landslide victory, he chose not to seek re-election in 1968. He assumed that he would die young, and even took up smoking again in retirement. He had previously quit on medical advice after a heart attack. He died in 1973 at the age of 64. Lady Bird died in 2007 at the age of 94. Both are buried in the grounds of the ranch. The Texas White House, or the home of LBJ, is now administered by the National Parks Service. Entry to the grounds is free, but there is a small charge to have a tour of the house. It is well worth it. The ranch is near Stonewall, 14 miles west of Johnson City, in East Texas.

Johnson City. The park includes his adult home, his family burial plot, a small CIA monitoring station, plane hangar and runway, and you can also drive around the large grounds of the ranch, on which you will find 'LBJ' branded cattle. I found the whole place absolutely fascinating [see The Texas White House Slice of Americana Pie].

At this point I was only around fifty miles from Austin, so I took some more time out to wander around the antique shops in downtown Johnson City, and to look up some potential places to stay in Austin. They all seemed a bit pricey, but I was determined to spend some time in Austin, a place I had wanted to visit for many years. As I approached the city, I had a slight sinking feeling that the laid-back vibe I was looking forward to might not be so apparent. This was truly a city, with many high-rise buildings and a busy road network. By the time I arrived in town I was getting tired, so I took a chance on one of the chain-motels I saw from the highway. It looked far enough out of town so as not to be too expensive, but close enough that I would be able to walk downtown. Luckily, I got it all about right, and it included free secure parking in the motel grounds. I was also lucky that the $75 I paid for the room was due to rise to $115 the following night, because Austin was about to host the American Formula One Grand Prix. I should have been aware of this but having spent the last ten days in another world I was completely oblivious.

I didn't need to head downtown Austin to find somewhere to eat because there were several places just across the highway from my motel, which you could cross by bridge. I also discovered a bike hire docking station just around the corner, which meant I could hire a bike the following morning and head off into town in no time. Early the next morning I did exactly that, using my credit card to secure my bike. I spent the morning touring around the town, including a visit to the very impressive Capitol Building; the campus of the University of Texas; and several secondhand shops in the hip area around South Congress (sometimes known as SoCo). As with all similar bike hire schemes there are numerous docking stations around the town, where you can drop off a bike and pick up another one when you are ready.

Austin is only 75 miles north of San Antonio International Airport, via I-35, so I didn't feel under any pressure to cut short my visit to Austin. I had got everything ready for the journey back to the UK the previous evening, so my luggage was all good-to-go, and I had checked in for my flight on the internet. Returning the hire car was simple and quick. From my experience, hire car return signs are always clear at airports and San Antonio was no different. The only slight panic is always whether there will be a convenient petrol station to make sure the tank is full up before you return the hire car. But I have got into the habit of looking for petrol stations at the beginning of a trip, and I knew, on this occasion, that I would have a good choice reasonably close to the airport.

My flight was an early evening one to Detroit and then a connecting flight back to Heathrow. Unfortunately, my initial flight was severely delayed. It looked like the majority of people on that flight would also be making transfer flights out of Detroit. All those flying onto Europe were reassured that our transatlantic flight companies were aware of the delay, and that we would all make it on to flights to our ultimate destinations that evening. The delay ended up being over four hours, but we were all given food vouchers, and I did make it back to Heathrow the following morning, even if it was closer to lunchtime than breakfast.

Conclusion

Texas had turned out to be a fascinating state to explore. I had travelled across Texas before – on a Greyhound bus, heading west from Houston – but had always harboured thoughts that this was not a state for me. I found its politically conservative – even reactionary – reputation rather off-putting. This was neatly encapsulated by a gay comedian, whose show I enjoyed one evening in a comedy club in Chicago. He joked that he was nervous about taking his show to Texas because he had heard that before settling on the state slogan 'Don't mess with Texas', they had considered 'Back up, Faggott!'.

My experience on this road trip had, thankfully, dispelled many myths about Texas. Yes, there are some scary looking guys driving around with bull horns on the hoods of their pick-up trucks, and the joke about chicken being considered a vegetable in Texas had played on my mind (because I'm a vegetarian). But every single person I interacted with was kind, generous, and interesting to talk to. And this even included the stern-looking border patrol guards who stopped me close to the Mexican border. They were only doing their job and once they could see that I wasn't carrying – or doing – anything suspicious, they politely entertained my questions about their job. At one point on the trip, while I was driving through the East Texas Hill Country, I even imagined that I could live in Texas..

And the driving! Texas is a real treat when it comes to road tripping. You get near empty roads, plenty of places to pull over and rest up, and wonderful vistas. All of this should provide enough opportunity to unwind, think big thoughts, and engage in quiet reflection, along with the prospect of looking for that next adventure and whatever else might come your way. Some of that could certainly be found in Big Bend National Park and The Guadalupe Mountains.

With a little bit of forethought you could extend this road trip to include a trip across the Texas-Arizona border to visit two parks I haven't made it to: Petrified Forest and Saguaro. Petrified Forest National Park is the site of thousands of fossilised remains, including crystallised trees. The preservation of Petrified Forest owes much to the efforts of John Muir [see John Muir Slice of Americana Pie]. The park is also on Route 66 [see Route 66 Slice of Americana Pie] so could be included on a road trip down that route or as an extension to the road trip featured in chapter 10. Saguaro National Park is home to over a million giant Saguaro cacti and can be found just north of Tucson, Arizona. Personally, I would consider both parks too much of a stretch for a Texas-based road trip: It's around 400 miles from Carlsbad to Saguaro, and a further 250 or so miles north from there to Petrified Forest.

Chapter 5

West Coast to East Coast via Yellowstone

National Parks: Yosemite, Yellowstone, Grand Teton, Glacier, Badlands, Wind Cave, Gateway Arch, Shenandoah
Other notable sites: Craters of the Moon National Monument, Battle of Little Big Horn National Monument, Mount Rushmore Memorial, Crazy Horse Memorial, The Bridges of Madison County

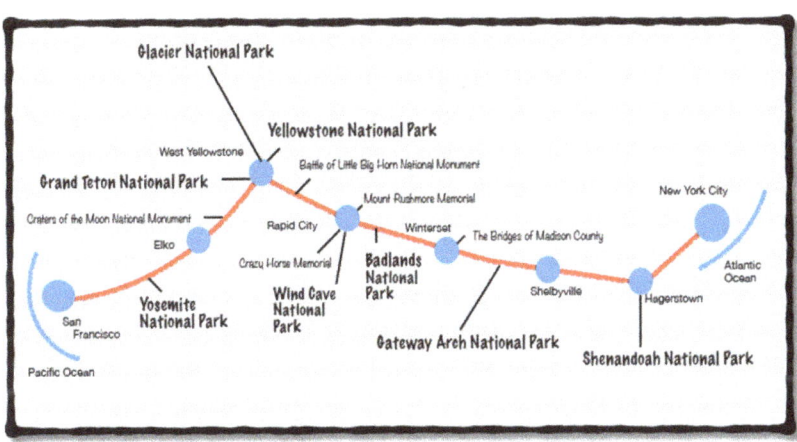

This chapter was composed while singing:

Six Days on the Road, as performed by Steve Earle and the Dukes (1987) and

America, as performed by Simon and Garfunkel (1968)

Introduction

In 2005 I was in the United States undertaking some research for a book I was writing on political correctness. I needed to interview some people in San Francisco and then New York. The obvious thing to do was fly from one city to the other, but I dismissed this option when I began formulating a cross-country drive, to include a visit to Yellowstone. The cartoon characters Yogi Bear and Boo Boo, in Jellystone, started popping into my head, but here was my opportunity to visit the real thing, and the most famous of the American national parks.

Cross-country drives

If you are considering a cross-country drive there are three obvious ways to do it. First, you could hire a car from any one of the car rental outlets. You will need to check that they will allow you to do this, because (unless you intend to come all the way back again) the trip will be one-way – with the car being dropped off in a different city from the one you hired it from. Most outlets will have no problem with this, but you will be charged an excess fee for a one-way drop off, so you will need to factor this in to your costs. You might also consider hiring a slightly bigger car than normal because you will be spending a lot of time in it. This could add to fuel costs, though.

Second, you could consider what is commonly called a 'driveaway', where you take someone's private car from one place to another. This is not unusual in the United States, and there are many companies facilitating the process. On their websites you will see lists of cars, detailing where they are located, where they need to be taken to, the date windows, and any restrictions which may apply. It's a bit hit and miss, and you may need to be very flexible in order to pull this off. Car rental companies are also now running similar 'transfercar' schemes, because they too need to relocate cars and you could ask the rental company you are thinking of hiring from if they need anything transferred to where you are heading.

The third option is to buy a car. This might sound a bit drastic and very expensive, but if you have the time and inclination it could be a good option for a number of reasons. For example, with this option you could look for a very distinctive vehicle – perhaps a classic soft-top, or a van with space to sleep. And you will be able to sell the vehicle when you finish the trip. If you buy a car from a dealer they may have an outlet in the city you are travelling to or know other dealers who might be willing to buy it from you. They might also be able to arrange insurance for you and ensure that the vehicle is properly serviced before you head off. In the process of driving all the way across the US you may well add 3-5,000 miles to the speedometer (odometer), but this is not a huge number by American standards, in which case you might find you could sell the car you have bought for almost as much as you paid for it. If you really like the vehicle you will also have the option of shipping it back to your home country. It costs around $3,000 to ship a car to Europe, but if the vehicle is distinctive in some way you might well find that it is worth a lot more in Europe.

If you live in the UK it is relatively straightforward (and cheap) to re-register an imported vehicle, so long as you have the original American paperwork. And if you have trouble answering some of the questions on the UK forms the internet should come to your rescue, because there are websites detailing the specifications for all kinds of makes and models going back over fifty years. I have done this, and I was pleasantly surprised how quick and easy it was. Within one week the new UK paperwork had arrived, along with a new UK plate number. You will have to get the actual number plates made, but this is cheap and easy if you take the relevant paperwork along to Halfords or any other local place authorised to do this. Naturally, you will need to arrange for an MOT test and get some UK insurance in order to be legal. The MOT garage should also be able to advise you about correct headlight alignment for the UK.

Leaving San Francisco

I started my cross-country Yellowstone road trip on 30 April. This was a rookie error for reasons which will become apparent later, but I had little choice because of my interview schedule. I headed north east from San Francisco on I-80, towards Sacramento and Reno. The apartment I had been renting in San Francisco was actually in Berkeley, so I was on the right side of the Bay, but if you were staying in San Francisco itself, it is relatively straightforward to follow the signs to the Bay Bridge (signposted Berkeley and Oakland) and you'll already be on the I-80 once you've done this. Some ideas for cheap or free things to do in

San Francisco are contained in 'Six things to do in San Francisco' at the end of chapter eight.

If you want to take advantage of driving across the iconic Golden Gate Bridge you could also leave San Francisco on the 101 (heading north), but you need to remember to turn right when you see the signs for The San Rafael Bridge (and the signs to Richmond). You can then pick up the I-80, going north, signposted to Sacramento. Sacramento is the capital city of California but doesn't really merit a stop off on such a trip, and Reno is only worth visiting if you want to give some of your money to the owner of a gambling casino. That said, it is close to Lake Tahoe, on the border of California and Nevada, and the lake is certainly worth seeing. I had been to Lake Tahoe before so didn't stop on this occasion.

Seeing the signs to Lake Tahoe did remind me of the time I followed a makeshift sign directing me to a time-share talk close to the lake. Not that I had any intention of buying into this life-changing opportunity, but it did say that all those who signed up for the talk would get two free nights in a lakeside hotel. Being a poor student at the time this was irresistible, but I wasn't in any way prepared for the seriously hard sell which was about to ensue. I had to endure nearly three hours of sales talk which explained how my life would never be complete until I signed on the line. It was quite easy to resist the pitch because I only had around $500 in my American bank account at the time. I mentioned this fact to one of the sellers in the hope that I might be granted early release, and on the grounds of good behaviour, but instead he took this as a challenge and simply upped his game. I was eventually ejected from the sales wringer, clutching my voucher, so I did get to spend two very pleasant nights in the hotel, as promised. The stay was only tainted by late-night thoughts that there could be a knock on the door, which would then initiate another mad sales loop, from which there would be no escape.

Yosemite National Park is easily within one-day striking distance from San Francisco, and it's a very pleasant route, if a little slow, particularly as you head up to the Yosemite Valley itself. Instead of heading north east out of San Francisco, you would need to drive due east. You still need to cross the Bay Bridge out of San Francisco, but instead of heading north at that point, you will need to turn south by picking up the I-580, which will eventually head east, out towards the west entrance to Yosemite. If you book in advance you could stay in any number of cabins or lodgings in the park itself, or just pull over and stay in one of many motels on the edge of the park. I have stayed in the inexpensive cabins in Yosemite, and never been so cold at night. So it's worth asking yourself what the temperature might be in the middle of the night (regardless of what it was in the day) and whether you have the money to upgrade to some heating. If you wish to head off to Yellowstone after Yosemite you need to exit on the east side of the park, and then head due north to Lake Tahoe and pick up the I-80, heading north and east.

Having visited Yosemite twice before this trip I kept heading north east on I-80, across, Nevada. I stayed overnight in the small town of Elko, at a nice looking, and, as it turned out, cheap motel. I was exhausted, having driven around 500 miles that day. If you have more time than I did the obvious thing to do would have been to split that into two days travel, and possibly include that stop at Yosemite (around halfway).

The next morning, I continued heading north east, but watching carefully for the Highway 93 turn off, so that I could get off the interstate for a while but still be heading in the right direction. This was a good decision and took me through the towns of Twin Falls and then Idaho Falls. On that road I spent some time at a fascinating place called The Craters of the Moon National Monument – which looked exactly as you might imagine from its name. The craters were formed by volcanic activity, along with lava tubes, which produce caves when the outer crust of the lava cools, enabling the inner core of molten lava to keep flowing. The seven-mile loop road could easily have been the conspiracy-theory site for those, so-called, faked Apollo moon landings. It was great being able to get some full-360 degree views, which were all fascinating.

On the road again, I enjoyed a very pleasant time driving through the salt plains (home of various land speed records – for obvious reasons). I arrived at Yellowstone early evening on the second day of driving from San Francisco. I had driven close to 1,000 miles between the two places, so, if you have the time, allocating 3-4 days for this part of the trip could be a good idea.

Yellowstone

Immediately on approaching Yellowstone, I realised the rookie error I had made, because there was snow everywhere, and I could see that many of the roads were closed; they probably hadn't opened from the previous winter. I had naively assumed that by the beginning of May things would be pretty much okay. Not surprising then, that the vast majority of visitors come to Yellowstone in June, July and August.

Yellowstone was the first national park, established in 1872. It occupies over two million acres, on the borders of Idaho, Wyoming and Montana. It is truly an extraordinary place to visit. It is roughly 1,000 miles from San Francisco and 2,000 miles from New York, but metaphorically it is a million miles from anywhere else on the continent. Several vistas offer the possibility of believing that you might actually be on another planet. It is called Yellowstone after the river which runs through it, and there is a famous view in the centre of the park where you can see the river spilling down a canyon, known as the Grand Canyon of the Yellowstone. There is an excellent visitor centre close by there, where you can buy food and souvenirs. You will definitely see wildlife in Yellowstone, including bison, who often wander along the road next to you as you drive. Wolves used to be common in the park but were all but destroyed before being reintroduced in 1995.

The weather situation presented advantages and disadvantages. On the advantages, it was easy to find accommodation and I had a very pleasant two-night stay at a very reasonably priced motel, close to the west entrance to Yellowstone. It also meant that I had the park pretty much to myself a lot of the time. This was a real treat, partly because I could wander around the landscape and take photos without fear of a family suddenly appearing in my shots, but also because I could experience the full eeriness of much of what was around me, including the famous bubbling pools. It also meant I could visit the famous Old Faithful geyser – so-called because of the regularity of its outpourings – without any parking problems, and with only a handful of other visitors. Weather-permitting, the road network will guide you around 150 miles of spectacular scenery and all the main sights are clearly signposted. But just pulling over at any point and taking a stroll is likely to be rewarding.

There were two main disadvantages brought on by the weather. I wasn't going to be able to visit the other national park which is close by, just to the south – Grand Teton – and you should certainly do this (my pass included both parks in one fee, but I don't think this is the case anymore). Grand Teton is a majestic granite mountain range, granted national park status in 1929, although not without controversy, due to the activities of the billionaire Rockefeller family. They bought up a lot of the land around the mountain range, in order to protect it, much to the annoyance of the locals. This stand-off took many years to formally resolve, but from the mid-forties an area of protected national park land had been clearly demarcated.

**The Grand Canyon of the Yellowstone River,
Yellowstone National Park, Wyoming**

The weather situation also meant that I needed to leave the park by travelling north and then east, effectively skirting the eastern side of the park, which was closed. This meant adding many more miles onto my journey than I had anticipated. That said, my route was spectacular, and I got to experience some of the wide-open spaces of Montana as well as Wyoming. If you have more time than I did this is the obvious point from which to continue north towards Glacier National Park, which, as its name implies, is a spectacular glacial landscape. The area became a national park in 1910 but required a lot of marketing due to its somewhat remote location. Even travelling up from Yellowstone you can expect to be on the road for around six hours, covering nearly 400 miles. In effect, you will have crossed the whole of the State of Montana, from south to north, and be on the Canadian border by the time you arrive in the park. Clearly, you should not undertake this journey lightly, particularly if, like me, you are travelling coast to coast. But if your intention is to remain in this part of the US, you could certainly visit Yellowstone, Grand Teton and Glacier comfortably in a week to ten days depending on where you start from. Bozeman, Montana has an airport and would be an obvious place to start and finish from.

My exit route from Yellowstone took me north on Highway 191, through a marvellous original stone gateway to Yellowstone, which had etched on it President Theodore Roosevelt's democratic statement about the national parks being 'for the benefit and enjoyment of the people'. I continued on to I-90, where I turned right towards Bozeman and Billings. If you wanted to visit Glacier National Park this would be the point where you would turn left to get on I-90 going west (towards Butte). For me, one of the nice consequences of my enforced detour was that I got to stop off at the Little Bighorn Battlefield National Monument (or Custer's last stand), which is directly off I-90 after Billings. The Battle of Little Bighorn took place in June 1876, when the American 7th Cavalry, lead by George Armstrong Custer battled with Lakato and Cheyenne Indians, led by Sitting Bull and Crazy Horse, in the vicinity of the Bighorn River in Idaho. Two years earlier, the Americans had pledged to protect the Indians, but a gold rush in the nearby Black Hills had brought an influx of white outsiders onto the protected land. A stand-off soon became inevitable, and the ensuing battle was won by the Indians, but, as we now know, they were not to win the war.

The Black Hills of Dakota

I was heading east towards Rapid City because I wanted to visit the famous Mount Rushmore National Memorial. This is a must-see on any cross-country journey particularly if you are travelling across the northern part of the country. The memorial features the heads of four American presidents, carved out of the rock face.

It was the brain-child of the historian Doane Robinson, who wanted to attract visitors to the Black Hills of Dakota and he approached the sculptor Gutzon Borglum with a view to carving something into the hills. The original idea was to celebrate the wild west, but Borglum suggested that it should be presidents because of the potential wider appeal. After the funds were secured the project began in 1927 and was completed in 1941. Completed may not be the right word, because by that time further funding was becoming problematic and plans to include the presidents' waists were abandoned. Borglum chose to carve George Washington, Thomas Jefferson, Theodore Roosevelt and Abraham Lincoln, because he considered them the most significant presidents.

Mount Rushmore National Memorial, Black Hills of South Dakota

Environmentally unfriendly and intrusive on the one hand, but a marvel of human ingenuity and artistic flair on the other hand, Mount Rushmore is so American it almost *had* to exist. For a start it's huge, and it's more than a little bizarre. It is there simply because it can be, and because of its commercial potential in attracting visitors. It's also *politically* controversial, because The Black Hills are sacred to Native Americans, so what *are* these carved presidents actually saying to indigenous people? All that said, I was certainly glad I experienced it first-hand and being a fan of Hitchcock films, I was irresistibly drawn to it, because some of the scenes from the film *North by Northwest* (1959) were filmed there. Not however the famous chase scene across the heads themselves, which Hitchcock could not get permission for – sacrilege of a white American kind this time – and anyway, he preferred 'lot' filming, so he had the heads reconstructed back in Hollywood [see Hitchcock Movies Slice of Americana Pie].

The Black Hills of South Dakota is a fascinating area to explore, and worthy of at least one week's exploration on its own. I stayed at a pleasant and relatively cheap inn, which was only a short distance from Mount Rushmore. Staying here also provided me the next morning with an opportunity to travel the seventeen miles south west to visit another spectacular carving – of the legendary Native American hero, Crazy Horse, from the Lakato tribe. The carving is more spectacular than Mount Rushmore for two main reasons. First, the carving of Crazy Horse is bigger than Mt Rushmore, and that's just his head; eventually the carving will include his horse. And second, it is very much a labour of love, overseen by one family. The scale is breathtaking. Crazy Horse's head is nearly 100 feet in height, and his outstretched arm is over 250 feet long. By comparison, Mount Rushmore is only 60ft from the top to the bottom of the presidents' heads, and I haven't even mentioned the dimensions of the horse. Lest you be disappointed, let me say that this monument is very much work in progress. Work began in 1948 and nobody knows when it will be finished. The original sculptor died in the 1980s and the project is now in the hands of his children and grandchildren, but still overseen by his surviving wife.

The Crazy Horse Memorial was commissioned by Henry Standing Bear, a Lakota elder, after his permission was sought by the local sculptor Korczak Ziolkowski, who had worked for a while on the Mount Rushmore site. It too is not without controversy, because some native Americans believe that elders must consult first with their tribes and there doesn't seem to be much evidence for this. In addition, from what is known about Crazy Horse, it is doubtful that he would have approved of his image being used in this way. And it is unclear how close the carving resembles the man anyway, because there is no photographic evidence. There is also that issue again of the Black Hills being considered sacred, and whether blasting away at the rock, in the ways required to complete the sculpture, is an act of disrespect. To cap it off, the family overseeing the project are not of the Lakota tribe themselves, which has naturally caused some discontent, and because the family are very protective of the project – and determined to work at their own pace – any talk of completion is highly speculative. By comparison, Mount Rushmore was completed in less than fifteen years.

The Badlands

Given the amount of time I spent at the Crazy Horse Memorial site, which I don't regret, it meant I needed to get moving. If you have more time than I did this is obviously the point from which to explore the Badlands National Park. You could stay in Rapid City, because from there it would be easy visit Mount Rushmore, Crazy Horse and Badlands (and even Wind Cave National Park, if you put your mind to it). But if, like me, you needed to get moving you could still position yourself on the I-90 heading east and get to experience some of the Badlands, particularly if you follow the Badlands Loop. To do this you will need to leave the interstate at Wall and head south on Highway 240. Make sure you start heading east rather than back into the main part of the park, and then head north to return back up to the I-90. This involves a thirty mile detour, and will obviously be much slower than continuing on the interstate, but by doing this you will be in the park itself.

The Badlands National Park was established in 1978, although it had been a national monument before then. It is a vast, inhospitable, but mesmerising, series of limestone spires. Inhospitable to humans but it is home to a range of hardy animals, including sheep and bison. Wind Cave National Park was established much earlier in 1903. It is exactly as its name implies, a giant cave where atmospheric pressure causes rushes of wind to emerge from its entrance. The park is only small but contains a wide variety of animals including bison and elk. You only need to pay an entrance fee if you go in the cave itself. Both Wind Cave and The Badlands are around sixty miles from Rapid City. For The Badlands you need to travel east on the I-90, but for Wind Cave you will need to head south from Rapid City.

If you want to visit Mount Rushmore, Crazy Horse and Wind Cave together in one day, you need to get on Highway 244 heading west from Rapid City, and then Highway 385 heading south. Each site is well signposted. One problem with a cross-country run is that there doesn't seem to be an easy route from Wind Cave across to the Badlands

National Park without first heading back to Rapid City. Some careful planning may be required if you want to visit both parks in one day. Due to my time limitations, I didn't head down as far as Wind Cave. I also hadn't found the time the previous day to visit the town of Deadwood (Wild Bill Hickok, Calamity Jane and all that). It's a short detour south on Highway 85, from the I-90 – but before you reach Rapid City, if were travelling east.

There's also a much longer detour available, due south from the town of Wall, to visit Wounded Knee (around 75 miles). The small town commemorates the last official battle in the so-called Indian Wars between the new American forces and the indigenous Native American tribes – in this case, the Sioux-Lakato (1890). It is also known to be the burial site for Crazy Horse, and was used in the title of the best-selling book by Dee Brown (1970), which charts the Native American experience of invasion by the armies of the new white settlers.

It is around this point on a cross country journey – if it has not become clear already – that you realise just how vast and intimidating the landscape of the United States can be. It also becomes crystal clear around this point just how resourceful and resilient the Native American tribes were, particularly those who inhabited The Badlands and surrounding lands. Equally, it is also clear just what a challenge it must have been for the various wagon trains, made up of ex-European would-be settlers, as they made their way westwards across the continent. Of course, the modern traveller not only has the car or Greyhound bus as long-distance road transport choices, but also the steel horse, and it is not uncommon to see a small fleet of them cruising along the highway [see Harley Davidson Motorcycles Slice of Americana Pie].

I pulled into a Conoco gas station and service area to fill up. I instantly loved the stark contrast on display: I was in the middle of a wild nowhere, but here was an edifice of American modernity. As I headed off to the restroom I was singing lines from Springsteen's *Badlands* (1978), but once inside I tuned into a loud conversation between three old Americans hunched over their urinals. They were reminiscing about how they used to be able to pee over a gate, but now had to push just to get a trickle. Once back in the car their conversation made my mind fixate on the line in the Springsteen song about the need to keep pushing.

As I steamed east on I-80, lost in my thoughts about the vastness of my surroundings, I suddenly found my road revelry rudely interrupted by the sight of kicked-up road dust in my rear mirror. It was a police car crossing the central reservation, now going in my direction, with its siren and flashing lights in clear view. It approached my small convoy of cars, in which I was last in line. Damn, it was me he wanted to pull over. There was no cop in sight, and then, out of the blue, there he was. The customary exchange took place, but not before I had seen him approach me on foot in my wing mirror, when I clocked that he could not have been more than seventeen years old (surely)? He explained to me that I was doing 89mph in a 75mph speed zone area and that he would have to 'ticket' me. I protested on two fronts: that all the other cars were going the same speed as me, and that the road was wide open and devoid of anything which could cause a problem. Naturally, it made no difference. Indeed, I think I made it worse for myself. He explained that untrained people are a danger when travelling at this speed. I replied by stating that I'd driven much faster on German autobahns. His face clearly indicated that he didn't like my reply. The fine was $99, but he explained that it only had the status of a parking ticket in South Dakota, from which I took some comfort. I also took some comfort from the fact that he didn't see the half-opened bottle of red wine I was saving for that evening. Technically, it's illegal to carry any alcohol in the passenger part of a vehicle and only unopened alcohol containers are allowed to be stored elsewhere.

The Mid-West

Trying to forget about the speeding injustice which had been metered out to me and, wondering how I was actually going to pay the fine, I continued at a very speed-legal pace towards Sioux City and Des Moines (childhood hometown of the travel writer Bill Bryson). My mood was lifted by reflecting on the unlikely road trip made by Alvin Straight in the summer of 1994. He travelled east from his hometown of Laurens, Iowa, (a little way north from my current location) to visit his brother, Henry, in Blue River, Wisconsin. The two towns are only 250 miles apart, but he made the journey on his John Deere lawnmower, which took six weeks to complete. The journey is dramatised in the David Lynch film *Straight Story* (1999).

A Slice of Americana Pie

A critical appreciation of: Harley Davidson Motorcycles

Talk to many bike enthusiasts and they will tell you that the Harley is not the best of motorcycles; far from it. Many of its models are cumbersome and not particularly fast – hence the nickname 'hog'. But culturally, what better symbolises the freedom of the open road than the image of someone cruising along on a Harley? The Harley has become synonymous with that freedom, along with some rebellion thrown in for good measure. And if there's one thing that the United States excels in, it has to be branding, and Harley is surely one of its most famous brands. The very name has an allure which is hard to beat, even if its detractors persist in derogatory name calling, such as 'Hardly Able Son'.

Even if we were to accept that the Japanese (even the English), on balance, perhaps do make better motorcycles, Harley Davidson was in the right place at the right time and was gifted some of its iconic status because of that. The company's rise coincided exactly with the growth in petrol engine transportation, along with its promise of freedom and adventure. What better country to promote this promise than in the wide-open spaces of the United States, steeped in a cowboy pioneer spirit of trailblazing and fending for oneself, unfettered by authority. Not surprising then that the motorbike quickly became referred to as a steel horse, replacing one horsepower with multiples. Yes, that other great American motorcycle company, Indian, could easily have taken on *the* American brand mantle, and perhaps it did for a while (at least until 1954, when the company stopped production), but the Harley won out – to become *the* cultural icon, if not as the perfectly engineered motorbike.

All that said, some of the most famous motorbikes to appear in American films were not Harleys, including the Triumph that Marlon Brando rides in *The Wild One* (1953), and the Triumph that Steve McQueen (anachronistically) rides in *The Great Escape* (1963). But Brando did at least own a Harley, and Peter Fonda and Dennis Hopper *were* riding Harleys in *the* most iconic of all the biker films, *Easy Rider* (1969) – even if they were highly customised. And Arnold Schwarzenegger was riding a Harley Fat Boy in the film *Terminator 2* (1991). But none of this really seems to matter that much, because ask any number of Europeans who might be contemplating riding the Lincoln Highway [see Lincoln Highway Slice of Americana Pie] or Route 66 [see Route 66 Slice of Americana Pie] and it would be highly likely that they would also be contemplating doing it on a Harley.

And who needs advertising campaigns when your product has celebrity approval? Trawl through internet images and you find the likes of George Clooney, Justin Timberlake, John Travolta, and Pink, all sitting proudly on their Harleys, and from the more glamorous period in Hollywood history, both Cary Grant and Elizabeth Taylor were known to love a Harley. The Harley was also the choice of bike for the famous stunt rider Evel Knievel when he used a XR750 to make his longest leap – over 14 Greyhound buses in 1975.

Harley Davidson are the surnames of the two friends who formed the company in 1903. They began work from a small workshop in Milwaukee, Wisconsin, where, today, you will find the Harley Davidson Museum. They were later joined by two of Davidson's brothers. But they didn't have the best of starts. It appeared to be hard to get a motorcycle up a hill, and for a while they flirted with bicycles, before finally fixing their attention on producing a decent motorbike for a growing consumer market. They specialised in producing big-engined bikes and were able to patent some of their design features. That said, many of the company's bikes over the years have been heavily customised by enthusiastic owners, and the bikes have become synonymous with the 'chopper' or 'chop' scene.

The company has proven to be remarkably resilient, in the face of some bad judgements, unfortunate government decisions, and some unpopular bikes. And there seems to have been a clear revival of fortunes in recent years. So much so, that the now iconic orange and black signage is unmistakable even to people who have never owned a motorbike, at dealerships and in the branded products found in department stores. The company also now seems much clearer about its products – producing lighter and better handling bikes, with more than a nod to classic motorbike styling. I wouldn't mind betting that even when one of these bikes is sat next to a better engineered bike on any street corner, who is not seduced – even if it's just for a moment – by the allure of jumping on the Harley and cruising off *outta* town? Count me in.

The cementing of the Harley brand in popular consciousness seems to have as much to do with the position of the motorbike in general as a rebellious symbol of unfettered individual freedom, as anything the company itself has managed to produce. But maybe the two things have always been riding 'hand-in-glove'?

It is difficult to mess with an icon, so it will be interesting to see how companies like Harley Davidson are able to navigate the new world of e-bikes and potential new markets – including a growing female bike culture. That said, as with so many examples of Americana, it is the very fact that they have a nostalgic appeal to a mythical past, which grants them their strong emotional attachments. And is it possible to ever take control and engineer these attachments? In the case of motorbikes, perhaps it's just too soon to think about dismantling a deeply ingrained Wild West image of a cowboy, living the life of an individual in the great outdoors unfettered by government interference? And perhaps we should remember just how easy it was to substitute a real horse for a steel horse in the popular American consciousness.

In conclusion, do we find here a good example of the contradiction often at play in the very concept of Americana: the symbolic appeal to something at the very heart of American culture, but the need to wear some rose-tinted aviator sunglasses to fully appreciate it?

I was heading towards the small town of Winterset (just a little south of Des Moines). By all accounts, it is a nondescript Mid-West town, but to me it held the prospect of a whole host of delights, including old unrestored diners, second hand shops, and old garages and filling stations. It didn't disappoint. I stayed overnight in a chain-motel, just outside town. I chose this particular town because I would then be in Madison County and close to the covered bridges made famous in the novel by Robert James Waller (1993) and the subsequent film (1995) starring Clint Eastwood and Meryl Streep. The now famous covered bridges – all seven of them – are scattered around the area, and I spent the following morning locating all of them. This included the Roseman Bridge – the one made famous by the books and film. I noticed that some of the local roads had been renamed after characters from the books, which struck me as a good example of life imitating art. Before I left Winterset, I popped along to see the house where John Wayne was born, which was certainly worth a photo.

I continued east, at first poodling along some very typical Mid-West highways (mainly Highway 34) with the obligatory corn fields and red barns on either side of the road. I then turned onto the interstate (I-74) in order to make up some time. I crossed the Mississippi River at Burlington, where it was difficult not to think of Mark Twain's *Adventures of Huckleberry Finn* (1884), and the dilemmas that teachers continuously face when dealing with aspects of racism. I was in the middle of writing a book about political correctness, and I quickly got lost in a string of thoughts about the n-word and whether publishers should remove that word when republishing literature from the past. I also found myself singing *Ol' Man River* (1927) – a tune which had its lyrics changed over the years for the same reasons. This was also the tune which I believe inspired Paul Simon when composing *Bridge Over Troubled Water* (1970). I was heading towards Indianapolis and Cincinnati. I stopping overnight at a chain-motel just off the freeway at the small town of Shelbyville, halfway between the two.

If you wanted to visit one of the newest national parks – Gateway Arch National Park – you would need to ensure that St. Louis, Missouri, is included on your cross-country route. It's a good idea because St. Louis is an interesting city, located on the Mississippi River, and the city where the famous Highway 61 [see Highway 61 Slice of Americana Pie] intersects the famous Route 66 [see Route 66 Slice of Americana Pie]. Down by the river you will find the famous 630ft stainless steel arch, known as the Gateway to the West, which honours President Thomas Jefferson's role in opening up the west of the country to white settlers, and the pioneering expedition of Meriwether Lewis and William Clark at the beginning of the 19th Century (known as the Lewis and Clarke expedition).

The Roseman covered bridge, Madison County, Iowa

It's a great trip up to the top of the Gateway Arch in a little tram car, and there's a viewing platform at the top. Originally known as the Jefferson National Expansion Memorial the whole area around the Arch has now been re-designated as Gateway Arch National Park (2018). It's the first urban-based national park, and it remains to be seen if more will follow. I had visited St. Louis several times before so didn't include it on my itinerary this time, but it can be easily reached by heading south on Interstate 55, which connects St Louis with Chicago (following the original path of Route 66). You would only need to allocate a couple of hours to visit the park, and it's well signposted, on the banks of the Mississippi River. There are lots of parking options around the area, but no car park at the park itself, so you may have to add some time for parking and getting to and from the park.

North and south

The next morning, after checking the map, I became aware that there was still a fair way to go to New York. I had arranged a meeting with someone at New York University a few days later and it began playing on my mind. I continued to watch the speed limit signs as I tried to get as close to the east coast as I could that day. My odometer indicated that I had covered over 1500 miles since leaving the north entrance of Yellowstone a couple of days before.

I continued on the interstate to Columbus, Ohio and I ended up staying in a reasonably priced chain-motel in Hagerstown (again, simply because it was convenient and because I physically couldn't drive any further). This was a further 500 miles from my previous night's stop. That evening, as I enjoyed a cheap Mexican meal, I checked the map because I wasn't sure what state I was in. Turned out I was in Maryland and before that I had been in West Virginia. I'd always considered West Virginia to be part of the south, so I was surprised to see how far north it stretched.

Critical Cultural Comment – The Concept of the American South

The question of what divides the north from the south in the United States is a complicated one. Yes, states like Arizona and New Mexico are in the south (geographically), but they are not states that would jump to the American mind when speaking of *The* South (whereas Alabama and Georgia most certainly would). And when Neil Young sang the tune *Southern Man* (1970) it was clear that this was a cultural reference, not a geographic one – and ditto for his scathing song *Alabama* (1972). To which the band Lynyrd Skynyrd famously provided The South's retort when they sang *Sweet Home Alabama* (1974), which celebrated The South and reinforced the cultural divide. The lyrics of the Lynyrd Skynyrd song initially appear to be somewhat reactionary, but there is a subtle subversive quality running through them. And in his autobiography Neil Young confirms his feeling that his original accusatory lyrics had been somewhat ill-conceived (Young, 2012). The controversy testifies to how complicated this cultural divide actually is.

> The South is sometimes called Dixie – a reference to the Mason-Dixon Line. This boundary line was surveyed by two British men, Charles Mason (an astronomer) and Jeremiah Dixon (a surveyor) and completed in 1767. Their story was celebrated in the song *Sailing to Philadelphia* (2000) where Marc Knopfler sings the lines for Jeremiah Dixon and James Taylor for Charles Mason. The song was based on the fictionalised account of the two men in the novel by Thomas Pynchon (Pynchon, 1997). Mason and Dixon were originally commissioned to undertake the survey work in order to settle the land border dispute between the States of Philadelphia and Maryland, and they laid stones to mark the boundary (some of which are still there).
>
> However, a wider cultural divide soon became apparent when the extended westward boundary started to be viewed as a demarcation line between the northern states who had abolished slavery, and the southern ones who hadn't. This culminated in the boundary signifying the two sides in the American Civil War (1861-65) – with The South comprising the confederacy of 11 southern states – Alabama, Arkansas, North and South Carolina, Florida, Georgia, Louisiana, Mississippi, Tennessee, Texas, and Virginia – who all wished to remain independent of the union of United States. The legacy of the Civil War was graphically retold through the eyes of black American experience in the novel *Beloved* by Toni Morrison (1987). Its subsequent acclaim and criticism attesting to how deep the cultural divide still remains.

Both Maryland and West Virginia were considered border states in the American Civil War, so it turned out that I had been accidentally following the boundary of the north-south divide, and the westward extension of the Mason-Dixon Line. The scenery was spectacularly green and rolling, and I wasn't surprised to see from the map that I was near the Appalachian Mountains. From Hagerstown it is possible to head due south on the I-81 into the Appalachians and Shenandoah National Park. For me, that trip was going to be for another day (this park features in chapter nine) You might also want to make the same decision if you are doing a cross country run because if you are going to visit Shenandoah it makes sense to combine this with a visit to the Great Smoky Mountains, and that will involve you heading some way south; very much into *The* South.

The other thing I had checked over dinner the previous evening was that I was now only 250 miles from New York City. I knew the journey into the city itself would be slow, but I thought I would still have enough time on my hands to take it relatively easy and arrive late in the afternoon. This turned out to be correct.

The next morning I left Highway 30 in Philadelphia and headed onto the famous New Jersey Turnpike (a toll road, with variable rates depending on where you enter and leave). Some maps show the road only as the I-95. The turnpike took me straight into New York City, after I had past signs to Gettysburg (location of the famous Civil War battle), Hershey (hometown of the famous American chocolate) and Trenton (home of the famous Ivy League university, Princeton). I also pulled over for a coffee at a sprawling truck stop, where I enjoyed taking some photos of the huge, and often decorated, rigs, which were parked up. The rest area had what appeared to me, at first sight, to be a rather bizarre church – within a small mobile port-a-cabin – along with a statue of Christ. But, on reflection, I concluded that this was perfectly reasonable: for truck drivers who may – after spending long periods on the road – find themselves in need of some spiritual (if only Christian) succour. I also liked it because it helped dispel the myth that long distance truck drivers only ever seek the pleasures of the flesh. I suppose a combo was also an option.

Entering New York City

From the New Jersey side, you can enter New York City via the Lincoln Tunnel or the Holland Tunnel, or, further north, across the George Washington Bridge – all of which will cost you money. Many people will advise not driving into New York City at all, certainly not into the borough of Manhattan, but I had no choice because I needed to return the rental car, and drop off my stuff at the apartment I had rented on West 21st Street.

If you avoid the obvious commuter times and have a sense of how the road grid pattern works, driving in Manhattan is not the nightmare it might appear. Essentially, the avenues head north-south, and the streets head east-west, and if a street is one way then the next one is likely to be going the other way. Some avenues and streets have names, but most just have numbers, with the low avenue numbers starting on the east side, and the low street numbers starting in the south. 5th Avenue determines the east-west divide; so, for example, West 21st Street (where I was heading) would be west of 5th Avenue. More advice and tips about spending time in and around New York City can be found in chapter seven, including airport information, and see 'Six things to do in New York' at the end of chapter seven for some cheap or free things to do.

My biggest problem turned out to be trying to find a gas station in Manhattan, so I could return the car with a full tank. Shouting my question at a cab driver through the car window while at a stop light got me a result, though.

Conclusion

I had been six days on the road in order to complete this cross-country road trip. I was pushing it a bit because I had commitments at the other end. It would be possible to undertake such a trip in five days if you just want the experience of being on the road, and certainly if you were sharing the driving. Allocating ten days would mean that you could be quite relaxed about the trip and still get to visit at least two or three national parks and some other interesting monuments. Yellowstone, Grand Teton and the Badlands would be the obvious ones, but you could fit in Shenandoah or Yosemite or Wind Cave as well, if you put your mind to it. If you wanted to extend the trip to fourteen days you would certainly be able to include both Shenandoah and Yosemite and Wind Cave, or you could be more adventurous and head north to include Glacier National Park. But I wouldn't underestimate the size of the detour to Glacier National Park.

Any cross-country trip is likely to involve between 3,500 – 5,000 miles of driving, depending on the number of detours to places of interest. As always, interstate freeways will get you places fast, but the old highways are often what makes the trip worth taking – particularly if you want to taste some on-the-road Americana pie.

For some of this road trip I was roughly following the old Lincoln Highway [see Lincoln Highway Slice of Americana Pie], particularly at the beginning (the San Francisco leg) and at the end (the New York leg). The middle part of the original Lincoln Highway included Chicago and headed across Nebraska, both of which would have been unrealistic for me given the places I wanted to visit and in the time I had. I have

A Slice of Americana Pie

A critical appreciation of: The Lincoln Highway

The Lincoln Highway was the first cross country highway in the United States, conceived by Carl G. Fisher, in 1912. Fisher was an early 'petrol head' and set about convincing similarly minded people that the automobile would not come into its own until it had decent roads to run on. He formed the Lincoln Highway Association in order to raise the funds for a transcontinental route, which would help put the car on the same footing as the train. It took a while to settle on the uncontroversial name for the project, and – perhaps surprisingly – it was not supported by Henry Ford who believed that such infrastructure projects needed government, not private, funding. After reconnaissance work from key members of the team – who attempted to drive the agreed route – construction began in 1913. The team were lobbied by town representatives along the proposed route, but the Association eventually settled on what they considered to be the most direct route from the east coast to the west, totally over 3,000 miles.

Like Route 66 [see Route 66 Slice of Americana Pie] it is no longer one single highway and some imagination and determination is required to follow the original route. Actually, it was never one single constructed highway but a series of upgrades to already existing roads and historic trails, interconnected by newly built sections. Although originally conceived to be completed by 1915, it wasn't effectively completed until the mid-twenties. Almost immediately, the federal government then decided to start numbering the main highways, State by State. The effect of this was to gradually lose the idea of the need for *national* highway routes.

There were other broader reasons for a loss of interest in national highways. Significantly, many of the new interstate freeways, built in the 1950s and onwards, did not upgrade existing roads but created brand new roads, 'free' from preexisting highway furniture, including towns. These new freeways were thus much faster routes, and as the general pace of life increased, it seems that many of the original highways just lost their allure. This was also, perhaps unwittingly, encouraged by the national obsession with the relentless pursuit of progress and celebration of the modern, without realising what was being lost in the process. Just as the Joni Mitchell song *Big Yellow Taxi* (1971) explains.

All that said, re-discovering the past has now become an enthusiastic pursuit of many American groups and societies, allied with the desire on the part of many individuals to recapture a past which appears better than the present, combined with a new-found nostalgic wish to preserve a heritage. The Lincoln Highway slots neatly into this narrative. The official start of the highway on 42nd Street, in the district of Manhattan in New York City, now proudly displays a red road sign, signalling not just the route but also its historic and cultural significance.

The highway's official finish is at the Legion of Honor in Lincoln Park in San Francisco, but the original roadway abruptly stopped along University Avenue in Berkeley (on the other side of the bay to San Francisco). This was because, until 1936, there was no road bridge connecting the two cities. Now the Bay Bridge, which spans San Francisco Bay – connecting the cities of Berkeley and Oakland with San Francisco – is an integral part of the Bay Area transport network. It is also part of Interstate I-80, which broadly follows the original Lincoln Highway route through Sacramento and up into Reno, Nevada.

There were also logistical problems at the other end, when leaving New York City, because both the Lincoln and Holland tunnels, which connect the island of Manhattan with New Jersey, didn't exist in 1913 (when construction of the Lincoln Highway begun). Early travellers would have needed to catch a ferry across the Hudson River to begin the road journey proper. That said, both tunnels were under construction and probably open by the time that many of the early drivers undertook their first transcontinental road trip. George Washington Bridge, which also connects Manhattan with New Jersey, was also open to traffic from 1931 onwards.

Thanks to the brilliant interactive map designed and created by the new Lincoln Highway Association, formed in 1992, the original route of the Lincoln Highway, along with its numerous changes over the years, can be driven or ridden, and studied. Heading 'out west', what the map shows is that the route broadly followed what is now Highway 30, through Philadelphia and Pittsburgh, Pennsylvania, and then headed north west up to the Great Lakes and the city of Chicago. From Chicago it headed due west, following what is now I-80 into Colorado and on to Salt Lake City, Utah. From here the route dropped south, away from I-80, and followed what is now Highways 93 and 50, towards Lake Tahoe and Reno, Nevada, before picking up the I-80 route again, down into Sacramento and on to San Francisco. If you were to follow the map's route you would have to make a decision whether you wanted to take the various detours, particularly the significant loop in Colorado. Doing this would most likely mean that you would have put many more miles on your odometer than the original Lincoln Highway Association anticipated.

In a modern car, you could easily complete a cross-country road trip comfortably in five days, particularly if you have a co-driver. So, spare a thought for the intrepid folk setting out on the original Lincoln Highway, who would have needed to set aside at least a month to get from one coast to the other. They would also have been lucky to manage more than an average 20mph and would have been constantly on the lookout for places to stay overnight and for places to fill up with gas. Modern motorists still need be on the look-out, probably for their favourite fast food outlet or favourite motel chain. In my case I would also be on the look-out: for some decent coffee, and for those sneaky highway patrol police cars, in case they were hiding behind road-side bushes.

been to Chicago many times and I would certainly recommend a visit there, and surely Nebraska is irresistible to anyone who has listened to the Bruce Springsteen album of the same name. In which case you might want to consider following the route of the old Lincoln Highway all the way across the USA.

You might also consider going coast to coast from 'Back East' to 'Out West' by following the Lincoln Highway from New York (starting on the New Jersey Turnpike) across to Chicago, and then following the route of the original Route 66, all the way to Los Angeles [see Route 66 Slice of Americana Pie]. This will take you to St Louis, Missouri (where you could visit Gateway Arch National Park), on through Oklahoma City, and then into the south west of the US, enabling you to visit both the Petrified Forest and the Grand Canyon national parks. When you hit California on Route 66, you could also visit Death Valley National Park and Joshua Tree National Park (see chapter ten for more details about this route and parks).

Whichever direction you drive, it's worth reflecting on the fact that a cross-country trip is likely to involve you travelling over parts of the Appalachian, Rocky, and Sierra Nevada mountain ranges. Most likely, you will be on a bus, in a car, or on a motorbike, unlike the original would-be new American settlers who set off from the east coast in search of new homelands in wooden wagon trains. Some of these would have made their way over all three of these mountain ranges.

However you decide to do it, a coast to coast road trip is certainly worth contemplating, and will, no doubt, stay with you for some time, whether you try get some of your kicks on that old Route 66 and/ or follow the path of those intrepid early petrol heads on the Lincoln Highway. Both routes will also give you access to a large number of national parks – even more if you consider making your own detours. Although I really enjoy driving in the United States, I have also taken the Greyhound bus all the way from New York to Los Angeles, stopping off at the Grand Canyon. On that trip I slept on the bus to save money on accommodation, and my ticket enabled me to jump on and off any cross-country Greyhound bus. I was half the age that I am now, so I doubt that I will do that again, but it's certainly worth contemplating if you have a good back; your finances are limited; and/or you can't, or don't want to, do all that driving.

Chapter 6

Rocky Mountain Way and the Wild West

National Parks: Rocky Mountain, Arches, Canyonlands,
Mesa Verde, Black Canyon of the Gunnison, Great Sand Dunes
Other notable sites: Red Rocks Park, Colorado National Monument

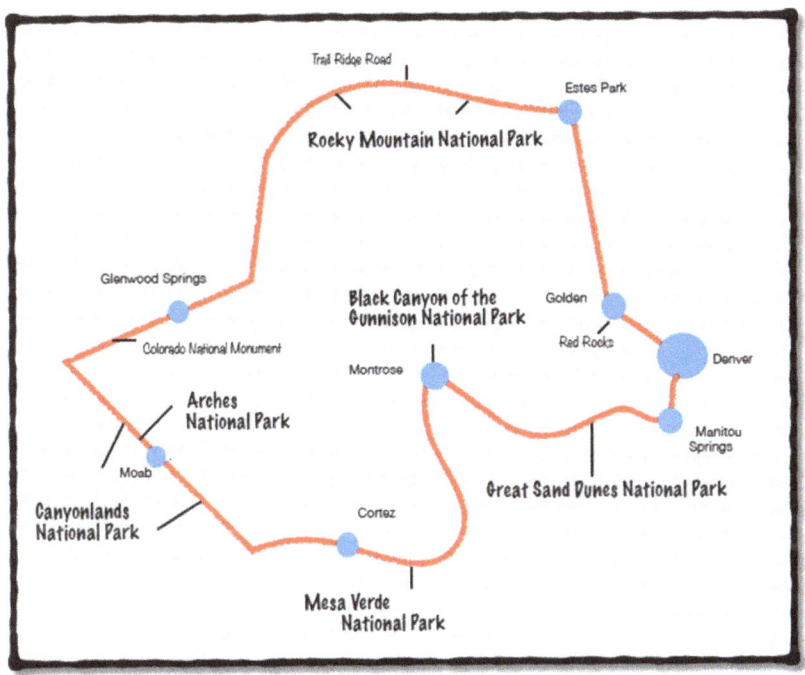

This chapter was composed while singing:
Rocky Mountain Way, as performed by Joe Walsh (1973) and
Ol' 55, as performed by Tom Waits (1973)

Introduction

I lived in California for a couple of years, where I spent a lot of my spare time exploring its hinterland, through a mixture of hiking, running, cycling, and driving. At the time I couldn't imagine there would be another State that could keep giving in the way that the Golden State had. Then, in 2010, I hatched a plan to loop around the State of Colorado. On that trip there were several occasions where I found myself thinking that here was a State which could hold its own in any competition with California. No wonder the bumper sticker on the pick-up truck in front of me as I drove out of Denver said: 'Colorado: It's all good', because it was.

At the end of the first week of September 2010, I was due to undertake some student recruitment work in and around Chicago, which gave me a week to complete my Colorado loop. That makes this road trip the shortest one in the book, but it was one of the most glorious. It could be easily extended to 10-14 days by staying longer in some of the places, and/or expanding the loop, and I would certainly have done this with more time. My broad aim was to visit as many of the national parks I could in this part of the United States. Colorado and Utah currently contain nine national parks between them, so for some of the time I would be crossing the border between the two States. I decided to start and finish in Denver because this was the obvious city to fly into. The trip was essentially an anti-clockwise loop, heading northwest from the mile-high city, until I eventually returned from the south east.

Arrival in Denver

I didn't get off to the best of starts. I arrived early afternoon at Denver airport and thought it would be nice to head downtown to experience the city of Denver before I launched off into the American great outdoors. It was one of those occasions where I found myself mentally unprepared for a drive that took me into a really busy urban environment. I suppose I had swallowed a bit of Jack Kerouac nostalgia, knowing that this was where he had stopped several times on his cross-country road pilgrimages [see On the Road Slice of Americana Pie]. As I got nearer the centre I was still harbouring thoughts that downtown Denver might look a little more like its wild west image, not necessarily with dusty roads and horses tied to poles, outside bars with swing doors, but at least a nod in this direction. I'm sure I could have found what I was looking for, but I was tired, and jet-lagged. I decided to pull over and look at the map. I could see that the town of Golden was not far away and roughly in the direction I would be heading, so I took off in the hope that this might be a better transition into what I was expecting from this trip.

After about an hour's driving (around 50 miles) I arrived in Golden, which was pretty much perfect. Driving downtown, it was easy to imagine how everything would have looked 100 years ago, because it didn't look that different today. I stopped off at a traditional hotel expecting to stay there overnight. Unfortunately, today's prices were over $100 for the night, so I decided to look around for something which had a little more like yesterday's prices. In the end I opted for an unassuming chain-motel. Even that wasn't as cheap as I was hoping for ($80), but at least it meant I wouldn't have to hold up a passing stagecoach the next morning in order to pay the bill. All I really needed that evening was a chance to check my maps and have something to eat. It turned out to be a good choice, and the young guy on reception gave me a good orientation around some local sites.

The burial site of Western hero Buffalo Bill (real name William Cody) was high on the list of local attractions, so after breakfast the next morning and a quick tour of the town again, I started winding my way up Lookout Mountain. The mountain was appropriately named because the view of the Great Plains from the top was glorious. No wonder Buffalo Bill wished to be buried there, even if some of his friends and family felt that he should have been buried in the town he founded – Cody, which borders Yellowstone National Park. I bought a dream catcher and had a coffee at the gift shop before looking around the museum which told the story of Buffalo Bill. Outside the museum was his burial plot.

Buffalo Bill was a Wild West figure, with mythical status, and here was a good chance to see something of the real man behind his legend. This included information about his Wild West tours, where he staged re-enactments of Wild West life. He brought those shows to Europe on and off for nearly twenty years around the turn of the century. Interestingly, he hired Native Americans to work on the enactments, enabling audiences to get a more rounded view of their culture than the one often presented.

Before heading up to the Rocky Mountain National Park I had one more personal must-see to visit. This involved a small detour of ten miles, down to Red Rocks Park and Amphitheater, the legendary concert venue. I became intrigued by this place after seeing Neil Young perform there in a thunderstorm, on his *Red Rocks Live* DVD, and also a young U2 on their *Under a Blood Red Sky* DVD. I was also aware that anyone who was anyone had played there, including The Beatles. I was surprised to read in the foyer that there had been concerts there for over 100 years, although the venue we now know was opened in 1941.

On arrival, I was pleasantly surprised to find that I could walk along the rows of seats, looking down on the stage. Preparations for a concert were happening on stage but I didn't get to hear any of the natural acoustics. From the top rows you could see the city of Denver in the far background. Before leaving I took the short, marked, hike around the actual red rocks which surround the venue. Pleased that my morning's worth of short detours had put me in a good state of mind, I returned to Golden, and then took Highway 93 north towards Boulder. The air felt clean and fresh, and the vistas were expansive, which made me want to yell 'Colorado', in the style of John Denver – *Rocky Mountain High* (1972). I stopped for lunch in Boulder, where it was easy to drive into town and park. I enjoyed a sandwich in the sun, visited a couple of second-hand shops, and had a quick look at the University buildings. The football field here was in the opening credits of the 1970s TV programme *Mork and Mindy*, featuring a very young Robin Williams – 'Nanu Nanu'.

The Rocky Mountains

It is less than a couple of hours drive from Denver to Rocky Mountain National Park (around 75 miles), so, even though I had made quite a few detours and stops, it was clear that I would be able to arrive near the park late afternoon. I planned to stop overnight at Estes Park, which looked to be on the park's border. After a quick tour around the town in my hire car I took a chance on an unassuming lodge. This turned out to be a good choice. The room was great, very reasonably priced, and after enquiring about hiring a bike, my very friendly host offered me one of his own bikes for free. I dropped my things off in the room and was soon on the bike doing the four-mile loop of Estes Lake, after which I wandered on foot into the town. It was a little bit twee, with some rather expensive looking gift shops, but I found a great place for dinner and a beer, after which I wandered along by the river until I came to an open-air concert performance by a country and western singer, Ron Ball. As the sun was going down, I returned to my room, now fully immersed in my Colorado state of mind.

The next morning, I was up at the crack of dawn, and after a very nice breakfast in town, I was soon heading up into the Rocky Mountains. I drove along Highway 34, following the Fall River until I came to the official park entrance. Rocky Mountain National Park is unusual in offering day passes as well as weekly passes. The day-passes didn't strike me as good value, so I ask the ranger at the booth why it cost so much to enter what appeared to the only road in the area. I also added that I was surprised not to have seen a sign mentioning this further back down the road. She saw my questioning as confrontational and called the head ranger. He quickly arrived and told me sternly, but politely – and in a manner indicating that he had been trained to deal with difficult customers – that this is the way it is. I politely replied that I was only asking, and after paying my money I was soon cruising along the road. I decided to stick rigidly to the 40mph speed limit just in case he had radioed ahead to other rangers to tell them that a reprobate had entered the park.

The scenery was so stunning that I quickly forgot about my entrance booth confrontation. I was on the Trail Ridge Road; a truly magical experience. This road leads all the way along the top of the park, right through the Rocky Mountains. The road sits between 10-12,000 ft up in the mountains, and is listed as the highest paved road in the United States – although the Mount Evans Scenic Drive appears to take you higher (14,000ft). Either way, you certainly couldn't get much higher – on paved road anyway. It was difficult not to keep stopping to take in the air and to take photos, and I decided to succumb to the urge at every obvious opportunity.

Rocky Mountain National Park was granted its status in 1915 after pioneering work by the naturalist Enos Miles. The Trail Ridge Road goes roughly east-west through the heart of the park, but the entire Rocky Mountain range goes north-south all the way through the United States, including large parts of Canada, and creates a natural boundary between the east and west of the United States, even if the Mississippi River represents a more central divide of the country. The mountain air was truly invigorating, with the highest peak in the park being well over 14,000ft feet – Longs Peak – which is in the southeast of the park, with a trailhead just off Highway 7.

As I drove slowly along Trail Ridge Road, I could see signs to various trailheads. At several points I stopped by the side of the road and climbed a while to take some photos. I stopped at the Alpine Visitor Center where I bought some postcards and souvenirs and studied the park brochure I had been given at the entrance. There was a great little hike that starts from the car park – The Alpine Ridge Trail. It's only around half a mile there and back but it offers great views, after ascending the appropriately named Huffers Hill. I then continued west on the Trail Ridge Road until I came to the Colorado River trailhead. The trail follows the river north to the abandoned ruins of Lulu City. It was a beautiful day and it was great being on the banks of the famous river. I thought the hike all the way to Lulu City would be too far, so I turned around after about halfway. I then continued south in the car towards Grand Lake where I left the park at The Lake Entrance booth. At this point the Trail Ridge Road becomes Highway 34 again, making the full length of the road through the park around 50 miles. I stopped to take a photo of the official Continental Divide marker; river water to the west of which drains towards the Pacific Ocean, and river water to the east of which drains towards the Atlantic.

I spent the late afternoon enjoying a glorious drive alongside the Colorado River, stopping for photos where the river was in full flow. At the town of Granby, I turned south along Highway 40 until I hit Interstate 70, going west. Time was getting on and I assumed I would be able to make good progress along this main thoroughfare, which turned out to be correct. I stopped off at Georgetown, which was signposted from the freeway as an historic 19th Century silver mining town. The town was beautifully preserved and worth the stop, which included a sandwich and coffee. Back in the car I continued west, hoping to get as far along the freeway as I could before dark. The freeway kept following the Colorado River, and I decided to stop for the night at Glenwood Springs. I had travelled around 100 miles since leaving Georgetown, which had taken me around two and a half hours. After a quick drive around I plumped for an old-fashioned inn/motel, which provided me with a nice room. The person on reception told me that there were hot springs in town (hence the name of the town) and an outdoor swimming area, so I headed off into town with my trunks. After an enjoyable splash around, I strolled into town and had dinner and a beer in a very nice bar.

The next morning, I had breakfast at the motel, then continued my journey west on I-70 until I hit Grand Junction. I stayed on the interstate heading towards the border with the state of Utah, but not before I had made the small detour to the Colorado National Monument. This was a fantastic introduction to a landscape I was about to become familiar with. That landscape was actually strangely familiar, it having been the backdrop for numerous wild west films, but actually being in it made you realise how alien it was, so much so that it almost defies description. Had political circumstances been different this national monument could easily have become a national park and perhaps it will be in the future. As is stands, it is administered by the National Park Service, requires a fee payment, and has everything you would expect from a national park. Its striking red rocks, monolithic towers, and deep canyons, along with the huge vistas, all typify the natural environment of Colorado and Utah.

Arches

I continued on I-70, crossing the border into Utah, and then I turned south on Highway 191 at Crescent Junction. I was heading towards Moab, not because I knew anything about the town, but because it was conveniently sandwiched between Arches National Park to the east, and Canyonlands National Park to the west. I arrived early afternoon after having covered 200 miles since leaving my motel early that morning. Moab didn't look as exciting as I was hoping for, but once I had a great room secured at an inn right off the main road, I was soon off once more, back up the road to the entrance to Arches National Park. I really wasn't prepared for what I was about to experience. The landscape was truly breathtaking.

I was surprised to read that Arches National Park was not designated until 1971. The park gets its name from the hundreds of stone arches which can be found around the park. The rocks are a beautiful shade of red, and from the road some of them look like they are so delicately balanced on other rocks that they could fall at any moment. The park was shaped by the relentless erosion of sandstone rock, caused by a combination of wind, water and ice. The main paved

A Slice of Americana Pie

A critical appreciation of: *On the Road* (1957)

The novel *On the Road*, by Jack Kerouac, was a linchpin for cultural change. It was anti-establishment, promoting new ways of thinking, acting and being. Kerouac called his new visionaries 'Beats', which became 'The Beat Generation'. So influential was this vision that it is unlikely that Bob Dylan would have developed his lyrical style without reference to it, and even the name of the most famous pop group of all time may well have been influenced by it (Turner, 2005).

The novel had its own beat in more of a literal sense. Its style was stream of consciousness, or spontaneous prose (as Kerouac called it), written as human thought naturally presents itself, without concern for the conventional rules of grammar. It is also lyrical in form, designed to sound like jazz music, and like so much of Kerouac's work, it is probably best read out loud, or, even better, listened to.

Kerouac was attracted to the subversive, sexual, and *jouissance* connotations behind jazz music, and he was a big fan of Slim Gaillard, who invented his own words, in keeping with his musical style, heightening the sense of going with the vibe, or being taken by it. In Freudian terms, this would be viewed as being guided more by the id rather than the ego and/or the moralistic super-ego. Here, the notion of being 'on the road' is very much a metaphor for breaking free from the stifling conventions of bourgeois life and being open to new forms of experience. Or, living in the spontaneity of the moment rather than by the expected norms of behaviour.

Kerouac was attracted to those groups in society, which a sociologist of the time called 'Outsiders' (Becker, 1963) – those who lived on the edge of society and the law. These are the people who are closest to a new vision, having little stake in the present order. "The only people for me are the mad ones, the ones who are mad to live", he says in the novel, displaying the double meaning. They are also 'beat', as in weary, but Kerouac saw the double meaning here as well, as in 'beatific'. The term stuck and began being applied to the artists who were giving voice to the emerging sensibility. This included Kerouac's friend Alan Ginsberg, whose poem *Howl* was considered obscene by the 1950s establishment, and William S. Burroughs, whose novel *Naked Lunch* was similarly received. Kerouac's closest friend was Neal Cassady, who he admired and looked up to. He was seduced by Cassady's disrespect for social convention, his sexuality, and nomadic lifestyle, and saw him as the epitome of The Beat Generation.

In the novel, Cassady becomes Kerouac's alto-ego in the form of Dean Moriarty; Alan Ginsberg becomes the character Carlo Marx; and William S. Burroughs becomes Old Bull Lee. Kerouac presents himself as the narrator, Sal Paradise. If fictitious names are no coincidence, then it is highly likely that Sal is a shortening of Salvation, inferring that this is what he is seeking. As the novel takes shape we meet these characters in search of enlightenment and salvation in a series of hedonistic encounters. Denver, San Francisco, and New York are key settings in the novel; three places where Kerouac spent a lot of his time.

The novel had a long gestation period, partly due to the difficulty in finding a publisher. It was eventually published in 1957, but the events he described in the novel were mainly based on his travels in the late-forties. Kerouac typed the novel on one continuous roll of paper, based on notes he took while on the road. Some of the typing was done in the North Beach area of San Francisco, where he started spending more of his time, along with similarly minded artists and counter-cultural figures, some of whom had moved out west from New York. The centre for their meetings and poetry readings was the City Lights Bookshop. Right next door is the Vesuvio Café, a popular watering hole for the Beats. The small street which separates the two is now fittingly called Jack Kerouac Alley.

Kerouac was born in Lowell, Massachusetts, in 1922, to French-Canadian, Catholic parents. Both of these things were important, because English was a second language for him, and he often claimed that spirituality was the essence of his work. He won a football scholarship to Columbia University in the late-thirties/early-forties, which took him to New York City, where he met Ginsberg, Burroughs and Cassady. Gravitating down from the Upper West Side to Greenwich Village, the Beats congregated in places like the San Remo Café, Le Figaro Café and Café Wa on MacDougall Street, where Dylan reputably played his first gig in New York. Kerouac was photographed many times in New York, where he can be seen in plaid shirt, Levi's and work boots – a look he didn't invent, but he certainly helped the look to become *de rigeur* for any self-respecting hipster, even to this day.

On publication, the novel received a mixed reception from critics, but its iconic status is now secure. Kerouac went on to publish a string of successful books, several picking up on the same themes, including *The Dharma Bums* (1958), and *Desolation Angels* (1965). His drinking was increasingly becoming a problem though, and it eventually killed him, at the age of 47, in 1969. Neal Cassady had died a year earlier, in Mexico. Four years earlier Cassady became the driver for Ken Kesey's Merry Pranksters, who took off around the United States in an old school bus. The bus was bought with the money that Kesey made from his novel *One Flew Over the Cuckoo's Nest* (1962), the title of which resonates with the challenge to the social order that Kerouac's original notion of Beat helped engender.

I was lucky enough to be in New York in 2013 when the original scroll of *On the Road* was put on exhibition, along with other memorabilia and artefacts from Kerouac's short, but hugely influential, life. Viking Press also published an extended version of the novel in 2007, based on this original scroll rather than the edited/censored version published back in 1957. Interestingly, the characters on the scroll had their real names.

There is now a small museum in San Francisco, just up the road from the City Lights Bookshop, which celebrates Kerouac's life. Centre stage is the Hudson car used in the film of *On the Road* (2012), starring Sam Riley as Kerouac. Some of the sites associated with Kerouac and the novel, in both New York and San Francisco, are pointed out throughout the road trip chapters of this book.

road through the park makes navigation very easy and trailheads are clearly marked from the various pull offs. I stopped to wander along several of the trails, totally absorbed by what I was experiencing. It was mesmerising. The total length of the paved road is only around twenty-five miles, which includes two side roads, so you will have only driven around fifty miles by the time you are back at the main entrance.

Windows in the rock at Turret Arch, Arches National Park, Utah

The most famous of the landmarks in the park are all accessible from parking areas followed by short hikes. Balanced Rock can be seen from the road and is easy to walk around, and is also accessible in a wheelchair. A couple of miles down a side road is Turret Arch, with its famous rock-formed windows. A couple of miles further along the main road is another turnoff to what is probably the most famous of the arches, Delicate Arch, the image of which is used in countless promotional material for the American great outdoors. Right at the end of the main road is the trailhead to Landscape Arch, so named because of its huge lateral arch (over 300 ft wide). This is a more strenuous, but hugely enjoyable, hike, and includes several other arches. I enjoyed every second of my time here, and the park kept giving as the sun began to set on my drive out. I finished the day in Moab, at a place which had great food and great beer.

Canyonlands

Next morning, I returned to the same place I had dinner the previous evening, because I saw from the menu that they did breakfasts. As the sun was coming up, I pulled away from the motel, alive with thoughts about Canyonlands National Park and whether it would be able to top what I had already experienced. Thoughts of ranking my experiences soon disappeared though, because, before long, I could see that here was a landscape which couldn't be compared with any other. The vastness of what was around me was truly awesome and almost unimaginable. The sheer scale of everything was disorientating; the normal rules of perspective didn't seem to operate here.

Towards the Green River from the Grand View Point Overlook, Canyonlands National Park, Utah

Like Arches National Park, I was surprised to discover that Canyonlands National Park wasn't designated a national park until well into the 20th Century (1964). Driving around the park, nearly 50 years later, it felt so remote that you could easily believe that you were the first person to stumble upon the place. I remember being startled when I saw another person suddenly appear on one of the trails. I hadn't seen the film *127 Hours* (2010) when I visited the park, which retold the story of Aron Ralston, who slipped and fell in Horseshoe Canyon (Ralston, 2011). When I did see the film, the lessons there were somewhat obvious: if you are going into remote areas, tell someone what you are up to, and/or stick to well-marked trails. The first of these is not so easy if you are a visitor from afar, but I suppose you could tell the motel receptionist, if you are returning to the same motel that evening, or just tell a ranger what you are planning. Carrying more water than you think you might need isn't a bad idea either, unless you like the taste of your own urine, of course.

The ever-handy guide I was given at the entrance booth told me that the park was comprised of three main areas: The Island in the Sky (to the north); The Maze (to the west); and The Needles (to the east). Each area was appropriately named, as would soon become apparent. Each area was clearly demarcated due to the confluence of the two mighty rivers in the centre of the park: The Colorado and Green Rivers. To get into the park in the first place I had to go back up Highway 191, past the right-hand turn to Arches National Park, until I came to the left turn onto Highway 313, which took me straight onto the Island in the Sky. I stopped first at the visitor centre to get my bearings, and then drove down to the fork in the road, where I stopped to take a short hike around Mesa Arch.

I then drove the five miles north to Upheaval Dome, and then back down to the original fork to drive the final five miles along to the Grand View Point Overlook. Wandering along the trail at this point it was easy to believe that you were on top of the world, even though you were actually only 6,000ft up. Such was the vastness of the landscape laid out before you could also believe that you were looking out on the whole of the continent. This is truly a must-see, as you look down on the canyons forged by the Colorado River and the Green River. I say look down; what you are actually doing is looking towards them because the scale is almost unbelievable.

After returning to the car and realising that I would not be able to access either the Maze or The Needles without first driving back up the road I came in on, I decided to head back into Moab for a coffee and sandwich. The Maze looked to be accessible only by a four-wheel drive vehicle, so it was an easy decision to continue south on highway 191 until I saw the signs to take me through The Needles area of the park (a right turn onto Highway 211). It was a long drive from the highway to the Needles Visitor Center (around 50 miles), but the drive was wonderful and I'm glad I took the time to stop at the various overlooks, which were all clearly signposted. I was also lucky to be listening to a National Public Radio (NPR) programme on the car radio, which explained the role of the Buffalo Soldiers in the formation of the early national parks.

Mesa Verde

I wanted to reach the town of Cortez that evening, because it was the closest town to Mesa Verde National Park, so I left The Needles part of Canyonlands late afternoon. I had to retrace my route along Highway 211 until I reached Highway 191 again. I then travelled south until I hit the left turn onto Highway 666/491 which took me straight into Cortez. From the visitor centre in The Needles to Cortez had taken me a couple of hours (around 100 miles). I stopped outside the visitor centre in town, which was just about to close, but the two helpful assistants told me that Mesa Verde was only twelve miles up the road, and that there were several places to stay overnight if I just continued up that road. From the main road (Highway 160) I saw a nice-looking Italian restaurant and then a few unassuming motels. The thought of a nice pizza overtook me, so I pulled into one of the motel car parks. The guy on reception was very pleasant and told me the rooms were all very cheap. Not surprisingly, my room was very tired looking, but knowing I would be up early in the morning I dumped my suitcase on the bed and headed off back down the road to the restaurant.

The Italian restaurant was great, and very reasonably priced, and not long after returning to my room I found myself drifting off to sleep, pleasantly reflecting on what I had experienced the previous two days. My revelry didn't last long however, because I was soon bolt upright on the bed listening to some considerable commotion outside my room. It felt like cops and robbers were right outside my room, but I couldn't be sure because I was too scared to peel back the curtains in case either a cop or a robber saw me. My suspicions were confirmed when my

A Slice of Americana Pie

A critical appreciation of: Burma Shave Signs

In a society built around the automobile and with what appears to be an insatiable appetite for consuming goods and services, there is a certain inevitability that these two things would collide in the shape of a giant road-side advertising hoarding. It's only when you get up close – by foot if you can – that you realise just how big some of them actually are. But they can appear quite small from the window of your car, particularly when they are competing for your attention amongst a sea of signage.

Road signage comes in many forms: from road information signs to cinema screen size hoardings, and giant pylons holding up neon logos. They sometimes display public information but the majority are actually private company signage competing for your attention and aimed at persuading you to consume a particular brand of good or service, including the gas, food, and accommodation – which may be just up the road.

At some freeway junctions there are now so many signs that you have to wonder whether they are a contributory factor in road traffic accidents, with drivers becoming distracted and confused by signage overload. But, so normal are these signs, it's more likely the case that everyone has subconsciously learnt to comfortably filter and process all this information. Signs also often perform a wider cultural function, beautifully illustrated in the Springsteen lyric from the song *Jungleland* (1975), which speaks about the gang meeting beneath the giant Exxon sign.

One of the most interesting forms of road signage are the Burma Shave Signs, which have become a cultural phenomenon; signs that tell a story, sign by sign, as you travel down the highway. They are known as Burma Shave Signs because the Burma Shave company had the idea as early as 1925; that they could advertise their new brushless shaving cream with a sequence of evenly spaced road signs, each with short text, and each rhyming with the previous one. The object was to tell a short story, with the denouement or punchline revealed on the last sign. Actually, the story would often finish at the penultimate sign, because the last sign was invariably the company's name.

> Modern Man – Spreads it on – Pats it in – Shaves it off
> – See him grin – Burma Shave

Usually, there would be six signs, evenly spaced along straight sections of highway. The idea was conceived by Allan Odell, the company owner's son and proved very popular. The company's profits rose almost immediately after the first sequence appeared in Minneapolis, the home of the company, and it wasn't long before the company was using them throughout the United States. In the 1960s the company was sold to the bigger Gillette company, who dropped the idea, but by then they were pretty much part of vintage Americana anyway, having been typical on the slower old highways, which were increasingly being replaced by high-speed freeways.

Odell apparently got the idea because he felt that some existing road information signage already appeared in the form of a story waiting for a conclusion; as in: Gas; Food: Accommodation; followed by the name of the Service Area up ahead. In Odell's early sequences the rhyming stories were designed to be humorous, and usually family friendly, because it was recognised that families travelling in cars enjoyed looking out for the signs. An interesting twist occurred when some of the stories started to include wider moral messages, thereby melding advertisements for products with public information messages. This strikes me as a fascinating aspect of American culture, as in:

> Past Schoolhouses – Take it slow – Let the little shavers grow
> – Burma Shave

The sequencing of billboards in this manner was also chillingly utilised in the film *Three Billboards outside Ebbing, Missouri* (2017).

The singer-song writer Tom Waits saw a deeper symbolic meaning for the Burma Shave Sign in his song of the same name (1992); a distinct sense that because all the sequences end in Burma Shave, they appear to point to a mysterious place, possibly a lost highway, a road to nowhere. Here is also our entry point into a wider discussion about whether the evocation to continuously consume goods and services as the way to achieve happiness, contentment, and meaning, is ultimately only going to end up in forms of disillusionment. Being on the road thus becomes a metaphor for alienation; people in search of enrichment, but which is more likely to bring disenchantment rather than enchantment.

Newer road signs often retain much of the corny humour seen in the early Burma Shave rhymes. Two of my personal favourites were road-side messages from local churches. The first was a sign I saw when I was driving through a boiling hot Alabama: 'Remember: in Hell there's no air conditioning'. The second one I came across when driving west through a small town in Texas: 'This is a God-fearing town, so don't drive like Hell through it'.

The metal signs themselves, particularly mid-twentieth century ones, have now become highly collectible, including all signs advertising a brand of oil or gas, and road direction signs. So popular are 'Route 66' signs [see Route 66 Slice of Americana Pie] there's now a small industry dedicated to manufacturing reproductions of the real thing. All the original 'Route 66' signs are probably now long gone – either stolen and now hanging in private homes and workshops, or removed by local authorities after the route was official decommissioned in the mid-fifties. With a little bit of homework it is possible to find the dates and locations of auctions where decommissioned signs and those deemed in need of replacement are sold off by local authorities.

Route 66 was a popular location for many of the original Burma Shave Signs, and some of them have now been reproduced at certain points on the original route. For example, just outside the town of Seligman, Arizona, you will find:

> You can drive – A mile a minute – But there is no – Future in it
> – Burma-Shave

Reproduced in the original stock red and white of the Burma Shave Company, and erected by the Route 66 Association, this particular sequence of signs neatly captures that nostalgia for a past life and hints at why it was better.

room started changing colour to reflect the light show from the top of a police car, which appeared to have parked right outside my door. There was a lot of shouting and fast-moving footsteps. I made the decision to move the wardrobe against the door in case someone came crashing into my room. Given the ease with which the wardrobe moved it was clear that its balsa-like wood construction was hardly going to offer much resistance. After which I hid on the floor on the other side of the bed. Luckily, it all went quiet after what felt like two hours but was probably only around twenty minutes. I knew it would be difficult to sleep after this, so I re-set the alarm for an earlier wake up. When that alarm went off, I showered as quickly as possible, moved the wardrobe back in place, dropped the key off in the reception letter box, and then drove off in the direction of Mesa Verde.

One of the things I love about being on the road in the USA is just how many diners there are right by the roadside, and how early some of them open. There it was on the road ahead, a shining citadel called Denny's, with its bright lights indicating that it was open, and pick-up trucks in the parking lot just to confirm. All the road needed was a few Burma Shave signs to complete the old all-American picture [see Burma Shave Signs Slice of Americana Pie]. As I walked in, I saw a table full of workmen, complete with plaid shirts, baseball caps, jeans, and work boots. The place felt comforting and I could see huge breakfasts being deposited on the workmen's table as I moved towards a booth. The breakfast I chose looked puny by comparison, but I'm not proud. Regardless, I was just pleased to feel safe, after the cops and robbers show the previous evening, and knowing that I would soon be on my way towards my next national park. As I drank my coffee, I vowed in future not to go below $60 for a room unless I had looked at it first.

Mesa Verde National Park was easily accessible, by following a well-signposted road off Highway 160, travelling east. It was still very early in the morning, so, after entering the park I pulled over at a fire lookout tower to take in the view. The wooden sign by my car told me I was at the highest point in the park (8,572ft). A little further along I could see the value of such towers because there was evidence to the side of the road that a fire had recently blown through – wild or controlled, I couldn't be sure. Before long I was at the visitor centre, where I was pleased to see that there were ranger-escorted tours. I was eager to learn more about this ancient site, and after driving a few more miles down the road, I was soon on a walking tour around some of the ancient dwellings. I was in a group of around a dozen other people, led by a very knowledgeable ranger, who was happy to entertain any number of questions from the group.

Mesa Verde was one of the earliest national parks, established in 1906. Although the natural scenery is impressive, the park mainly celebrates and protects the work of the human architects who carved out a series of cliff-hanging dwellings, immediately underneath giant sandstone rocks.

Ancient cliff-hanging dwellings, Mesa Verde National Park, Colorado

The United States is often held up as an archetypal modern (even post-modern) society, so it was great to witness the existence of thriving communities hundreds of years before even the notion of a United States of America was conceived. The evidence suggests that the ancient Anasazi or ancestral Puebloans, as they are sometimes called, lived here for over 700 years, before they mysteriously moved on around the turn of the 14th Century. The ranger explained how complete this ancient society was, with brick and mortar-built homes, family gathering places (kivas), along with evidence of sophisticated farming methods, tools, manufacturing, and trade. Like many Roman ruins in Europe, very little was actually ruined; testimony to the skills of these ancient builders. In my tour group was a descendant of the ancient Puebloans, who, at several points, stopped to play his handmade pipe, in order to spiritually connect with his ancestors.

The main buildings and dwellings around which the guided tours wind are at the end of the road called the Chaplin Mesa. After the tour, I wandered around and took photographs of the canyons that the dwellings majestically looked down on. The rim of the whole area constitutes a giant loop, so, back in the car, I made my way down the other paved road towards the Wetherell Mesa, at the end of which more dwellings could be visited. All of the main sites can be comfortably visited in 2-3 hours, which enabled me to be back on the road before lunch.

The Black Canyon of The Gunnison

I had one final park to visit on this trip – The Black Canyon of the Gunnison – and a good amount of time to reach it before the end of the day. I continued along Highway 160, travelling east, until I reached the large town of Durango, where I needed to head north. Durango was only around 30 minutes from Mesa Verde, so I stopped there for lunch. I'm glad I did, because here was a town with all the Wild West trappings of the past, sitting alongside all the creature comforts of the present. I spent a very pleasant hour wandering around the place, before heading north on Highway 550.

A further hour up the road was the town of Silverton, which looked to be straight out of the 19th Century, and was certainly worth the short stop I made. Once parked up I was pleased to see a very rare Airstream motorhome [see Airstream Trailers Slice of Americana Pie], and a row of modern Jeeps for hire, all ready for off road adventures. I was also pleased to see that you could make a roundtrip journey to Durango on an old steam train – much as you would have done one hundred years ago. With more time I would certainly have made that journey, but time was against me now, so I continued north on Highway 550, arriving at the entrance to the Black Canyon of the Gunnison, a couple of hours later, around 5.30pm. The very helpful ranger at the entrance booth explained that I would certainly have enough time to see a main feature of the park – The Painted Wall – and then return in the morning to see the rest of the park.

The Black Canyon of the Gunnison didn't become a national park until 1999, although it had been a national monument since 1933. It's only a small park, but its main feature, the sheer granite walls of the gorge, are spectacular. Here is yet another example of where the scale leaves you a little disorientated. It also leaves you with the dilemma of whether it's worth taking a photograph, because that scale plays havoc with the perspective provided by a camera lens. Nonetheless, I tried to capture the grandeur of the granite walls opposite me, along with what appeared in my lens as a tiny glistening streak at the bottom of the canyon. This was actually the mighty Gunnison River. It's called the Black Canyon because its drop of around 2,000ft, along with its narrow walls, gives the impression of light having been sucked out of the gorge. The viewing point for the Painted Wall offered up a spectacular sight: a sheer granite wall streaked with lines of crystal, in a marble effect.

I was glad to be in the park at this time of the day (which was now around 7.00pm) because I was pretty much alone, and I could also see that I was going to witness a great sunset. I drove the five mile rim road, stopping for photographs, and then witnessed that sunset at the appropriately named Sunset View. After which it was definitely time to drive out of the park before it closed, and back towards the town of Montrose (15 miles away). I needed to find a room for the night, but I wasn't too concerned because, having been through Montrose to get to the park, I had already clocked several motels. I ended up at a nice looking chain-motel, in a nice room.

Unfortunately, by the time I had settled in, I realised that most restaurants would now be closing. The flip side of diners opening up early in the morning is that they close up early in the evening. Americans do seem to believe in that old motto 'early to bed, early to rise, makes you healthy, wealthy, and wise'. It's not unusual to see Americans entering restaurants between the hours of 5-6pm, and you might also see unsuspecting Europeans peering into the windows of a restaurant around 9pm, wondering why it's closed, and maybe even someone from the Mediterranean wondering whether it might actually be about to open. In my case, the person on reception told me that

I was in luck because the local Pizza Hut didn't close until 10pm. Although I was pleased to hear this, the thought of pizza for two nights running was a little disappointing. That said, at least I knew the motel I would be returning to was hardly likely to be seeing any police action that evening.

The next morning, I returned to the park, revisiting some of the places I had stopped the previous evening, but this time in order to take some short hikes. I then drove down to what is called the East Portal, at river level. I parked up by the Gunnison Tunnel and Diversion Dam, a significant engineering project from the turn of the 20th Century, which involved digging a 5.8-mile tunnel. I wandered along the riverbank watching the fishermen, before making my way back to the Highway 50, going east, for the journey back across to Denver. I knew I would have to be on the road for most of the day because I was due to catch my flight from Denver to Chicago O'Hare at lunchtime the following day. I had around 250 miles to cover, so I relaxed into the drive knowing that I would still have time to stop for lunch and for anything else that looked interesting by the side of the road. The town of Gunnison was only an hour or so along Highway 50, so I stopped there for lunch at a great traditional diner right in town.

Back to Denver

After lunch in Gunnison and a quick stroll along the main street, I then continued on Highway 50 until I hit Poncha Springs, where I turned left and north onto Highway 285. With just one more day added to my trip I could easily have turned right and south at Poncha Springs and made my way down to Great Sand Dunes National Park (designated in 2004) – a vast stretch of giant, drifting, sand dunes sitting below the towering Sangre de Cristo Mountain range. Certainly, a 10-14-day road trip would make this short detour (less than 100 miles from Poncha Springs) easily achievable. After which, you could travel east on Highway 60 until you hit the town of Walsenburg, where you could turn left and north onto Interstate 25, which would take you straight up to Denver. For me, I travelled north on Highway 285 until I hit Johnson Village, where I turned right and east, following Highway 24 all the way to Colorado Springs.

By the time I arrived in Colorado Springs it was late afternoon, so I decided to stop there for the night, and just make the short – 80 mile – journey into Denver the following morning, straight up Interstate 25. Unfortunately, Colorado Springs didn't have the allure that its name conveyed so I headed back to the much smaller town of Manitou Springs, which I had driven through to get to Colorado Springs. I had clocked several nice looking motels there on the way through. After consulting my map, I decided to drive through The Garden of the Gods to get back to Manitou Springs. This huge public park contained large numbers of those red sandstone buttes I had become very familiar with over the previous week. Arriving in Manitou Springs, which had a long, winding main street, I decided to pull into a nice-looking old fashioned inn/motel, where I secured a great room at a reasonable price. I then wandered through town, stopping at some gift shops before having a great dinner in a Western-style restaurant. After returning to my room I packed everything ready for my onward flight the next day, and then relaxed on the rocking chair, which was sitting outside my room.

The next morning it was a very straightforward drive up Interstate 25 into Denver. As ever, the airport was clearly signposted, as were the rental car drop-off signs. All I needed to do was look out for a gas station to fill up the car, which is easy when you are on a freeway because their giant neon signs are clearly visible at almost every freeway turn off.

Conclusion

This trip was only eight days long because of my work commitments. I wished it had been longer. Colorado and Utah contain nine national parks between them, and with some careful planning they could all be visited in one road trip. Alongside the parks I had visited, a slightly longer road trip could easily include Great Sand Dunes National Park, and with a bit more planning, could also include Bryce, Zion and/or Capitol Reef National Parks, which are all within striking distance if you head further west from Canyonlands National Park. For me, those parks were part of another road trip (see chapter ten).

Colorado really was 'all good,' and Utah was mesmerising. The natural landscapes were truly Wild West, and in many of the towns you could get more than a glimpse of the human Wild West. Although I was never a fan of the Western genre of films, this trip also made me want to revisit some of those films, many of which were filmed in Utah and Colorado, from *Stagecoach* (1939), directed by John Ford (see chapter ten), to *The Hateful Eight* (2015), directed by Quentin Tarantino.

Chapter 7

Up the Country to Acadia and Upstate New York

National Park: Acadia

Other notable sites: Niagara Falls State Park, Mount Washington State Park,

Home of Franklin D. Roosevelt National Historic Site, Woodstock Festival site

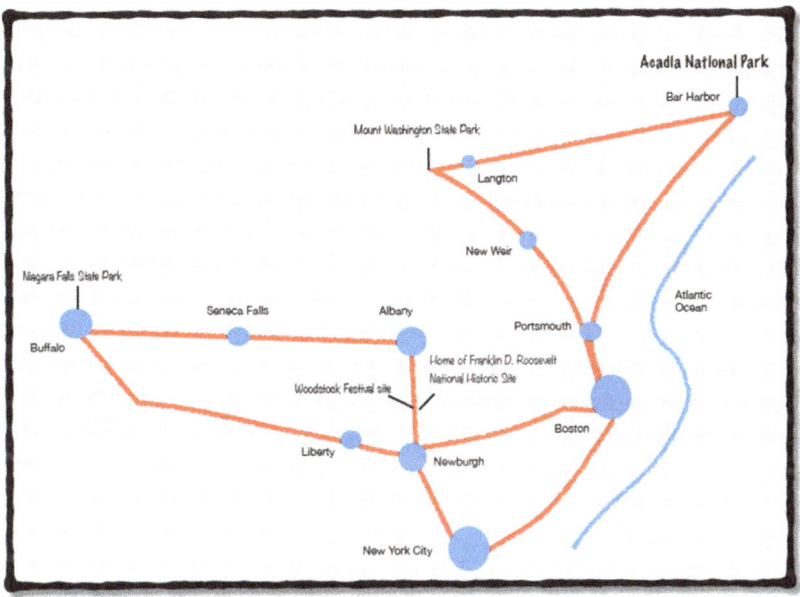

This chapter was composed while singing:

Born to Run, as performed by Bruce Springsteen (1975) and

Up the Country, as performed by Canned Heat (1968)

Introduction

Acadia National Park is in the far north-east corner of the United States, towards the Canadian border. It is around 800 miles from its nearest neighbouring park (Shenandoah, in Virginia) and because of that it might seem like an odd choice if your time is short and you want to visit several parks in one trip. A trip up to Acadia is well worth it though, and could be combined with a circular road trip around the states which comprise New England, and a visit to Niagara Falls, in Upstate New York.

I undertook this road trip in May 2016, but I have tagged on a section to include Niagara Falls, which I had visited a couple of times before. Spring is a great time to be in New England, and there should still be plenty of snow around Niagara Falls, although they are spectacular whenever you visit. There is also a good case for visiting New England in the Autumn (Fall) because of the spectacular gold and red leaves on show.

Arrival and orientation in Boston or New York City

I started in Boston with an international flight to Logan Airport, but you could easily begin this trip from New York. If you land at John F Kennedy (JFK) airport in New York City, you will be in the Queens borough, enabling you to head quickly north out of the City and without having to navigate the traffic around Manhattan. Most transatlantic flights fly into JFK, but you could arrange to arrive at La Guardia (also in Queens) or Newark, in New Jersey, if you are planning to spend some time in New York City first. It's just as quick into the heart of Manhattan from Newark or La Guardia, but Newark airport would be a good choice if you are heading out west and want to avoid NYC altogether.

If you hire a car from Newark, you will be able to drive straight out onto the old Highway 9, which winds down through New Jersey one way, and up alongside the Hudson River into Upstate New York the other way. And this is the road which is immortalised in the Springsteen song, *Born to Run* (1975). If you intend to go upstate you will need to cross from New Jersey into New York on the impressive George Washington Bridge, at the top end of Manhattan (which means you will avoid the traffic chaos further down Manhattan Island). This is the only bridge which crosses the Hudson River onto Manhattan Island. All the bridges and tunnels which take you onto Manhattan Island have tolls, unless you cycle or walk across a bridge. I have walked and cycled all the main bridges and enjoyed every minute.

You might choose to spend time in New York City before you head off into the American great outdoors, but, perhaps better, you could visit the City at the end of a road trip. This way, you could return your hire car to the airport, then head off by bus, train or taxicab. There are many websites offering advice on getting from the airports into the heart of Manhattan. Over the years I have done it by all means available. Key questions to ask yourself are: how much luggage will I have and what time of day will I be leaving the airport?

The cheapest way to get around NYC is by subway train but it's not easy dragging luggage around subway stations. That said, a taxi ride could be very slow and expensive at peak traffic times. A taxi from JFK airport on to the island of Manhattan will cost around $75 (2022), and the driver will expect a tip. Uber and the like might actually be more expensive, so it's worth checking carefully. A major advantage of a taxi is that it will drop you exactly where you want to go, which is really useful if you are tired and a little disoriented. But you need to compare that with a one-way subway journey which costs less than $3 (plus the AirTrain fare to connect you to the Subway system – around $10), and you may well get into the heart of Manhattan in less time than a taxi might take (depending on the traffic).

If you want to take the train from JFK it's worth doing your homework, because the fastest route is likely to be a combination of Air Train, LIRR, + subway (all well sign-posted), depending on where you want to arrive in Manhattan. The average cost of this combination of travel will be between $10-$15, depending on which combination of trains you take. Naturally, if you are travelling with companions the taxi could start to become something of a bargain, particularly given its convenience. There are also other minibus shuttle services available, which I used once and really enjoyed. They sit – cost wise – between the train and taxi. At peak times it can take a taxicab or mini-bus up to ninety mins to get from JFK into the heart of Manhattan (45 mins if the traffic is good). Newark and La Guardia airports also have express bus services.

Whichever airport you fly into there will not be a great deal of difference in cost to get into Manhattan – depending on which mode of transport you choose. Although La Guardia is closest (then Newark, then JFK) there won't be much difference in time taken either, particularly if you travel above ground. If you decide to use the subway, it's worth spending some time beforehand studying a subway map. It's a complicated network and locals will often only know their own journey, so may not be able to help. Some of the bigger stations, as well as having ticket machines, will also have attendants selling tickets, who will guide you – maybe a little abruptly! If you watch the train as it comes into the station you will see its line letter (A, C, etc.) on the front of the train.

You certainly don't need a car to explore the five boroughs of New York City: the island of Manhattan and the neighbourhood of Harlem, which begins above 110th Street, at the northern end of Central Park – and which featured in the song and the film *Across 110th Street* (1972); The Bronx to the north of the island; Queens to the east; and Brooklyn and Staten Island to the south. There is a road bridge onto Staten Island, but most people take the Staten Island ferry, which leaves regularly from the terminal by Battery Park at the southern tip of Manhattan. This is certainly a must-do, and surely ranks as one of the best free rides in the world, because of its view of the Manhattan skyline, and the Statue of Liberty.

The grid layout for each borough makes navigation and orientation relatively straightforward – and most streets have numbers rather than names, which also makes things easy. As mentioned in chapter five, Manhattan is particularly straightforward because streets go east-west from low to high as you go up the island, and the Avenues go north-south with the low numbered avenues to the east. East Manhattan means anything east of 5th Avenue, and West Manhattan means anything west of 5th Avenue. The only exception is Broadway, which follows the path of the original trail across Manhattan Island and cuts diagonally through the grid network from northwest to southeast. This makes for some interesting intersections, for example: Columbus Circle – where Broadway hits the southwest corner of Central Park; the neon extravaganza at Times Square – where Broadway crosses 7th Avenue; and the triangular shaped Flatiron building – where Broadway crosses 5th Avenue, at 22nd Street.

I have been visiting New York City most of my adult life, sometimes twice a year, and there was a time when I was quite nervous about straying beyond Manhattan, but over the years I slowly began exploring the other boroughs, often by hiring a bike and just venturing off. It's great fun cycling across the famous bridges, including: Brooklyn Bridge and Manhattan Bridge, which take you into Brooklyn; Williamsburg Bridge, which takes into the hip area of Williamsburg, in Queens; and the Queensboro Bridge which takes you further north into Queens. To the west of NYC – across the Hudson River – is the State of New Jersey, and it's just as easy to hop across there as it is to hop across the East river on the other side of Manhattan. For example, you can catch a PATH train (Port Authority Trans Hudson) from several places in Manhattan and visit the childhood home of Frank Sinatra in Hoboken. Further afield, you could visit many of the locations from the famous TV series *The Sopranos* (in and around Elizabeth) and make a trip to the birthplace of Bruce Springsteen, Asbury Park, with views of the ocean from its boardwalk. You could also have a beer or coffee in the Stone Pony music club – where Springsteen first played.

There are lots of places to hire a bike for the day (or longer), and each time I have visited NYC I've found more and more cycle lanes and safe cycle routes. One day I cycled all the way down through Manhattan from 125th Street in Harlem (the street where you will find the famous Apollo theatre), across the Brooklyn Bridge, and ended up at the famous amusement park, Coney Island, at the southern tip of Brooklyn. I've also cycled out across the Queensboro Bridge – immortalised in the Simon and Garfunkel *59th Street Bridge Song* (1966) – and ended up at the home of the famous jazz musician Louis Armstrong, in the Corona district of Queen's (34-56 107th St) which is now a great museum. From there it was an easy trip up to the Flushing Meadow complex (famous for tennis championships), where you will find Queen's Museum and a remarkable huge model of the whole of New York City. Further cheap or free things to do in NYC are included in the 'Six Things to do in New York' at the end of his chapter.

There are literally thousands of places to stay in NYC, to suit all budgets, but a budget hotel in New York could still cost an arm and a leg and some of the cheapest places to stay can be flea pits. I say this because it is not uncommon for fleas to be found in hotel rooms, although I've never had this experience. My advice is to decide on a district you like the sound of and then do your homework.

It sounds tempting to pound the streets of Manhattan but it's worth remembering that it's around ten miles from the southern tip of the island at Battery Park up to the heart of Harlem. Personally, I like the Chelsea district (around 23rd Street on the West side). I lived here for a while. It's very relaxed in the day, and lively at night, and is well-known for its gay vibe. Greenwich Village has a similar feel, with its mixture of students and arty types, but can be quite expensive. For that reason, many hipsters have now moved into what is known as the East Village. I have rented apartments in this area and stayed in reasonably priced bed and breakfast options. For many years I helped to organise student tours of NYC and often booked everyone into a great old hotel in Mid-town Manhattan. The staff there were always very welcoming, and the rooms were a good price for such a great location – close to the United Nations complex and Grand Central Station.

Once you have decided whether, and where, to stay in New York City (either at the beginning or end of a trip) it's worth spending a bit of time looking at a map of the whole state of New York, which stretches a long way north, up to the Canadian border – hence the term 'Upstate NewYork', and the reason why people like to say 'New York, New York' because it's a city within a very varied and interesting state. This postal address also prompted the song of the same name by Gerard Kenny (1979), with the subtitle: *so good they named it twice*.

Before venturing north into Upstate New York, you could first explore Long Island by heading east towards The Hamptons – home to the rich and famous who live on the east coast of the USA, and/or those who can afford a summer house away from the hustle and bustle of NYC. But at some point you will need to turn around, so you might prefer just to get to the interstate going north as quickly as possible. If you look at a map of the whole State of New York, you will see that New York City is right at the southern tip, and includes Niagara Falls in the north-west, which borders Canada. But you might consider heading north-east first, into so-called New England, which is the collective name for the States of Maine, Vermont, New Hampshire, Massachusetts, Connecticut and Rhode Island. To get into these New

England States you need to follow the signs to Boston, which is in the State of Massachusetts. To do this you head north-east from NYC by following the signs to the I-95, which you can either join from Manhattan or by heading north out of the borough of Queens.

Up the country into New England

Having started this trip in Boston I was already just over 200 miles north-east of NYC. Boston has nowhere near the pull of New York City but is an interesting city to explore and might well merit a stopover either at the beginning or end of a road trip particularly if you are flying in or out of Logan (Boston) airport. It's very pleasant walking around the oldest part of the city, with its lovely townhouses, and there are great views to be had from the top of the Prudential Tower. You can also enjoy a re-enactment of the 1773 Boston Tea Party protest down in the harbour, when imported tea from Britain was dumped in Boston Harbour as a protest against the British parliament's tax levy on colonial sales – what the protesters saw as an example of 'taxation without representation' because those in the colonies had no political rights in Britain. The protest now plays an important symbolic role, as a reminder of the fight for American independence from British rule, which was formally ratified in the Declaration of Independence, signed three years later.

For most of this trip I was going to be in New England, heading north towards the Canadian border (it's only around 100 miles north from Acadia National Park to the border post at Calais). If you want to visit Niagara Falls from Acadia you would then need to head south and west into New York State.

Logan International Airport is to the north of the city of Boston, so it's relatively straightforward to leave the city limits, following Highway 1 to interstate 95. If you had driven up from NYC, you could also avoid the city by staying on I-95 as you enter from the south because it acts as a ring road around Boston. From here you can alternate between Highway 1 and the interstate, depending on how quickly you want to travel north. I wanted to explore the coast, so I stuck to the old Highway 1, which was slow, but not desperately so. As I drove I began singing lines from the Jonathan Richman song *Roadrunner* (1976).

A Slice of Americana Pie

A critical appreciation of: McDonald's Restaurants

The name Ray Kroc might not feature on any official lists of the most influential Americans of the 20th Century, but when he bought into the hamburger operation run by the two McDonald brothers in San Bernardino, California, in the mid-fifties, and then set about establishing an expanded franchise under the name of McDonald's, he was about to become astronomically significant.

The two brothers who ran the original hamburger joint that Ray Kroc was so impressed by, did not, though, appear to be particularly impressed by him. The brothers wanted to be efficient in order to better serve their growing number of customers, not just as the means to build a business empire. Kroc eventually bought them out and went on to oversee what became a blue-print for similar operations. Indeed, this incredibly popular chain of restaurants is now so famous that it has become a concept and metaphor. McDonaldization is now regularly used as a term to describe a range of activities and processes which follow the core principles that Kroc adopted in order to expand the McDonald's franchise.

Those core principles were summarised by George Ritzer as: efficiency, calculability, predictability, and control (Ritzer 2000). Everything in The McDonald's operation is stripped down – no action is a wasted one; everything is ergonomic to the extreme. Everything is known in advance, even what is said, and every hamburger is identical (every bun is 3.5 inches in diameter). The workers are, to a very large extent, mere appendages of the machines; nothing is left to chance (for example the drinks dispenser will automatically shut off, and the French fry machine will trigger when the fries are ready). These things might now seem somewhat obvious, but McDonald's certainly raised the bar when it came to these work practices, and then took them to another level. The process is now a cornerstone of most franchise practices.

Whereas Henry Ford was well aware of how an assembly line could control the pace of work, and the productivity of workers, according to Ritzer, the process of McDonaldization also began to see the advantage in controlling workforce speech, through forms of scripted communication: "Would you like large fries with your meal?"; "And would you like an apple pie with that order?"; "Have a nice day!". It also sought to regiment the customer by marshalling a range of behaviours: e.g., restricting choices to those from a stripped-down menu; precisely determining when breakfast and lunch starts and finishes; and demanding that the diners themselves clear up after eating.

In essence, the process of McDonaldization understands perfectly the capitalist need to control the output of workers and the need to act in a completely rational way in order to maximise the efficient use of resources, including time, and, thereby, to raise profit margins. These ideas had been analysed and critiqued by the founding fathers of Sociology in the 19th and early 20th Centuries – particularly in the work of Karl Marx and Max Weber. The activities would not only enhance profitability, they were also the key to ensuring that no competitors would be able to keep pace. This would then establish the foundation for endless expansion, opening new franchises from the profits of existing ones. This model of expansion has been copied relentlessly by numerous food and drink retail companies.

The principles of McDonaldization can now also be seen in a wide range of very unlikely places. For example, George Ritzer looked at how funeral directors have sought to adopt the principles, and many people have taken Ritzer's lead and looked at how schools and universities have also adopted many of the principles.

In the case of universities, this can be seen in the stripped down 'bite-sized' choice of course combinations for students, and the attempts to rationalise the teaching process, resulting in all teachers acting and speaking in the same ways – and in the process losing their individuality. This analysis also coined the term 'McJobs' – those jobs where workers have little control over their work, and who can be easily replaced by other workers, with little training required. Naturally, this would be more troubling for professional people, when they feel too that they are being de-skilled in this way. After all, who wants to train to be a professional only to find out that you will have little control over how you will plan and execute your work tasks?

Max Weber also pointed out – over one hundred years ago – how, although all this may be efficient, it is also extremely disenchanting, and will inevitably result in what he referred to as an 'iron cage of bureaucracy'; a world where everyone feels trapped by conformity to the rules (Weber, 1921). This is beautifully satirised in the film *Brazil* (1985), directed by Terry Gilliam.

The process of McDonaldization is a fascinating one because it is always double-edged, something that Max Weber was also clearly aware of. On the one hand, the world becomes increasingly disenchanted – routinised and boring – but on the other hand, who wants to tolerate the inefficient use of scarce resources? And who hasn't been on the road, tired and hungry, longing for a bite to eat and a cup of coffee, but also very nervous about pulling over and entering a strange looking cafe or restaurant? Particularly when you know that just down the road is a franchise chain – signalled by a giant neon sign by the side of the road – which can be entered in the full knowledge of what to expect. And here is where some of those dangers of predictability instantly become extremely comforting.

The site of the original McDonald brothers' hamburger joint is actually on Route 66 [see Route 66 Slice of Americana Pie], but little remains of most of the original franchises and the early restaurants started by Kroc. This was probably inevitable, given the desire generally in American society to be seen to be forward looking and modern, resulting in a semi-permanent cycle of construction, demolition, and reconstruction.

An interesting variant on the modernising cycle was the decision to reconstruct one of Kroc's early McDonald's restaurants in Des Plaines, Illinois. As I drove past that particular restaurant it was easy to conjure up nostalgic images of that enduring American pleasure of driving down to the local diner for a burger, shake and fries. Because of that, McDonald's restaurants and all the others that followed suit, seem to be able to simultaneously capture what many people feel is very cold about corporate America, but alongside the warm feeling that many people get from indulging in simple pleasures.

I made my first stop at the coastal town of Portsmouth, on the border between New Hampshire and Vermont. You will find that a large number of towns throughout New England have borrowed their names from the original English town names. I could have travelled further north, but I wanted to rest up in order to be up at the crack of dawn the next day, in order to reach Acadia National Park in good time. I stayed at one of the many chain-motels, which was very pleasant, and it was a short walk to a very nice restaurant, where I also had breakfast the next morning. I love the classic American diner, but it's such a disappointment when it doesn't turn out quite how you expected (maybe the interior wasn't what you were expecting, or the food or service wasn't that great). I had none of that here, but I can see why McDonald's and the like came to dominate the fast food diner market, because at least you always know what you are going to get [see McDonald's Restaurants Slice of Americana Pie]

After a quick early morning drive around the waterfront I started making my way up the coast on Highway 1. Just like the more famous Highway 1 which hugs the whole of the Pacific west coast, the Atlantic east coast version stretches all the way from the tip of Florida (see chapter eleven) to the Canadian border. My first stop on the highway was at a large second-hand car garage because I could see many classic cars gleaming in the sunshine. The owner was great to speak with and showed me a couple of old type 2 VW camper vans he had for sale [see VW Camper Vans Slice of Americana Pie]. I told him I was heading up to Acadia and he said that his favourite hike there was the Beehive Trail, which I dutifully noted. I also stopped for a coffee at Old Orchard Beach because the beach looked very inviting as the sun glistened on the gentle tide rolling over the sand.

I stopped for lunch at a very nice diner, by the river, at the town of Wiscasset, and then re-joined Highway 1 until I saw the signs directing me to Acadia National Park, from the town of Ellsworth. This took me down Highway 3 and after about ten miles I hit the Thompson Island crossing which took me onto Mount Desert Island, where the park is located.

Acadia

Acadia National Park sits on a peninsula formed by glacial action. Hills and mountains fall away to the Atlantic Ocean, where craggy cliffs intersperse with sandy coves. It was officially designated a national park in 1919 when some of the then landowners, including the Rockefeller family, started donating their land to the fledgling National Park Service in order to prevent over-development and to preserve its natural beauty. The determined efforts of one man, George Dorr, were vital in ensuring that the work of donation was coordinated. The park had several alternative names before Acadia was agreed on, meaning idyllic place, and with reference to the original French settlements in the north-eastern USA. Cajun is an American contraction of Acadian, and is used to refer to the popular style of music (see chapter eleven).

I was heading to the small town of Bar Harbor, on the eastern side of the island, which was ten miles further on from the crossing onto the island. I stopped at the Hulls Cove Visitor Center to get orientated and pay my park entrance fee. The afternoon journey hadn't been very fast, but it had been an enjoyable drive. I had driven 300 miles since leaving Boston. I arrived in Bar Harbor, on the edge of the park, just after 4pm, and started to look for the inn I found on an internet search. It was on Cottage Street, a street within walking distance of everything the small town had to offer. The owner was extremely friendly and helpful, and I booked in for three nights. The room was fantastic and very reasonably priced, given its comfort.

I instantly liked the town of Bar Harbor. From my walk around the town I could see plenty of places to eat which seemed reasonably priced, and you could enjoy home-made ice-cream by the waterfront. I also discovered a bike hire shop close to my accommodation, and after a really nice breakfast the next morning I was soon on a really snazzy road bike. I chose a road bike because I wanted to head up Cadillac Mountain and then ride the loop road around the national park. I'm an experienced hill climber so I didn't find the early morning ride up to the peak of the mountain – at 1,500 ft – too strenuous. Catching the sunrise here means you one of the first on any day to see the sun in the United States. I hiked around at the top and enjoyed some glorious views across the sea towards Canada. The mountain was named after the French explorer Antoine de la Mothe Cadillac, who knew the area well. He went on to found what eventually became the city of Detroit – motor city – and the Cadillac car brand was named after him.

After freewheeling down the mountain I went back on myself for a mile or so to join the one way 27-mile loop road around the national park, stopping to take photos as I went. I saw the sign to Sand Beach, which the car salesman the previous day had told me was where I would find the trailhead he recommended. But I had already decided that for was for tomorrow. I cycled on to Thunder Hole, where I met a fellow cyclist who was 80 years old. She told me she loved the area and regularly cycled here. There was also a small visitor centre close by, where I chatted with the young employee who explained that this was her summer posting and that she was pleased to have got the job.

Towards the Atlantic Ocean from the top of Cadillac Mountain, Acadia National Park, Maine

After the short break I continued along the almost deserted winding coastal road, pausing at the cliffs at Otter Point and Little Hunters Beach before stopping for lunch at Jordan Pond House. I spent a very pleasant hour there in the sunshine on a wooden chair overlooking the lake, after which I spent the early afternoon completing the loop. At several points you will come across some of the original stonewalled carriage paths and bridges which were commissioned by the Rockefeller family, to encourage well-to-do visitors to come to the area and enjoy the vistas.

After returning my bike I walked back to my accommodation and enquired about the sauna room, which was available to guests. You had to pay extra to use it, but I found it irresistible, so I was happy to pay the extra dollars. That evening I strolled into town and enjoyed a beer and dinner while I chatted to a group of Americans who had travelled across from Texas to enjoy the national park. Afterwards, I headed off for an ice cream, before returning to my room.

The next morning, I drove back down the loop road to find The Beehive Trail, but before that I enjoyed half an hour or so on the deserted and beautiful Sand Beach. The trail walk was fantastic, including some very pleasant sections through the woods and also some quite strenuous climbing before I could enjoy the fantastic views from the top. The trail was 2 miles long and involved 500 ft of climbing. I then drove further round the loop road and stopped to hike to Bubble Rock and then onto Eagle Lake. That morning I had checked the location of the light house which features on many images of Acadia. This involved a further drive, to Bass Harbor, where I spent a pleasant half an hour or so scrambling around the rocks to get a good photo of the lighthouse. I then drove through the town of Seawall, which was exactly as its name implies, and then I stopped for a sandwich lunch at a typical American gas station, which had a nice bench overlooking the crossroad on which the station sat.

In the afternoon I hiked up Acadia Mountain to enjoy more fantastic views. On my return to the car I then realised that the reason I hadn't seen any other people was because the trail I had been on was closed (so as not to disturb nesting birds). I hadn't seen the sign on the way up. I then continued on, making a short stop at Echo Lake, and then headed back to my room. That evening I enjoyed another great meal in the pleasantly buzzing town.

Mount Washington

The next morning, I was up at the crack of dawn, packing up, and then enjoying a lovely breakfast at the cafe across the street, before heading off on a short hike across to Bar Island. This is a lovely little unspoilt island, accessible from the beach at low tide. Back on the mainland I then wandered along the Shore Path, before heading back to my accommodation, where I had left my hire car. I said goodbye to my great hosts and then headed off to Bangor, then got on Highway 2 to Lancaster. I stopped at a slightly bizarre but very enjoyable Dutch-inspired lunch stop, and in the afternoon, I bought some old New England car license plates and looked at some vintage Spartan trailers (a rival company to Airstream) [see Airstream Trailers Slice of Americana Pie]. I then entered the State of Vermont and drove on Highway 3 towards Bretton Woods and Mount Washington State Park. I wanted to climb to the top of Mount Washington, but I was also intrigued by the hotel complex at Bretton Woods. My University degree was in Political Economy and I was well aware of the significance of this place.

Critical Cultural Comment: The Bretton Woods Post-War Economic Settlement

The Bretton Woods Agreement was signed in 1944. It was the document aimed at encouraging international trade by stabilising currencies. In effect, leading trade countries pegged their currencies against the American dollar, which was in turn pegged to the value of gold. At the hotel complex you can see photos of Winston Churchill striding around the place, and a photo of the economist John Maynard Keynes, who had been instrumental in conceiving the Bretton Woods Agreement, and promoting the idea of a World Bank. He was also the man responsible for devising what became known as Keynesianism – the demand management system aimed at enabling economies to maintain full employment. Most western nations ran their economies using these ideas well into the 1970s before what became known as Monetarism began competing for the attention of leading politicians (including Prime-Minister Margaret Thatcher in the UK, and President Ronald Reagan in the US).

I decided to visit Bretton Woods the next day because I needed to find accommodation for the night. After a lot of driving around I settled on a lovely little place with cabins, in the town of Langton. My cabin was great and included a cooked breakfast. That evening, I had a lovely dinner at a restaurant which was just up the road.

The owner of the cabins told me that if I could get back to the foot of Mount Washington by 9.30 the next morning, I would be able to take the cog railway all the way to the top of the mountain. This was a three-hour round trip, with time for lunch at the top. The railway was fascinating, like a fairground ride, which took you through the snow up to the 6,000ft peak. The Observatory at the top of the mountain – the highest in the north east of the United States – has recorded wind speeds of over 200mph. At the top there were plenty of hikers, a few of whom, most likely, would have been hiking some (or even all) of the Appalachian Trail – the 2,200 mile trail which winds up from Mount Springer in Georgia, through 14 States, to Mt Katahdin, in Maine (see chapter nine for more information on this famous long distance trail). I discovered that the cog railway had been transported from Acadia National Park, because it had originally scaled Cadillac Mountain before being dismantled and transferred.

The cog railway as it approaches the summit of Mount Washington, New Hampshire

After returning to my car I then made the short drive back to Bretton Woods, which turned out to be a very exclusive hotel complex, but it was possible to park up and visit the room where the Bretton Woods Agreement had been signed off. I also had lunch there, after which I enjoyed a fantastic drive across to Interstate 93, and then down through the lakes where filming for *On Golden Pond* (1981) took place.

I ended up at New Weir and stayed in another cabin overnight. That evening I enjoyed dinner at a local bar and restaurant.

The next morning, I was up early in order to make the most of my drive back towards Boston. After coffee on the patio of my little cabin I set off in search of a breakfast stop, which I found in a great little diner in the town of Lacona. I then stopped off briefly in Canterbury to see a preserved Shaker Village – an ex-community of shaking Quakers, so named because of their physical movements during worship. Their celibate lifestyle no doubt contributed to their steady demise. I then couldn't resist a stop off in Salem, New Hampshire (not witch Salem, Massachusetts) to visit what was billed as America's Stonehenge. I thought this was probably over-egging it, but it turned out to be a fascinating place, and did have a network of stone structures designed to align with the path of the sun.

After a quick sandwich lunch, I then headed south towards the town of Lowell. I wouldn't normally stop off in such a busy town (unless I was spending a night or two there), but I was drawn to it because it was the birthplace of the famous Beat writer Jack Kerouac [see On the Road Slice of Americana Pie]. In the centre of town, I found the nicely executed memorial, which consisted of several upright marble slabs on which a selection of Kerouac's writings had been etched. After a quick trip to a couple of second-hand shops I then drove out of town singing *Hey Jack Kerouac*, by The 10,000 Maniacs (1987), and started heading towards the coast. I arrived in Hampton Beach, but eventually ended up back at the town of Portsmouth. Exhausted at that point I plonked myself back at the motel where I had started the trip. Perhaps because the manager was on reception, I managed to negotiate a room $20 cheaper than the first time. I also went back to the same restaurant for dinner and breakfast the next morning, before heading off back to Boston. My flight was not until early evening so I decided to hug the coast and had a pleasant time exploring some small towns, stopping off to have coffee and lunch and to visit some second-hand shops.

Across New York State

This had been a ten-day road trip for me, but it could be extended to two weeks (or more) to include a trip across to Niagara Falls. The obvious way to do this would be to trek west from Boston along interstate 90, towards Buffalo, New York. The Falls are just a few miles further north and are clearly signposted. It would be possible to do this in one hit because the interstate is fast and there are no diversions, but it is 450 miles from Boston to Buffalo, so you might want to break the journey roughly halfway, perhaps at Albany. Albany is the capital city of New York State, not New York City, which is worth remembering in case it comes up in a pub quiz. If you don't want to visit the city itself there are plenty of motels hugging the interstate on the outskirts of town.

If you want to follow the route I took around Upstate New York on a previous trip, you should follow I-90 from Boston until you come to I-84, then follow that road south west to Newburgh. As you approach the town you will cross the Hudson River. I stayed at a very pleasant chain-motel close to the junction of the I-84 and I-87, which had a great bar/diner close by. The next morning you could just head north on the I-87 to Albany, sandwiched between the Hudson River (on your right) and the popular Catskill Mountains (on your left), but you could do some exploring around this area first. For example, around twenty-five miles north of Newburgh you will find the former country home of President Franklin Delano Roosevelt (FDR). You will need to cross the Hudson River to the east side (via several available routes). The house is just a few miles north of Poughkeepsie and is a National Historic site and is a mine of information about the President and his wife, Eleanor.

Critical Cultural Comment – The FDR years

President Franklin Delano Roosevelt (FDR) won an unprecedented four General Elections (in 1932, 1936, 1940, and 1944). He led the nation through the Great Depression with an ambitious programme of federal funding (known as The New Deal), and then went on to lead the nation through the Second World War. Some of the events which took place at FDR's house in 1939 (at the outbreak of the Second World War) were dramatised in the film *Hyde Park on Hudson* (2012), starring Bill Murray as FDR. He contracted polio before he became president and lost the use of his legs, but he didn't like to be seen in public in a wheelchair, which would have been easier in a time when politicians were more likely to be heard than seen. In later life the events of the War appeared to exact a heavy toll on his health. By 1944 he was suffering

> with many complaints and died in 1945, just a few months into his fourth term as President. He will always top the list of longest serving presidents because legislation was passed a few years later restricting presidents to two terms (unless that legislation is revoked, of course). FDR, like his cousin and former President, Teddy Roosevelt, was also a great champion of the American national parks and encouraged all Americans to visit them. He was instrumental in ensuring that the Everglades, in Florida, Big Bend, in Texas, Shenandoah, in Virginia, and The Great Smoky Mountains, in Tennessee and North Carolina, all became national parks.

If you are up for more exploring, you could head north on Highway 9 from FDR's house (the same Highway 9 from New Jersey), then left, back across the Hudson River on Highway 299, into the Catskill Mountains (across I-87). Here you will find the little town of Woodstock, which was to be the original location for the famous Woodstock music festival in 1969 [see Woodstock Slice of Americana Pie]. The festival eventually ended up sixty miles further south west in the little town of Bethel, when the dairy farmer Max Yasgur agreed to lend his fields to the festival organisers. You can go on a search for the exact location, which now houses a permanent music venue close by – run by The Bethel Woods Center for the Arts. The town of Woodstock itself trades on its association with the festival and is a pleasant place to stop for a coffee and look around its various second-hand stores, which have some nice Americana items.

Between Bethel and Woodstock, you will find the huge Ashokan reservoir, one of the reservoirs which provides the water for New York City. New York City had an active reservoir in the northern part of Central Park (now called the Jackie Kennedy Onassis Reservoir) but such was the demand for water in NYC (currently with a population of over eight million people), that Upstate New York now has several reservoirs meeting that demand. The Central Park reservoir, long decommissioned, still has its water. It was the location for the back-cover photo of Simon and Garfunkel on their *Greatest Hits* album and is also the training route that Dustin Hoffman uses in the film *Marathon Man* (1976).

Niagara Falls

Driving north, you can skirt the edge of Albany by following I-87 until you hit I-90 heading west. It's round 300 miles from Albany to Buffalo and Niagara Falls. When I took this route I decided to break the journey just over halfway, at Seneca Falls. I chose here because I imagined that the so-called Finger Lakes, which are close by, could be an interesting place to explore. I stayed at a nice inn, in a very nice room, and I had a pleasant wander around the top of the biggest lake the next morning. It didn't merit a long stay so I was soon on my way heading further west on I-90, to Buffalo. Nearing Buffalo you need transfer to the I-190. Niagara Falls are just a few miles north from Buffalo on the I-190 and are clearly signposted. As you approach the Falls you will find yourself passing a plethora of places to stay overnight – including some original 1950s style motels. I find these places fascinating, partly because you never quite know what you might get if you book a room. On one of my trips to the area I arrived in time to see the Falls that day and then drove on out of town, but on another occasion I had a very pleasant overnight stop at a chain-motel, which was close to the Falls, and, surprisingly, was very reasonably priced for the area (with free car parking).

Niagara Falls was never granted national park status but is a State park. Had the Falls been granted national park status around the time of Yellowstone and Yosemite (late 19th Century) perhaps some of the commercial growth we now see in the area would have been stopped, but some of that commercialism had begun even earlier than that, so it is difficult to work out what might have been. That said, the immediate area around the Falls is largely untouched and you can therefore enjoy the Falls themselves in all their natural splendour. There are some great viewing platforms and you can also get very close to the water as it gushes over the top of the Falls. I found it fascinating to wander back up the river at the top of the Falls because from there it is difficult to predict what is about to ensue as you approach the edge of the drop. The volume of water and the volume of sound can only really be appreciated first-hand. The Falls are actually three separate waterfalls – The American, The Bridal Veil and Horseshoe Falls. You can get a great view of all three Falls by walking across the bridge into Canada (passports will be stamped).

A Slice of Americana Pie

A critical appreciation of: Woodstock

The Woodstock Music and Arts Fair took place over the weekend of the 15th-18th August 1969. It became so legendary that just the name conjures up images of late sixties hippy counter-culture. The hurriedly prepared logo, which featured a white dove perched on a guitar head, also included the strap-line: '3 days of peace and music', which perfectly captured the mood.

The story of Woodstock is a fascinating one. It nearly didn't happen, and when it did, it ended up 60 miles from the of town of Woodstock in Upstate New York. The organisers were keen to put on a festival close to the town of Woodstock because Bob Dylan and other free-thinking artists and musicians had set up home there. But the town council wouldn't allow it, and neither would anyone else, until the diary farmer, Max Yasgur, stepped in and offered the organisers some of his hay fields close to the small town of Bethel. The name Woodstock stuck because the organisers had already set up the investment company 'Woodstock Ventures', and the town of Woodstock still trades on its association with the festival. As it turned out, Dylan never played at the event – he was making plans to play at the Isle of Wight festival in the UK.

With hindsight, the somewhat chaotic nature of the event seemed to be in keeping with the notion of it being 'a happening', but the organisers *were* trying to be organised. They did print programmes and did issue tickets, but the ticket booths weren't ready before around 50,000 people had already entered the site, so they had little option but to make the event free. The early estimates that around 150,000 people might attend soon rose to three times that. The ensuing traffic chaos also made it difficult for many of the acts to arrive on time and the agreed running order soon went out of the window. Richie Havens, the first act on stage early Friday evening, was not apparently the scheduled one. Havens played on until other acts were ready. So the story goes, his song *Freedom* (1969) was improvised on stage because he had run out of material at that point.

At the other end of the festival – which was scheduled to finish on Sunday evening – the headline act, Jimi Hendrix, actually took to the stage just after nine o'clock on the Monday morning. Doubtless, many people will have missed his performance, particularly those who needed to be at work on Monday morning. Sandwiched in between Havens and Hendrix were (amongst others) The Who, The Band, Santana, and Crosby, Stills, Nash and Young – who were playing one of their first concerts together. All of this was captured on the four-hour film of the concert, which a young Martin Scorsese worked on. Notable for her absence was Joni Mitchell, but she still managed to capture the mood with her song *Woodstock* (1970). The agreed unofficial anthem was *Going Up the Country* (1968) by Canned Heat, who played it at the festival. The tune also captured the mood, which was the band's remake of a much earlier tune.

The film *Woodstock* (1970) is the official record of events, but a lot of the human stories which surrounded the event were neatly captured in the fictitious retelling of events in the Ang Lee directed film, *Taking Woodstock* (2009). In that film a lot of the spontaneity and innocence of all those involved in the unfolding saga of the weekend is humorously depicted. The film also provided insight into how events often become legendary – through retellings and reinterpretation; very little of which will be in evidence at the time. The social theorist C W Mills once said that the power of TV had become so great in the US that sometimes people would wait to hear about the meaning and significance of an event from TV News, even when they were there at the event (Mills, 1956).

With the benefit of hindsight it is possible to view the festival as something of a last gasp from the mouth of the sixties; an attempt to keep alive an anti-materialist, counter-cultural lifestyle built around more communal forms of living. The 1967 Summer of Love had hinted at these possibilities, but 1968 brought huge social upheaval and dislocations – including the assassinations of Martin Luther King Jr and Bobby Kennedy (the brother of JFK); televised unrest at the Democratic Party convention in Chicago; and the defiant black power salute by the two athletes at the Olympic Games in Mexico. At the beginning of 1969 the Vietnam War was still dominating the news and the American social mood certainly seemed one of disillusionment. *But,* in that summer, there was Woodstock – a breath of fresh peaceful air; a small hint of hope for a more caring, loving future.

Some of that peace and love was captured by the photograph which appeared on the gatefold sleeve of the double album of music from the festival. It featured a young couple in the foreground, who are standing in the festival field with a muddy blanket wrapped around themselves. That couple have been traced and are still together today (Hamilton, 2018). Their recollections of that weekend also seem to confirm that an event's meaning and significance is often not apparent at the time. There must surely have been many people at the festival who just saw it as a weekend trip, not the search for an alternative lifestyle.

One can only speculate about what might have been had subsequent Woodstock festivals taken place. The attempted West coast equivalent, which did take place just a few months later, was marred by four deaths.

The Glastonbury experience in the UK throws a more optimistic light on the festival experience, which started – coincidently – when another dairy farmer, Michael Eavis, gave over some of his land to hold a small festival in 1970. His farm is also some distance from the town which bears the UK festival's name. The big difference though is that there has been a Glastonbury festival pretty much every year since. Its history is another story, but its gradual accommodation to more commercial and corporate influences has meant that, for some at least, it has now lost touch with its more counter-cultural roots.

The fields in which the Woodstock festival took place, and the surrounding land, were bought up in 2005 to establish the Bethel Woods Center. Many bands have played there including Crosby, Stills, Nash and Young. A stop off in the small town of Woodstock is a fun thing to do, and where you might find some authentic and/or kitsch reproductions of artefacts of hippy Americana from the Woodstock era.

In some of the gift shops you can buy postcards which will show you a completely frozen Niagara Falls. This happened to the American Falls, in exceptionally cold weather in 1912. You can also buy images of a completely dry American Falls, because in 1969 the Niagara River, which feeds the Falls, was dammed, sending more water towards Horseshoe Falls. This was to enable a team of engineers and geologists to study the local erosion. Once the river flowed again the usual tons of water began cascading down again – a drop of nearly 100ft. Horseshoe Falls is said to have a drop closer to 200ft. Niagara Falls is definitely a must-see, even if the contrast between its natural beauty and its commercial hinterland is somewhat incongruous.

Horseshoe Falls, Niagara Falls State Park, New York State

Niagara Falls sits between two of the Great Lakes (which feed it), so, if you have the time and inclination, you could drive the short distance north from Niagara Falls to the edge of Lake Ontario, at which point you will be looking straight across to the Canadian city of Toronto (a great city to visit, but that's another story).

To the south of Niagara, back in Buffalo, you will also be able to look west, down Lake Erie, at the other end of which you will find Motor City,

Detroit, and the home of Motown records. Unfortunately, Detroit is now more famous for its 'rust belt' status – a reference to post-industrial decay and deprivation. If you make these two short excursions you will be driving close to the Canadian border, but at no point would you have actually crossed into Canada.

If you want to do more exploring around this area you could book accommodation for two nights. Whatever you decide, on your morning of departure, you will need to start heading east in the direction of Boston and New York. When I last did this trip, in order to avoid retracing my driving steps, I decided to turn my trip into a loop, by heading south out of Buffalo – where the I-190 meets the I-90. I turned right (heading south) onto the I-90, then took Highway 400 (heading east). Once I was on Highway 400, I relaxed and enjoyed a great day's driving, stopping for coffee, lunch, and every time I saw an interesting roadside place selling second-hand items. I then turned east on Highway 20, then south on I-390 and then east on I-86 until I hit Highway 17, heading east. I was determined to get as far as I could and ended up enjoying a lovely early evening drive along Highway 17, which was following the river. Exhausted, I stopped at a chain-motel in the small town of Liberty, which was cheap and cheerful, and had a nice diner right next door. I had driven close to 300 miles since leaving Niagara Falls that morning.

The next morning, I continued along the road until I arrived back at Newburgh, completing my Upstate New York loop. From there I joined Highway 9 going south and followed that road down the Hudson River, stopping by the river at Yonkers for lunch, before heading into New York City that afternoon. If you are in a hurry you could head into NYC on the Palisades Parkway (a toll-road), which you join by leaving Highway 9 on Highway 6 until you see the signs to the parkway, and then follow the signs to I-95 and onto JFK (or La Guardia or Newark airports).

If you are heading back to Boston from Newburgh, you just need to cross the Hudson and follow your route back up I-84 until you hit the I-90 going east into Boston, and then follow the signs to Logan International airport. Newburgh to JFK airport in NYC is about 75 miles (and will take around 2-3 hours, traffic and route permitting). Newburgh to Logan airport in Boston is about 200 miles (and will take around 4 hours).

Conclusion

Acadia is the only national park in the north east of the United States, and is close to the Canadian border. It is well worth the journey, particularly if you combine it with a tour around the states of New England, and possibly also include an extension into Upstate New York and Niagara Falls.

This road trip also provides a great opportunity to explore New York City, offering the prospect of experiencing some of the most spectacular examples of modern human architecture, alongside Nature's ancient architecture, to be found further north in Upstate New York. As the Gerard Kenny song title said: *New York, New York (so good they named it twice)* (1978).

Six things to do in New York City – which are free or relatively cheap

New York City has five boroughs – Manhattan (which includes the neighbourhood of Harlem), The Bronx (to the north), Queens, (to the east), Brooklyn and Staten Island (to the south). Most visitors spend most of their time in Manhattan, but it's well worth exploring all the boroughs, particularly if you have spent time in Manhattan before. You can also easily cross the Hudson River into New Jersey, which includes Hoboken (birthplace of Frank Sinatra). Unfortunately, many of the attractions are expensive and you could end up with quite a substantial credit card bill by the end of your trip. Here is a list of suggestions for places to visit and things to do which are are either free or relatively cheap. And some of them include paths which are less trodden. A combination of walking, cycling and subway can be a great way to spend a day.

1 A trip on the Staten Island ferry from Manhattan

The ferry regularly leaves from Whitehall Terminal, just by Battery Park at the southern tip of Manhattan. The trip offers one of the best views of the Manhattan skyline, and it passes the Statue of Liberty in New York Harbour, and it's free. You have to get off on Staten Island, but you can jump straight back on again – if Staten Island doesn't appeal.

Nearest subway: Bowling Green – on exit, head for the waterfront and look for the bright orange ferries.

2 A walk across Brooklyn Bridge from Manhattan

There's a dedicated footpath on the bridge which rises above the traffic. For me, a brilliant experience. Time permitting, turn right after the Bridge and head towards Brooklyn Heights – the promenade has a fantastic view of Manhattan – and then on to Atlantic Ave and catch the subway back. If you want to make a day of it, catch the subway to the end of the line at Coney Island, and enjoy the famous seaside community.

Nearest subway for Brooklyn Bridge: Brooklyn Bridge/City Hall – on exit, turn left and look for the pathway that goes between the two traffic lanes.

3 A wander in Central Park

Enter the park from 59th Street. Wander past the zoo, and the ice rink (if it's winter time) and then across to Strawberry Fields Memorial. If you leave the park just by W72nd Street you can see the Dakota building, where John

Lennon lived with Yoko Ono. He was murdered just outside. If you hire a bike you could go all the way through the park, across 110th Street to the north and on to the heart of Harlem on 125th Street.

Nearest subway: 59th St – which marks the southern boundary of the Park.

4 A wander around Greenwich Village

Greenwich Village is the heart of the Bohemian part of New York and home to many artists and musicians. Many parts feel like a village, with tree-lined streets and numerous coffee shops. There are many bars and clubs with live music playing every night [see On the Road Slice of Americana Pie]. Washington Square Park by New York University is a significant landmark. Stay between Bleecker Street and 4th St. if you lose your bearings.

Nearest subway: W4th St., or 8th St., or Christopher St-Sheridan Square, for the West Village.

5 A visit to Grand Central Station

The station is on W42 Street at Park Avenue. Go below ground onto the main concourse and look up at the ceiling and the chandeliers, as well as the departure lists. You can catch subway trains from here to Yankee Stadium (in the Bronx) – the home of the New York Yankees baseball team. Or you could further venture north up the Hudson River to Poughkeepsie and back, on a mainline train. Once out of the station, back on the street, look up at the Chrysler Building – the one with the bright silver top – and head there to get free entry to the Art-Deco lobby, but there's no access to the top.

Nearest subway: 42nd/Grand Central.

6 The Tenement Museum

A wonderfully presented museum and guided tour, which centres on a preserved tenement building in the Lower East Side, and which gives an excellent impression of what it was like for 19th Century European immigrants, many of whom would have arrived here straight after immigration clearance from Ellis Island. Tickets can be bought on the day or in advance (not expensive). Closed Mondays. Tours start at 108, Orchard Street.

Nearest subway: Delancey Street – on exit, turn away from the Williamsburg Bridge. Orchard Street is between Delancey and Broome Streets

Chapter 8

The Oregon Coast Highway and the Fire Mountains

National Parks: Redwood, Mount Rainier, Olympic,
North Cascades, Crater Lake, Lassen Volcanic

Other notable sites: Muir Woods National Monument, Big Basin Redwoods State Park,

Humboldt Redwoods State Park, Mt St Helens, Mt Shasta, Mt Tamalpais,

The Pacific and Oregon Coast Highways

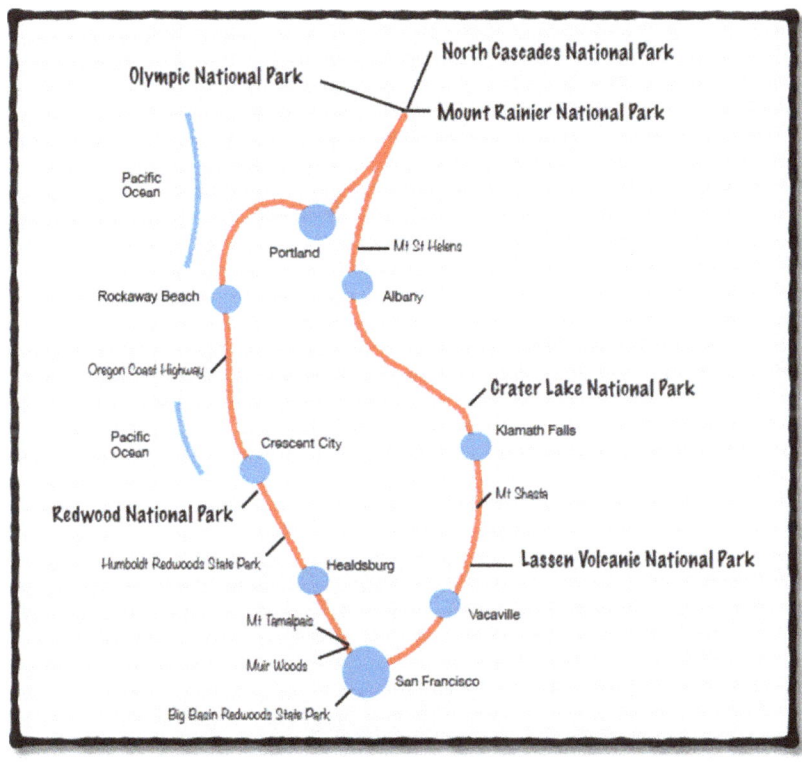

This chapter was composed while singing:
Everyday is a winding road, as performed by Sheryl Crow (1996) and
Me and you and a dog named Boo, as performed by Lobo (1971)

Introduction

I was particularly excited about the prospect of undertaking this road trip. I had previously driven up the Californian coast from San Diego – on the Mexican border – to San Francisco – in northern California – but never any further north. It's around 500 miles from San Diego to San Francisco, but actually around 800 miles from San Francisco to Seattle, up near the Canadian border. This trip was designed to explore those 800 miles and the national parks that are located in the north-west of the US.

For a lot of this trip I would be on Highway 101 – the coast road that winds up through the states of California, Oregon, and Washington. Technically, the coast road in California is actually Highway 1, but the roads intersect at various points, and when people talk of travelling along the Californian coast this could refer to many combinations of routes along Highway 1 and 101, depending on time available (Highway 1 is generally slower) and the places people want to visit. Several sections of the highway are also designated as the Pacific Coast Highway (PCH) in California, and the Oregon Coast Highway in Oregon. If you take Los Angeles as the official start of the 101 and the Canadian border as the finish, we are talking about around 1,500 miles worth of road (or pavement, as Americans prefer to call it).

If you have around six months to spare you could walk the entire length of California, Oregon and Washington along the Pacific Crest Trail (PCT) – over 2,600 miles of marked trail. This is the trail that Cheryl Strayed hiked in order to find herself. She recounted the journey in the book *Wild* (Strayed, 2012), which subsequently became the film of the same name, starring Reese Witherspoon (2014). This long-distance trail is also the sister of the east coast Appalachian Trail (AT) (see chapters seven and nine). Both trails traverse several national parks – seven on the PCT: Sequoia, Kings Canyon, Yosemite, Lassen Volcanic, Crater Lake, Mt Rainier, and North Cascades.

I undertook this in trip early September 2011. My intention was to spend ten days travelling up the coast from San Francisco and then looping back by travelling inland. Arriving in San Francisco is relatively straight forward. The airport is much smaller than Los Angeles Airport (LAX), and much easier to navigate because of that. It also means you should be on the road much quicker if you choose San Francisco over Los Angeles for a West Coast road trip. Either way, you will not be able to avoid the ten-hour plus transatlantic flight time. Because of that, it's a good idea to choose an airline company you particularly like when planning a West Coast trip (even if it is slightly more expensive than a competitor) because you will be enjoying their hospitality for some considerable time.

Arrival in San Francisco

If you've never visited San Francisco you might want to add some days at the beginning or end of a West Coast trip. San Francisco is a fascinating city and definitely worth exploring. You will find some free or cheap things to do in San Francisco and the wider Bay Area – which includes all the towns and cities which surround San Francisco Bay – at the end of this chapter [see Six things to do in San Francisco], but you should certainly do some homework on cheap places to stay. But It is easy to get around the city, by foot or by bus – and the obligatory cable car ride (a must-do). There is also a very efficient Bay Area Rapid Transport (BART) train network, which will take you underneath The Bay to the cities of Berkeley and Oakland.

Critical Cultural Comment – The Legacy of 1960s Student Radicalism

The city of Berkeley is the home of the University of California, Berkeley (UCB), which was at the centre of student radicalism in the 1960s and beyond. A significant flame was lit when the Free Speech Movement was begun there in 1964, when students openly defied the university's ban on the support for political causes. A famous speech by one of the students at the time, Mario Savio, can still be found on YouTube.

The movement proved to be a serious threat to the establishment, challenging deference to authority throughout American society. The university went on to become a west coast centre for a range of anti-establishment causes, including anti-Vietnam war protests, calls for racial equality, and the women's liberation movement, ranging from support for Betty Friedan's case for equality (1963) to Shulamith Firestone's much more radical manifesto (1970).

> The Free Speech Movement was loosely aligned with a previously existing organisation, Students for a Democratic Society (SDS), which had 'chapters' throughout the American university network. In its Port Huron Statement of 1962, drafted by Tom Hayden, it sought to strengthen ties between students and workers, and the fight for civil rights. More broadly, it advocated for greater participatory democracy and civil disobedience.
>
> Many of these causes were at the heart of what is often referred to as The New Left in American society, which began a shift away from an exclusive focus on the exploitation of manual workers, and more towards a wider range of social groups, in what started to be referred to as 'identity politics'. This shift saw the rise in universities of courses in Black Studies, Women's Studies, Queer Studies, etc.
>
> On a more light-hearted note, I remember once looking for the People's Park (a little way from the UCB campus) because I was aware that this had been a significant meeting place for radical students. I couldn't help but smile at the number of rules that the local authorities have since posted up at the entrance to the small park.

I lived for a short time in Berkeley and bought a bike to get around. It's easy to hire a bike in The Bay Area, and it's well worth it because of the many bike paths that huge the water's edge. That said, some of the hills in the heart of San Francisco itself are incredibly steep, so plan routes carefully (you can avoid the hills) or be prepared to push your bike on occasion. This is not as bad as it sounds because although some of the hills are steep, they are not long.

There are some lovely old hotels in San Francisco, but they can be expensive. I have undertaken study trips to the Bay Area with groups of undergraduate students and been very pleased with the hotels we stayed in. One year we had a good deal on a hotel very close to Union Square (right in the heart of the city) and on a couple of occasions we stayed halfway down Market Street, at a lovely old hotel with hundreds of rooms and very pleasant staff. That hotel was also just a stone's throw from the famous City Hall building, which often features in films set in the city, including *Dirty Harry* (1971) and *Milk* (2008).

If you look at a map you will see that Market Street is a main thoroughfare which cuts right through the downtown area, roughly from south to north, finishing at the main ferry terminal. At the north end of Market Street you will also find the large swanky department stores, and to the left (west) you will find the heart of the downtown area, including Chinatown. At the junction of Market Street with Powell Street you will find the much-photographed terminus of a famous cable car route. Cable cars from here will take you on a fantastic fairground ride along some of the steepest streets in the city.

As you head south down Market Street it starts to appear more run down, and you will find more homeless people. Indeed, the whole area to the east of Market Street has a much grittier feel, and I know that many of my students have felt less safe there. I love exploring every part of a city and have never experienced any problems, but, naturally, it pays to have your wits about you in any urban environment. If you continue south down Market Street you will eventually come to the bustling area known as The Castro – the area which became popular with the gay community, when they gravitated from the Haight-Asbury part of the city in the 1970s [see Six things to do in San Francisco].

San Francisco is a very cosmopolitan city and there will be lots of people advertising short stays on websites like Craigslist or Airbnb, so it's definitely worth doing some internet surfing if you want to find an interesting, quirky, or cheap place to stay. Because you don't need a car to get around the immediate Bay Area, you could finish a road trip by returning the car to the airport and then use the BART to get into the heart of the city. If you're lucky you might be able to find accommodation close to a BART station, so you won't have to walk far with your luggage. One of the reasons I liked that hotel in Market Street was because you could jump on the BART at the airport and jump out right next to the hotel. Time your journey into the city from the airport because that's the time you'll need to get back to the airport. You could also look to save some money by getting the BART into the city from the airport when you first arrive and then hire a car once in town – remember, it's always cheaper to hire a car from a town rather than an airport.

The Redwood Highway

Having spent a lot of time in San Francisco in the past, I decided to head north of the city as soon as I got in the hire car. San Francisco is nowhere near as busy as New York or Los Angeles, so you don't need to plan a route which completely avoids downtown. With that in mind I drove north from the airport straight out on to Highway 101, heading towards the downtown area. As you approach the city you can fork right and switch to the I-280, which will drop you on the Embarcadero (it's clearly signposted). The Embarcadero is slow, but you are right in the heart of the city and following the Bay round towards the Golden Gate Bridge – also clearly signposted. As you drive along the Embarcadero you will see the famous Coit Tower to your left, and Alcatraz Island in the Bay to your right, along with the numerous piers which jut out into the Bay, finishing at the bustling Fisherman's Wharf. After that, you will be on the road heading directly towards the Golden Gate Bridge (which is still Highway 101). The Bridge is free if you are travelling north (out of the city), but you pay a toll if you are heading southbound (into the city). It's definitely worth asking about paying bridge tolls at the car hire rental desk. Payment systems are constantly being upgraded. The first time I crossed the bridge I had to throw coins into a bin. Now you have the option of paying online up to 48 hours after crossing.

If you don't have plans to walk or bike the Golden Gate Bridge it's certainly worth stopping for a few minutes at the turnoff on the other side of the bridge. Here, you will get some fantastic views back along the bridge and across the Bay, back towards the city. San Francisco Bay appears to be a calm inlet of water, but its currents are notorious, and the whole area around the bridge can be covered in mist and fog, even in the height of summer.

The Golden Gate bridge was completed in 1937, and still stands as one of the wonders of the modern world. Several workers died in the construction of the bridge, which contains two enormous towers, acting as anchors for the suspension cables. You will certainly appreciate both the beauty and the engineering when you get up close, including some art-deco features. And many people in the Bay Area certainly appreciated the new thoroughfare when it first opened, because, if you didn't want to catch a ferry, it used to be a long road journey around the Bay to get to Marin County – which lies immediately across the bridge.

After crossing the Golden Gate Bridge, you will see signs to Muir Woods. I stopped off there at the end of this trip, but you could certainly consider stopping off at the beginning, if only to pay your respects to the 'Father of the National Parks', John Muir [see John Muir Slice of Americana Pie]. Muir was not only instrumental in establishing the need to preserve areas of outstanding natural beauty in the United States, but also in helping to preserve the large clusters of Giant Sequoia and Giant Redwood trees, which were being cut down at an alarming rate by loggers during Muir's lifetime (1838-1914). Sequoias and Redwoods are native to California and renowned not just for their huge size but also their age; 'Nature's Cathedrals', as Muir called them.

Although Giant Sequoias and Giant Redwoods appear very similar, the trained person will instantly know the difference. Sequoias can be found inland, on the slopes of the Sierra Nevada Mountains (see chapter three), and Redwoods tend to hug the coastline. Redwoods also tend to grow taller (sometimes well over 300 ft), while Sequoias often have thicker trunks and live longer (often over 3,000 years). On this trip I would be in the company of Redwoods for much of the first few days. I love these trees, and love nothing more than following the trails that take you through some of the woods where they can still be found. Two such places are very close to San Francisco – the above-mentioned Muir Woods, just to the north, and Big Basin Redwoods State Park, just to the south. Either or both locations are certainly worth a stop. When I lived in California, I was prone to tension headaches, one solution for which was a tablet, another solution (which worked) was a walk amongst the Redwoods, so, if you are feeling at all anxious, I recommend a stop off.

If you had turned left to Muir Woods you would have found yourself hugging the coast on Highway 1 (a slow, but beautiful stretch of this old road, which features at the end of this chapter). I stayed on Highway 101 to get some faster miles under my belt, but you could also consider turning right when you see signs to Napa Valley – California's main wine region. It's such a pleasant drive through both Marin County and into the Napa Valley. Well, it is once you get past the right hand turn off from the 101, for the San Rafael Bridge and San Quentin prison. If you have seen the film *Dirty Harry* (1971), it's surely difficult to shake the image of the villain, Scorpio (Andy Robinson), as he hijacks the school bus and has it driven up this section of the highway. Until, of course, he sees the massive figure of Inspector Harry Callahan (Clint Eastwood) standing on the flyover at the San Rafael Bridge turnoff, Magnum 44 at the ready. If you can avoid the temptation to take that turn off and look for some of the locations used in that film, you will soon find yourself settling into a very pleasant drive north. I bypassed The Napa Valley this time, but on a previous occasion I remember spending a lovely afternoon driving from vineyard to vineyard, spoilt only by the fact that I couldn't swallow the wine I was tasting. You could stop off anywhere in the Valley and look for a motel. But it is unlikely to be cheap: this is a well-to-do area; irresistible, though, if you have watched the film *Sideways* (2004).

I pulled off at the town of Santa Rosa. I wanted to stop to photograph the train station because this was the location for the arrival of Uncle Charlie in Alfred Hitchcock's film *Shadow of a Doubt* (1943) – his best film, according to Hitchcock. He liked Santa Rosa, seeing it as a perfect example of small-town USA, into which he was only too happy to inject some jeopardy. This part of California was a favourite filming location for him, perhaps because he owned a house just south of San Francisco, near Santa Cruz [see Hitchcock Movies Slice of Americana Pie]. If you'd have stayed on Highway 1 as you drove north out of San Francisco, you would have been following the route that Melanie Daniels (Tippi Hedrun) took in the film *The Birds* (1963), to deliver the love birds to Mitch Brenner (Rod Taylor) in the coastal town of Bodega Bay. The Bay and the schoolhouse are still just as they were in the film. San Francisco and the surrounding area was also the location for perhaps his most famous film, *Vertigo* (1958), in which you will see a scene where Scottie Ferguson (James Stewart) and Madeleine Elster (Kim Novack) are walking around a cluster of Giant Redwood trees. This was filmed at Big Basin Redwoods State Park, which was close to Hitchcock's house.

As the sun began to go down, I pulled off Highway 101 (known as The Redwood Highway at this point) at the small town of Healdsburg and stayed in a chain-motel. The motel was more expensive than I was expecting, but the person on reception explained that this part of California was expensive because of its proximity to the Napa Valley. It was late and I didn't want to drive around putting him to the test, so I paid up. I had driven 100 miles since leaving the airport. There were some good options for dinner and the motel had a decent breakfast offer, included in the price.

I continued along Highway 101 the next morning until I came to the left fork for Highway 128. This road would take me across to Highway 1 directly on the coast. I was up very early, because I wanted to spend as much of the day as possible on this slower coastal route. Highway 128 turned out to be a very pleasant drive. The sky was azure blue, the air was warm and fresh, and I was soon in my own California state of mind. I couldn't resist pulling over to take a photo of the sign displaying 'The Mendocino County Line', and then spent the rest of the day singing the words to the song of the same name by Willie Nelson and Lee Ann Womack (1992). I decided to stop in the town of Mendocino, where I spent a nice reflective time on a short cliff walk, overlooking the ocean. I was beginning to settle into this road trip, living much more in the moment. There's an irony here, because Highway 101 is one of the best roads to forget the 101 things which are usually on one's mind.

Pretty much as soon as I hit the coast, I got the sense that I was now off the tourist map. I loved living in California, but I spent most of that time somewhere between Los Angeles and San Francisco, where I often felt penned in by the sheer business of that part of the coast. Driving north of San Francisco it soon became clear that this is probably much more what the whole coast of California looked and felt like 100 years ago.

Redwoods

I stopped at Fort Bragg for a coffee and some map reading. It looked like I would be able to spend the rest of the day hugging the coast until I hit my first national park – Redwood. My rate of progress was improved when Highway 1 took a turn inland to hit Highway 101 at Leggett, and from there I made good progress to Eureka where I stopped for lunch, but not before I had driven through the Avenue of the Giants in Humboldt Redwoods State Park. You can't miss the park because the highway goes straight through it, and the Redwood trees are so spectacular that you just have to pull over and spend at least a few minutes in their company. There are also three 'drive-thru trees' in this area. These are obvious tourist traps, and you pay for the privilege of driving through the base of the trees. I still found it irresistible, so I took the opportunity to drive through what is probably the most famous of them – The Chandelier Tree – in the appropriately named Drive-Thru Tree Park – which is signposted from the town of Leggett.

A Slice of Americana Pie

A critical appreciation of: Hitchcock Movies

An Englishman born in the East End of London at the turn of the 20th Century is an unlikely candidate for a slice of Americana, particularly road related, but we are not so much talking here of the man, but his films, particularly those he made in the 1950s and 1960s, where travel was often a significant motif.

By the time that Hitchcock had moved to Hollywood in the late 1930s he had already made a mark as a director, but he naturally wanted the opportunity to work on a bigger scale with bigger budgets. He was successful with a number of films in the 1940s but came to resent the lack of control he had over his work. With a stubbornness bordering on arrogance but with a belief in what he could produce he set about maximising artistic control of his work, and for a ten-year period (roughly 1954 to 1964) he produced a string of films which helped shaped movie making as an art form, and particularly the role of the director/auteur in that process.

Hitchcock was lucky in the sense of being in the right place at the right time. The 1950s saw Americans keen to cash in on their increased leisure time and at a time when going to the movies was as natural as watching TV was to become in later years. He was also keen to experiment with what a cinematic experience might be and seemed intuitively aware of how human emotions could be evoked and manipulated through the medium of film. He was called the master of suspense, but he was also the master of his art form. So much so that it is now routine for directors to doth their caps in his direction, and to study his cinematic techniques. For example, Martin Scorsese once said that the famous fight scene in *Raging Bull* (1980) reproduces almost exactly the movements and editing used in the infamous shower scene in *Psycho* (1960).

When I first watched those Hitchcock films I was entranced by the technicolor look and the glamorous settings. There was Scottie (James Stewart) gliding around the streets of San Francisco in his beautiful American car, pursuing the mysterious and glamorous Madeleine Elster (Kim Novak) in the film *Vertigo* (1958). There was Roger O. Thornhill (Cary Grant) tearing across the Mid-West towards Mount Rushmore in *North by Northwest* (1959). And in *The Birds* (1963) there was Melanie Daniels (Tippi Hedren) in her sports car, driving north from San Francisco up the coast to Bodega Bay to deliver two love birds.

But there was always a darker side to everything that Hitchcock put on screen, much of which spoke to the fear behind the thin facade of everyday American life. Perhaps because he was English he was able to expertly exploit this, often in very subversive ways. For, example, there is surely a certain sacrilege in having people running over the four Presidents' heads on Mount Rushmore National Memorial. Hitchcock must have known that he wouldn't get permission to film those particular scenes on the stones themselves, but he always preferred to recreate settings back in the studio anyway, where he would have more control. That said, some of the filming did take place at the National Memorial.

Hitchcock liked to put ordinary Americans in extraordinary positions, again exploiting the idea of things being able to fall apart very quickly. Hitchcock entrapped Mr. Everyman James Stewart on several occasions – through injury, in *Rear Window* (1954); through infatuation, in *Vertigo* (1958); and through mistaken identity, in *The Man who Knew too Much* (1956). Hitchcock enjoyed the mistaken identify ploy, and the transfer of guilt which can ensue. This was perfectly exemplified by Henry Fonda in *The Wrong Man* (1956). He would sometimes put a whole community in jeopardy, like the poor residents of Bodega Bay, who come under attack by those birds. In *The Birds* (1963), the locals blame the newcomers who have travelled to the small town, heightening the sense of invasion by outsiders. In all of these cases Hitchcock was able to feed off the idea that stability could crumble at any moment, which perfectly mirrored the fears that many Americans harboured at the time concerning the Cold War with the Soviet Union, and the threat of nuclear attack.

Hitchcock was subversive in other ways too. He seemed to revel in battling with the film censors, trying to get one up on them. In a classic example, he told the censors that no knife had actually touched Janet Leigh in the *Pyscho* (1960) shower scene – it was all in the imagination of the viewer. In actuality, of course, it was careful montage editing, mixed with Bernard Herman's soundtrack of screeching violins. By distracting the censors he thereby managed to get the first toilet pan on screen. Hitchcock liked the O of the pan to signal personal demise and his imperilled characters often had an O in their name. He also liked the O to appear in the title of the film. He also loved sexual metaphors (the train entering the tunnel, for example), and the subversive hint of homosexuality in his male characters. Anthony Perkins as Norman Bates being the classic example, but he had also hinted at this much earlier; for example, in the film *Rope* (1948).

Hitchcock's films teach us a lot about aspects of American cultural life, particularly the role of fear in establishing order and threatening disorder. For example, a whole community could be threatened by the presence of one stranger in town, like the arrival of Uncle Charlie, played by Joseph Cotton, in Santa Rosa, California – in the film *Shadow of a Doubt* (1943). Individuals could also be threatened by travelling into unfamiliar territory – the road being used as a metaphor to signify disorientation. For anyone who has seen the film *Psycho* (1960), who can also forget that terrifying first glimpse of the Bates Motel sign from the highway; which was perfectly exploited in the TV series of the same name.

On a happier note, I love the way Hitchcock's films help to define so much of what now comprises the nostalgia for the 1950s and 1960s – those colourful settings, the big cars, and the glamorous actors – perfectly epitomised by Cary Grant and Grace Kelly. In this regard, it is not so much real life which is remembered, but its manufactured version on the celluloid screen, and herein lies a key ingredient of Americana: it is steeped in an imagined nostalgia for the past, which Hitchcock films perfectly exemplify.

After lunch I made steady progress along the coast on the 101 until I hit the largest collection of Redwoods on the Californian coast. This includes three Californian State Parks, stretched out along the coast – from south to north: Prairie Creek Redwoods State Park, Del Norte Coast Redwoods State Park, and Jedediah Smith Redwoods State Park. In 1968 these State parks were encircled by the newly designated Redwood National Park. This was extended in 1978 to further protect and preserve what is now also a UNESCO World Heritage site. You can get orientated at the Kuchel Visitor Center, which is directly off Highway 101. As someone who loves being in the company of these trees, I could easily have spent a week in this area, but half a day to two days is more than enough to capture something of the gentle energy emanating from these woodlands.

It's almost fifty miles (about an hour's drive) from the Kuchel Visitor Center up to Crescent City, where I stayed. By the time I got to Crescent City I had driven around 300 miles in total. This is a convenient town to stay over because there are a number of motels. If you feel you've had your fill of Redwood trees you could just stay over for one night, but if you want to chill out in the area you could easily spend two to three nights here. I stayed at a lovely old inn right on Highway 101. It was difficult to fault this location: the owner was great, the room was nice, and there was good food and lovely beach walks within a stone's throw. Given that you would now be fifty miles from the first of the State parks I would recommend exploring further south *before* you venture north to find accommodation. There are lots of trailheads starting directly off the 101, and you will also see signs to the Lady Bird Johnson Grove, named in honour of the wife of President Lyndon B. Johnson [see The Texas White House Slice of Americana Pie]. As you head north you can also leave the highway and take the more scenic drive through the woods by forking left when you see the sign to the Newton B. Drury State Parkway, which rejoins the 101 around ten miles further north.

If you decide to spend just one night in the area you could easily explore the northern state park – Jedediah Smith Redwoods – the following morning, and if you wanted to stop over for two nights you would have time to go back down the coast and enjoy parts of the coastal trail walk. Whatever you decide to do, on leaving Crescent City you will only be ten miles from the Oregon border. I always get up at the crack of dawn on these road trips, so I found myself in Oregon very early on a misty/foggy morning. I was pleasantly surprised to see that I was still amongst Redwood trees. The trees are often said to be native to the Californian coast, but, naturally, they do not respect the man-made border. The fog was beginning to lift and after coffee I decided to head down the road to Loeb State Park to take an early morning stroll. I'm glad I did. The trails were short, but beautiful, and I was pretty much alone in the woods. I was now in a good state of mind and ready to enjoy Oregon for the first time.

On the Oregon Coast Highway

I was around 300 miles from Portland, a city I was keen to explore, but ahead of me I had a coastal drive along the Oregon Coast Highway (still the 101). The next one and a half days were absolutely sublime. It was one winding road after another, with glorious views across to empty beaches, which all had beautiful white horse waves landing gently on the glistening shoreline. I was completely absorbed by it all, even more so when I pulled over at every opportunity to wander around some of the coves, and along some of the expansive beaches. My longest stop was at the Oregon Dunes National Recreation Area, where I stopped to eat the sandwich lunch I had bought a little earlier. The sand was brilliant white, and the place was completely empty, apart from a young family I spotted in the distance as I walked along the beach. If, like me, you have enjoyed the California coast, but disliked a lot of the hustle and bustle, this is definitely the place to be.

As I made my way up the coast, I began to see signs directing me inland to Portland, but I wasn't ready to make the turn, so I continued north, still enjoying every minute of the drive, until I reached the small town of Rockaway Beach. Not the beach that The Ramones (1977) had sung about – that one was 3,000 miles away, due east in Queen's, New York City – but a good tune to be singing nonetheless. I was surprised by how expensive some of the places to stay were, but I managed to find an unassuming inn which was reasonably priced. Time was getting on and I appreciated the owner taking time to tell me about the places to eat. The sun was beginning to go down, so on my way to eat I took a detour down to the wide beach to watch the sun disappear over the Pacific.

The next morning, I checked the map and decided to continue along the 101, hugging the coast until I had to turn inland at the estuary of the

Columbia River. From there it was a fast drive into Portland once I'd joined Interstate 5, heading south. I was surprised to see I-5 because I was used to seeing signs to it when I lived in southern California. The Interstate was completed in the 1950s, which I'd always thought was simply to shorten the drive time between Los Angeles and San Francisco, but in fact it stretches all the way from the Mexican Border to the Canadian border, to include Portland, in Oregon, and Seattle, in Washington State.

View from the Oregon Coast Highway, Oregon

Driving into Portland caused me to pause, reflecting on whether I wanted to be in an urban environment after what I had been experiencing the last few days, but I did want to visit Portland, mainly because of its laid back, liberal reputation. I had read that the hip place to be was around Hawthorne Street, so I headed straight there. I thought it would be a good idea to find accommodation first and then spend the rest of the day exploring the city. I stopped by a couple of hip looking places but both were fully booked – most likely because they were relatively cheap and did appear to have a good vibe. Undeterred I continued my search. The roads were easy to navigate, and there were no high-rise buildings, which I later read was a deliberate policy. It was also before lunchtime, so I wasn't too concerned about the time. In the end I pulled into a chain-motel, a couple of blocks away, and booked a relatively cheap room. The room was very nice and knowing that I wouldn't need the car to explore the city, it was also great that there was secure parking on the premises.

To make the most of the day I was soon on my way into the downtown area. I combined walking with catching buses and trams which were readily available. I started off in the Pearl District because I wanted to visit the famous Powell's City of Books. The cobbled streets were fun to walk around, and had I lunch in a trendy cafe. By coincidence, I was reading the book by Robert Penn – *It's All About the Bike* – where he documents how he built a bike from famous manufacturers of components around the world (Penn, 2011). I had reached the point in the book where he was describing his visit to Chris King Precision Components, which is in Portland. After lunch, I continued my tour of the downtown area, eventually ending up back on Hawthorne, where I looked in some secondhand shops, before enjoying a beer and a cheap Mexican meal in one of the many bustling eateries. The whole vibe was great, and I enjoyed my walk back to my motel, where I promptly feel asleep.

Mount Rainier

The next morning I was keen to get on the road up into Washington State to visit my next national park, Mount Rainier. I took the I-5 up to the junction with Highway 12 and then drove east towards the park. This road will take you to both the southeast and southwest entrances. The southwest entrance looked to be closer, so I headed north on Highway 7 from the town of Morton, until I hit Highway 706 going east. Before long I was at the Nisqually Entrance. Nisqually is the name of the river I had been following for the last few miles. I arrived around 10.30 in the morning, the journey from Portland having taken me around three hours. I drove slowly towards the Henry M. Jackson Memorial Visitor Center, where I found the usual collection of souvenirs, and a good selection of food options. I bought a sandwich in anticipation of a picnic lunch on the slopes of the mountain.

Mount Rainier was one of the first designated national parks, in 1899. John Muir described Mount Rainier as the noblest of the 'fire mountains' on the American Pacific Coast, and this quote greets you on the outside wall of the visitor centre. The complete Pacific Ring is known as the ring of fire because of the frequency of the earthquake activity and the volcanic eruptions. Mount Rainier is one such volcano, as is Mount St Helens, also in Washington State, and Mount Fuji, in Japan. Mount Rainier shakes from time to time, but there has not been a violent eruption for over 1,000 years. However, geologists who study the Pacific North West are well aware of the dangers from these sleeping giants, and a lava flow from Mount Rainier could reach the city of Seattle, on the Pacific coast.

Mount Rainier, Mount Rainier National Park, Washington State

From the parking lot at the visitor centre, Mount Rainier stood before me, its snowcapped peak glistening in the warm sunshine. It was perfectly formed and the whole scene looked to be straight from a picture book. The ever-handy brochure I was given at the entrance was displaying a number of trails, so I was keen to get on the slopes as soon as possible. The peak of the mountain stands at over 14,000 ft, and the brochure told me that it should only be attempted by experienced climbers, with climbing equipment. It also told me that there were a wide range of trails of varying lengths, the majority of which were not strenuous. I decided to take a stroll before lunch on the Nisqually Vista Trail (1.2 miles), which enables you to get up close to one of the many glaciers in the park. Armed with my picnic lunch I then set off on the more strenuous 5.4-mile Skyline Trail, through Paradise Park, up to Panorama Point at 6,800 ft. This was a fantastic hike on the slopes of the mountain, which included close-up views of beautiful meadows, and far-distant views across the State of Washington. I also got the chance to chat to people on the slopes, who were from all over the United States and beyond. After spending around four hours on the mountain slopes, which included my lunch break, I arrived back at the visitor centre.

I left the park via the southeast entrance, which turned out to be a fantastic drive, passing lakes and rivers until I arrived at the Stevens Canyon Entrance and the Ohanapecosh Visitor Center. I then made my way down Highway 123, before turning west on Highway 12, back to Morton, where I had been that morning. It would have been nice to turn east on Highway 12 towards Yakima onto Interstate 82, and then south on Highway 97, but I had spent so much time in the national park that time was now against me. It was late afternoon and it looked like the I-5 would be my best bet to get some serious miles under my belt. If you have more time than I did I would certainly recommend Highway 97 because it would eventually take you straight down to Crater Lake, the next national park on my list.

If you have even more time – perhaps a road trip of two weeks or more – Mount Rainier would be the obvious place to launch off from to visit two more national parks in the far north-west of the United States – Olympic National Park, to the west of Seattle, and North Cascades National Park, up on the Canadian border. These two parks were out of my reach for this road trip but with more time and a little planning you could easily reach them. Olympic Park would certainly be a possibility within a two-week road trip up from San Francisco, which could also include a visit to Seattle. Olympic Park was designated a national park in 1938. Like Acadia in the far north-east (see chapter six) it spills down to a long length of coastline. Its main geological feature is Mount Olympus, which is surrounded by protected rain forest, all located within a huge peninsula. Interestingly, if you wanted to spend the whole of a road trip on Highway 101, you will find that this highway actually encircles the park.

North Cascades National Park was designated in 1968. Because of its location, in a remote part of the north west of the US, way up on the Canadian border, it is one of the least visited of the national parks. Like its sister park, Glacier National Park, in Montana, it comprises a large number of glaciers and glacial lakes, which are continuously being topped up by waterfalls, from which the park takes its name. One highway leads you through the park, but it's a long way north on I-5 until you hit Highway 20 going east into the park. You could be on the road for around five hours if you drove from Mount Rainier directly to North Cascades. With that in mind, you could consider starting a road trip around the Pacific North West from the city of Seattle, which has a major international airport.

Making my way west on Highway 12 instead of east had one distinct advantage; I would be able to get some great views of Mount St Helens. In order to take some photos, I stopped at the Hopkins Hill viewpoint, the large sign at which announced that I was 24 miles from the crater. It also stated that the major eruption in 1980 had blasted one cubic mile of material into the air, reducing the height of this very active fire mountain from 9,677 ft to 8,300 ft. After my stop I continued along Highway 12 until I hit I-5 going south. I made it to Albany before the sun set, where I pulled off the freeway and booked into one of the many chain-motels for my overnight stay. One of the nice things about being on an interstate is that the major intersections will always have a selection of motels and neighbouring diners and restaurants. This can be very useful when you are feeling tired, because all you have to do is look across to the giant neon signs, and make your choice from the seat of your car.

Crater Lake

The next morning, I continued along I-5 going south until I hit the city of Eugene, the capital city of the State of Oregon. I was keen to get to Crater Lake, and I didn't fancy navigating my way around a large city. That said, I had heard that Eugene was a great place to live, so I pulled off the freeway and followed the signs to the University, which many Americans had told me was also a great place to study. It was easy to park on the roads just by the campus and I spent a very pleasant hour in the sunshine drinking coffee and looking around the bookshop. I cut my stop short because I wanted to be at Crater Lake before lunchtime. I left the interstate just south of Eugene, heading south-east on Highway 58, until I met Highway 97 going south. The drive was lovely, and the road was fast. I turned right onto the dead straight Highway 138, which was signposted to the national park. The North Entrance to the park was then a left turn from Highway 138. It had taken me around two and a half hours to get from the University of Oregon to the national park (around 130 miles).

The crystal-clear Crater Lake, Crater Lake National Park, Oregon

It is difficult to describe what you see when you first look into the water of Crater Lake. To say it is spectacular would not do it justice. It's a feast for the eyes. It's so vividly blue that it quickly becomes mesmerising.

The lake is a dormant volcanic crater, formed by a massive eruption from the then 12,000 ft Mount Mazama, which is now filled with crystal clear glacial water. It has long been considered an area of outstanding natural beauty and became one of the first American national parks, in 1902, three years after Mount Rainier. The lake is 8,000 ft up and five miles wide. It is also the deepest lake in the United States (nearly 2,000 ft deep). Navigation is easy because there is a 33-mile loop road, with signposts leading you up to mountain trails and down to the shoreline. There's also a great visitor centre, and all amenities are available at Rim Village, which has plenty of places to sit, inside and out.

I spent the afternoon driving the whole of the loop road, stopping to take it all in, and trying to capture a perfect image of the lake on my camera. My longest stop was to climb up the marked trail to Mount Scott, the highest point in the park, at nearly 9,000 ft. This trail is on the east side of the lake. It starts off gently but becomes more strenuous as you climb to the viewpoint at the top. The views across the State from the top were well worth the climb. It's around two miles to the top, but you have to come back over the same two miles to get back down again. Although I only spent the afternoon exploring the park, I didn't feel I'd missed anything significant. Apart, perhaps, from a boat tour, which stops at Wizard Island, the small volcanic cone protruding from the lake. I left the national park from the south, passing through Mazama Village, down along Highway 62, until I hit Highway 97 again, going south. The drive from the park down to Klamath Falls was a lovely early evening drive, for twenty-five miles of which I was following the shoreline of Upper Klamath Lake. I stayed overnight at a chain-motel in Klamath Falls.

Mount Shasta and Mount Tamalpais

I awoke to find a misty morning and a distinct lack of breakfast options, apart from some nasty tasting motel coffee, some cakes in plastic wrappers, which looked like they had a shelf-life of 500 years, and some fruit, which I popped into the car. I was sure that I would find a nice diner along the road, so I set off heading further south down Highway 97. The mist began to lift as the sun rose in the sky and I soon found myself enjoying a wonderful road revelry. As Mount Shasta began to loom in the distance, I pulled over to take a photo. The air felt slightly damp and fresh, and once back in the car I found myself singing lines from an old favourite song by Lobo, about being a free man (1971). I did indeed feel like a free man, as I crossed the border from Oregon into northern California. Needing to fill up with petrol I stopped at the amusingly named town of Weed, which had a fantastic all-American diner where I finally got that breakfast I was looking for.

As I pulled out of Weed back onto I-5 heading south I had a distinct sense that I had settled into living in the moment. I made a snap decision to turn off and take a look at the town of Mt Shasta, in the shadow of its namesake – the 14,000 ft 'fire mountain'. There was a classic car show right in town, so I spent a wonderful hour looking at everything on display. As I was drinking some decent coffee, I became taken by the sign opposite, which was advertising bike hire for Mt Shasta. Being a keen cyclist and not having been on a bike during this trip I made another snap decision to get out on a bike on the slopes of the mountain. It was now a beautiful Californian morning and within a short time I was cycling towards the mountain on a great road bike, but not before I had taken the fruit from the car and bought a bottle of water. I'm a competitive person and I knew I wouldn't be satisfied with just a short ride. I ended up climbing until the road pavement stopped at around 8,000ft. Naturally, it was a very pleasant freewheel back down again.

Back on the road again I continued south on I-5 heading towards San Francisco. Had I not stopped at Mt Shasta I might just have had enough time to visit Lassen Volcanic National Park. I didn't have this on my itinerary, so I wasn't too concerned, and I was pleased by how my mood had relaxed into living in the moment. That said, and with the benefit of rational hindsight a quick visit to it would have completed my list of Californian park visits. The park can be accessed by turning east on Highway 44 at the town of Redding. Lassen Volcanic became a national park in 1916, while the volcano was still very active, and a huge eruption of this 'fire mountain' had occurred just one year earlier.

I made it to Vacaville as the sun was going down, after having left I-5 to join the I-505, which links the I-5 with the I-80 – the main freeway joining San Francisco with the state capital city of Sacramento. I pulled off the freeway and booked into a chain-motel. I had driven 300 miles since leaving Klamath Falls early that morning. The other reason I didn't visit Lassen Volcanic National Park was because I wanted to spend the end of this road trip in Marin County, just to the north of the Golden Gate Bridge. I had very happy memories of

A Slice of Americana Pie

A critical appreciation of: *Zen and the Art of Motorcycle Maintenance* (1974)

The book *Zen and the Art of Motorcycle Maintenance* reputedly holds two records: it is the biggest selling philosophy book ever (around 5 million sales) and it was rejected by more publishers than any other book (reputedly,121). Its author, Robert Pirsig, only wrote one other book, *Lila* – on similar themes – and remained reclusive throughout his life, rarely giving interviews.

The *Zen* book was first published in 1974, and although it hardly gets mentioned in formal philosophy circles, it completely resonated with the zeitgeist of the time. Indeed, it helped to define it, being part of a New Age movement, which combined aspects of Western and Eastern philosophies. Particularly in the United States, the book also resonated with the anti-war, hippy, counter-culture movement, which by 1974 was losing direction. Although the last American troops didn't leave Vietnam until 1975, the war was long over, and lost. President Nixon had resigned from office a year earlier, in disgrace, and in the year the book was published. Clearly, much of the accompanying disillusionment with those in authority was in need of resolution.

The book has a universal appeal, but it is all-American in many respects. Fundamentally, it works on two levels. First, it celebrates that all-American wanderlust, to be out on the road in the American great outdoors in search of fulfilment (and on a motorcycle). Second, it incorporates elements of anti-materialist Eastern mysticism in the search for personal enlightenment. In a society where institutionalised religion was increasingly being implicated in the anti-authoritarian sensibility, and where the idealism of left-wing politics had little real purchase, personal journeys of enlightenment seemed to hit the right note. Pirsig was aware of this when he agreed that his own personal journey, which he documents in the book, just happened to coincide with the same journey that many others were making, or seeking to make.

The actual motorcycle route undertaken in the book takes Pirsig, his son, and two friends, on two bikes, out west from Minneapolis towards Bozeman, Montana, and then on into Oregon and south to San Francisco. Two national parks are on the route – Yellowstone and Crater Lake. Their road exchanges speak to a fundamental difference, between those who have a mere means to end relationship with machines and technology – with little interest in how machines actually work, only that they do – and Pirsig's own view of the importance of understanding not just motorcycle maintenance, but how this can unlock the door to a more fulfilling and meaningful relationship with the world and its objects.

More significantly, the road journey and accompanying conversations are the rhetorical device to explore deeper issues concerning Pirsig's own past, and his quest to explore the concept of Quality. At the core of which is his need to reconcile the subject-object dichotomy which he feels has dogged Western consciousness, and, in the process, prevented personal enlightenment. It speaks to the need to reconcile the I – the person's mind – with the objects we experience around us. For Pirsig, the Western mind – from Plato onwards – has persisted in believing that what is objectively the case must be separated from what is subjectively felt. This division is a limit on human Reason (or better, Western Reason) which Pirsig grapples with throughout the book.

The title of the book now also begins to make sense. For, in societies which are technologically advanced, with modern production processes, there is a danger of humans becoming lost or alienated, resulting in what Pirsig's contemporary thinkers called a 'homeless mind' (Berger, Berger and Kellner, 1974). A distinction emerges between those who are able to accommodate themselves to this feeling of alienation, and those who are compelled to dig deeper. Motorcycle maintenance is usually experienced as rational and scientific, so the question becomes one of how might we rediscover our spiritual – Zen – relationship with it?

As we read, we become aware of a shadowy figure in the book – Phaedrus – who speaks as a former self of Pirsig. We learn that Phaedrus' philosophical digging had put him so at odds with society, such that 'correctional' action was deemed necessary. The parallel at this point is with Ken Kesey's novel *One Flew Over the Cuckoo's Nest;* raising the question of what to do with people and groups who cannot conform to society's norms (Kesey, 1962). Three main tools appeared to be at the disposal of the authorities at the time: forms of mass manipulation (media messages aimed at conformity); forms of physical force (in response to street protest); and forms of institutional rehabilitation (to help individuals re-conform). But, chillingly, in the case of Kesey's McMurphy – famously portrayed on screen by Jack Nicholson in the film of the same name (1976) – and for Pirsig's former self, the individual rehabilitation took a medical route.

We are now halfway through the book – ingredients all laid out – and moving forward, literally, to San Francisco, but also spiritually, towards a reconciliation with Pirsig's past, and trying to solve that Quality problem at the heart of Western Reason.

Physical journeys are often deeply symbolic, pointing to spiritual journeys. The US seems to be almost uniquely able to combine these two aspects, in being a nation with a vast outdoors, built on a foundation of modern transport networks and infrastructure, and a population often grappling with a rootless, modern (even post-modern), sensibility. No surprise therefore that European thinkers like Jean Baudrillard were drawn to analysing this in narrative form (Baudrillard,1989), and film directors like Wim Wenders were drawn to exploring this on screen. In *Paris, Texas* (1984), for example, the character Travis (played by Harry Dean Stanton) appears as a lost American Everyman. The Road Movie genre, in general, might also be considered a significant American invention, and equally at home in comedy form – e.g. *Planes, Trains, and Automobiles* (1987) – as well as in action adventure form – e.g. *Vanishing Point* (1971).

I have read the book three times, with long gaps in between, and got something different from it each time. This could be one of the reasons why the book works for so many people: It is not so much Pirsig's own solutions to the questions he raises, but what he is able to spark in readers, in their own quests for enlightenment and understanding. Sometimes, just being out in the American great outdoors can help us all to recuperate, regenerate, or even reinvent. Sometimes, as with Pirsig, that experience can then become a gateway: to help us come to a deeper understanding of ourselves and the world around us.

cycling in Marin County and had not been back since. My stop over at Vacaville, just north of San Francisco, meant that I would have the bulk of the next day to chill out there before I caught my flight out of San Francisco airport.

The next morning, I continued south on I-80 and then followed the road round the top of the Bay, crossing the San Rafael Bridge on Highway 580 (signposted to Richmond). This brought me back to Highway 101, from which I then followed the signs to Muir Woods on Highway 1. My day panned out beautifully. After a leisurely walk around the Redwoods in Muir Woods [see John Muir Slice of Americana Pie], I made my way down to Stinson Beach on a wonderful stretch of this coast road. From there I drove to the town of Fairfax, where I had a very nice brunch. The town of Fairfax is northern California writ-large – laid back and liberal. It's also home to the Fairfax Cyclery, which, by a double coincidence, Robert Penn had visited to buy his cycle frame in the book I was still reading. The relevant chapter reminded me that here was the spiritual home of the mountain bike. I own two Marin bikes – which used to be made in the county before they transferred manufacturing abroad. When I lived in California the mountain bike as we now know it didn't exist and it was virtually impossible to climb any significant mountain off-road by bike.

Given that Mt Tamalpais was a short distance away from where I was sitting, I decided to head off to the Fairfax Cyclery. I hired a state-of-the-art Marin mountain bike, which got me all the way up the mountain. Towards the top I almost came off on the increasingly stony path, but I made it, completing a route I could only have dreamed of making when I lived in California. The view from the top of Mt Tamalpais is stunning, with the whole of the Bay Area laid out in front of you. This also inspired the tune *Tamalpais High* by David Crosby (1971). Rest assured, you don't have to do what I did, because your hire car will take you to the top in no time. For me, on that mountain bike, it was a fantastic way to finish this road trip.

If you need a one-night stop over before leaving San Francisco there are several reasonably priced chain-motels at the airport. I've used these motels on several occasions.

Conclusion

This had been a spectacular road trip. Not only had I been in the company of 'Nature's Cathedrals' – the mighty Redwood trees – but I had also been on the glorious Oregon Coast Highway (the 101), where every day was indeed a winding road. To cap it off, I had been in the vicinity of the literal caps of several fire mountains, located in the Pacific North West. The whole experience had been breathtaking, including my cycle rides, which were literally breath-taking. My only regret was that I didn't stop off at Lassen Volcanic National Park, but I certainly don't regret allowing myself to live in the moment for a lot of this trip.

With a little more time and planning this road trip could easily be extended to include visits to Olympic and/or North Cascades national parks – although both are some way north from San Francisco, making Seattle a possible alternative starting point. That said, it is certainly worth considering spending some time in and around San Francisco, either at the beginning or the end of any planned road trip to the west coast of the USA.

Six things to do in San Francisco – which are free or relatively cheap

The good news about San Francisco is that it's easy to get to places on foot and many of the streets are a hive of activity. If you want to take the weight off your feet, it's really easy to jump on a cable car. And if you want go further afield the Bay Area Rapid Transport (BART) trains are fast, efficient and clean. The city of San Francisco itself is quite compact, but the whole Bay Area is huge and includes Marin County to the north, the cities of Oakland and Berkeley to the east, and San Jose to the south. If you want to explore the whole Bay Area, a hire car is probably the best bet. There are a huge number of places to visit and things to do in the Bay Area. Here are some of the cheaper and quirkier options, including some paths less trodden.

1 Wander through Chinatown and surrounds

The official entrance to Chinatown is the huge gate on Grant Street. You can wander from here through to Columbus Avenue. At the junction of the two streets you will find the famous City Lights Book Store, and Vesuvio's Cafe – a spiritual home for the Beats in the early-sixties [see On the Road Slice of Americana Pie]. Keep going and you will come to Telegraph Hill, and Coit Tower, with fantastic views of the city (small fee to go to the top). Look in the sky for the famous wild parrots of Telegraph Hill.

2 Catch the Powell Street cable car from Market Street to Fisherman's Wharf

The cable car goes right through the heart of the city, past Union Square, and up some of the steepest San Francisco Streets, before descending to the Bay. It's a fantastic, cheap fairground ride. The start point, halfway down Market Street, is impossible to miss. There are always people milling around, some of them just watching the cable cars being turned around before they make this journey. At the other end, it's just as busy, as you make your way down to Fisherman's Wharf – which is full of tourist shops and restaurants, and the place to get the ferry to visit Alcatraz Island (which is not cheap).

3 Catch a bus and wander around Haight Street and Golden Gate Park

The junction of Haight and Ashbury is a famous landmark of late-sixties hippiedom, and the emerging gay community. The house at 710 Ashbury was where the rock group The Grateful Dead lived from 1966-68. Jimi Hendrix, Janis Joplin, and the band Jefferson Airplane also lived close-by in the late-sixties. Haight Street still has many ethnic shops and a café culture. Golden

Gate Park was a focus for many psychedelic events in 'the summer of love' (1967) and has a Japanese tea garden at its centre. The peace and love mood was captured in the song *San Franciscan Nights* (1967) by The Animals.

4 Hire a bike, catch the ferry to Sausalito, and cycle back.

Bike hire places are easy to find, and bikes travel free on the ferries. You can catch a ferry from the Ferry Terminal at the end of Market Street, or from Pier 41. Once off the ferry in Sausalito – a small Bay-side town in Marin County and reputed to be where 'the dock of the bay' can be found, as in the song of the same name by Otis Redding (1968) – you can cycle back across the Golden Gate Bridge (about 2-3 miles from Sausalito). From the Bridge you can either head back to Fisherman's Wharf (about 5 miles following the coast), or venture into the Presidio (along Lincoln Avenue) and into Golden Gate Park (along 25th Avenue).

5 Take a trip across the Golden Gate Bridge to Marin County

You can do this by bus, but best if you use a hire car. After crossing the Golden Gate Bridge, stop off at the signposted viewpoint. Then take Highway 1 and head to Muir Woods (also signposted). This is a haven of tranquillity, with paths around Giant Redwood trees [see John Muir Slice of Americana Pie]. From there you can follow the winding road to Muir Beach and Stinson Beach and up Mt Tamalpais for great views of the Bay. If you have time head for the laid-back town of Fairfax for lunch, and then hire a mountain bike from the Fairfax Cyclery to tackle Mt Tamalpais – tough going, but well worth it.

6 Explore some famous film locations around San Francisco

Many famous films were shot in San Francisco. Frank Bullitt (Steve McQueen) in the film *Bullitt* lived at 1153 Taylor Street, the same street where a lot of the famous car chase was filmed [see Steve McQueen Slice of Americana Pie], and Scottie (James Stewart), in *Vertigo* (1958), lived at 900 Lombard Street. Key scenes in *Dirty Harry* (1971) feature the Saints Peter and Paul Church at 666 Filbert Street. And the film *Milk* (2008) – about the politician and gay activist Harvey Milk – features Castro Street to the south of the city. A lot of the gay community emigrated here from Haight-Ashbury.

Chapter 9

The Blue Ridge Mountains of Virginia and on Top of Old Smoky

National Parks: Shenandoah, Great Smoky Mountains, Mammoth Cave, New River Gorge

Other notable sites: The Blue Ridge Parkway

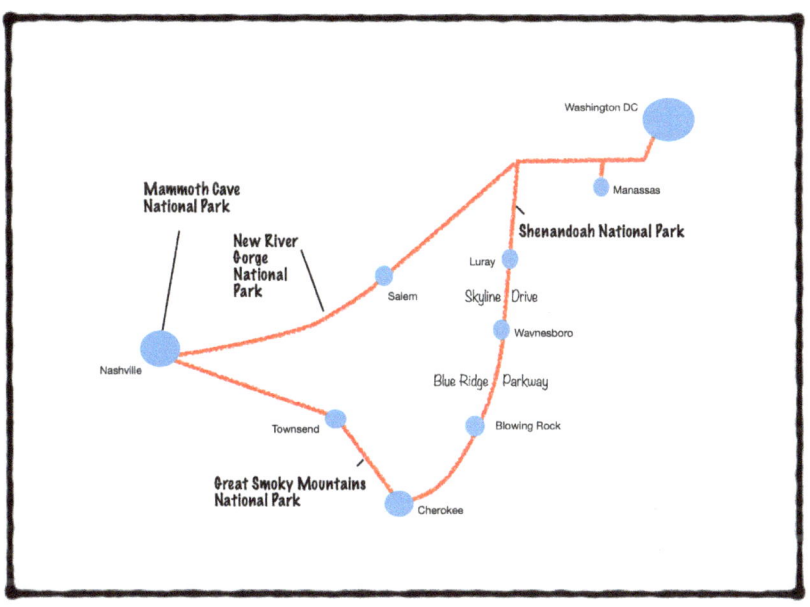

This chapter was composed while singing:

Take me Home, Country Roads, as performed by John Denver (1971)

and

Tennessee Homesick Blues, as performed by Dolly Parton (1984)

Introduction

There are far fewer national parks to the east of the Mississippi River than the west, but two of the most popular are within easy striking distance from Washington DC. I was due to catch a flight from DC in early September 2014, to St. Louis, Missouri, so this was an ideal opportunity to spend ten days before that on the trail of Laurel and Hardy's lonesome pine (1937). Shenandoah and the Great Smoky Mountains National Parks are connected by the Blue Ridge Parkway, but to avoid having to retrace my steps I created a wider loop back to DC, which included a visit to Nashville, Tennessee.

Arrival and orientation in Washington DC

Washington DC is the capital of the United States but is not part of any State. It exists in its own right in the federal District of Columbia (hence, DC). It sits between the States of Maryland and Virginia. It should not be confused with the State of Washington on the Pacific North West. I did once read about someone who booked a flight and confused the two, so it's worth checking twice if you are doing an internet search for cheap flights late at night or when you are tired.

One of the most striking things about DC is that it feels very different to New York, so combining a visit to both could make for an interesting contrast. If you don't want to drive between the two cities there are regular trains, and very cheap buses (e.g. Bolt Bus) as well as the more familiar Greyhound buses. It takes around four hours on the bus, traffic permitting. DC is nowhere near as hectic as NYC, and the downtown area is easy to navigate on foot once you have found your bearings. The majority of the government buildings are relatively close to each other, including the Capitol, and the Supreme Court. The White House though is a couple of miles down Pennsylvania Avenue. If you don't want to walk between any of the buildings there are a number of little tram-like tour buses which circle the main area. There are also a large number of interesting museums – including the National Museum of the American Indian (which I recommend) – all within easy reach of each other – and a trip to the Library of Congress is well worth it.

If you plan to stay in DC for a day or two, a selection of some cheap or free things to do are included in the 'Six things to do in Washington DC' at the end of this chapter. Accommodation can be expensive so it would certainly be worth doing some serious internet searching before you leave home. I have conducted many student tours of DC and we normally stayed at a wonderfully old and rambling hotel on 11th Street, between Capitol Hill and The White House. This area is also close to downtown, and close to the headquarters of the FBI. I love these old American hotels. I see them as authentic slices of Americana pie, but I appreciate that they are not for everyone.

The Blue Ridge Mountains and Shenandoah

Having visited DC many times before, I headed off from the airport towards my first national park – Shenandoah. The city's airport – Dulles – is pretty easy to navigate and isn't as busy as you might expect. Everything is clearly signposted, and it wasn't long before I was out of the airport environs, heading south on Highway 28, and then west on I-66. The airport is located to west of the city, and because Shenandoah is to the west, I didn't need to go anywhere near the downtown area. I arrived at the town of Front Royal – the gateway to Shenandoah – only an hour after leaving the airport, having driven around 60 miles. Front Royal was significant in the American Civil War (1861-1865) as the location where the celebrated Confederate General 'Stonewall' Jackson (representing the southern states who wanted to keep their independence – and slavery) led and won a battle against the northern Union forces (representing the one nation United States – and anti-slavery).

Shenandoah National Park was designated in 1935. Before then, its canopy of trees and trails had already been an escape for many Americans living in and around the eastern seaboard. It's a world away from the urban and industrial landscapes of cities like Baltimore, Pittsburgh and Washington DC, and although it would not have been easy for working class/blue collar families to access its recreational possibilities during the Great Depression of the 1930s, these possibilities became increasingly open during the 1950s and beyond. Workers *were* in and around the park in the 1930s, though, as part of President Roosevelt's New Deal economic policies which funded an ambitious programme of road, trail, and cabin construction, which generations of people have benefited from ever since.

The 2,200 mile Appalachian Trail (AT) also runs through the park, and its distinctive markers can be seen at several points. This makes the AT accessible to park visitors for short distances, who may then find themselves mingling with the more hardy folk who will have put aside the six months necessary to walk the whole trail from Springer Mountain in Georgia, to Mount Katahdin in Maine (or vice versa). Had you been on the trail in 1996, you might have bumped into the travel writer Bill Bryson and his friend Steve Katz. But possibly *not* – for reasons which are explained in his book *A Walk in the Woods* (Bryson, 1998), which was later turned into the film of same name (2015).

After paying the park entrance fee at the official north entrance, I was pleased to be handed my park brochure, which explained that I would be able to drive all the way through the park on the Skyline Drive. This 105 mile road would take me across the top of the Blue Ridge Mountains, but at a leisurely 35mph. I did wonder if this route would be the perfect motorcycle ride, but I'm not sure whether many bikers would enjoy being so speed-restricted. For me, I quickly reconciled myself to the speed limit, relaxed into a sedate driving position, and made my way up the winding road. I had hardly got going when I found myself at the Shenandoah Valley Overlook. I was 1,390 ft up according to the marker, and I spent some time there in quiet reflection as I looked down towards the Shenandoah River, which was gently glistening in the distance. It was also at this point that I started singing the greatest hits of John Denver, surprising myself about how well I had absorbed the words over the years.

By the time I got to the Hogback Overlook I was now not only 3,470 ft up, but also in a position to see why the Blue Ridge Mountains are so-called. It was a wonderful sight, as I looked west, because the sun's rays were shining through the clouds and landing on an expansive landscape of gently rolling blue-coloured hills. Time was getting on though, and I could see that there was no opportunity to stopover on the Skyline Drive itself, so I turned right (west) at the Thornton Gap Entrance Station onto Highway 211 and after only ten miles I was in the small town Luray, where I checked into a chain-motel.

Knowing that I would soon be restricted to 35mph again, I set off early the next morning with the expectation that I would get to the end of the Skyline Drive that day. I found it difficult not to keep stopping at the overlooks in order to take photographs, so I'm not sure whether I would have got much beyond 35mph even if I had been allowed to. I stopped at the area known as Skyland, which included a marker for the highest point on the road (3,680 ft). I then took an early misty-morning stroll along one of the trails where I spotted my first AT marker. I then made a longer stop at the Byrd Visitor Center where I had coffee and bought some food for later. In the parking lot there was a statue to commemorate the work of the Civilian Conservation Corps (The CCC) – the people who had worked in the park as part of President Roosevelt's New Deal to boost economic activity in the 1930s. Interestingly, the accompanying plaque referred to the possibilities for 'recreation and re-creation' in the park. I then strolled to the Dark Hollow Falls, which were exactly as their name implies.

I continued down Skyline Drive, spending the afternoon winding around endless sweeping bends in the road and looking across at the blue-coloured mountains. The mist in the valleys enhanced the expansive landscape, but as the sun slowly began to dominate the sky, the rays – once again – created beautiful patterns as they hit the mountain tops. Late afternoon I found myself descending towards the junction with I-64 and the official end of Skyline Drive. At that junction I turned right on Highway 250 and made the short journey to the little town of Waynesboro, where I was pleased to see some motels. Unfortunately, the one I chose was a good example of where looks can deceive. The room had a nice little porch, with a pleasant view, but I soon realised that you get what you pay for, and because I hadn't paid much I certainly didn't get much. It would be harsh to say that the room was a flea-pit (it certainly didn't have any fleas) but I did vow that I would spend a bit more money on accommodation the following day. The evening was saved by being able to walk to a pleasant Mexican restaurant for dinner.

The next day turned out to be a repeat of the previous day, except this time I would be on the Blue Ridge Parkway, the road which links Shenandoah National Park with the Great Smoky Mountains National Park. I returned along Highway 250 to get back to Rockfish Gap, where I had left Skyline Drive the previous day. I then turned right straight onto the Blue Ridge Parkway, which begins exactly where Skyline Drive ends. If there hadn't been any signs you would believe you were still on the same road. I was pleased to see that there wasn't a fee to travel on the parkway, only nice looking, helpful, wooden signs, to keep you on track. I was also pleased that the speed limit had risen to a heart-stopping 45mph. I parked up at the Humpback Rocks Visitor Center, to get my bearings and picked up a really helpful brochure, which looked like a national park one. It marked all the key features of the parkway, including the overlooks and the trailheads, and told me that it was 469 miles long. It also pointed out that you could lodge at the Peaks of Otter Visitor Center (around halfway down the road). I assumed this would be booked up, but made a mental note that this could be an option in the future.

As with the Skyline Drive, it was clear that there were many small towns just off the road, so I wasn't concerned about finding accommodation, only that I would be looking for something a bit more up market this time. I decided to stop at the Peaks of Otter Visitor Center anyway, and I'm glad I did. It was a big complex and I enjoyed a cooked breakfast. The view from my table was lovely, overlooking Abbott Lake and Sharp Top Mountain. It turned out that there was a one mile loop trail around the lake so I had a wander before getting back in the car, but not before I bought some food for a picnic lunch.

Just a little further down the road I stopped at a large AT sign near Bear Wallow Gap, where I was lucky to see a small family of deer. I then spent a lovely few hours winding down the parkway until I came across a little Appalachian hamlet of cabins which had been renovated to recreate their original look and function. It turned out to be Mabry Mill, which was once a working sawmill and blacksmiths, and all its workings were on view. Hand-held ploughs and horse drawn carts had been strategically placed to complete the look. I sat by the small lake to have my late lunch, looking at the mill wheel on the side of one of the buildings. The sun was now shining bright and it was a lovely way to spend an hour. I spent the rest of the afternoon in a manner to which I was becoming accustomed – driving around bends and stopping to take in the views. I crossed the state border between Virginia and North Carolina, and as the sun began to set I pulled off the parkway and drove the short distance into the town of Blowing Rock. I was very pleased to see some nice looking motels and inns, and after wondering if they might be a bit expensive, I took a chance on one of them. I was in luck: the room was big, with lovely furnishings, and wasn't that expensive. The owner explained that downtown was within easy walking distance, where I would be able to find several places to eat. It was a beautiful, warm evening and the sky turned a wonderful gold and red as I made my way downtown, where I enjoyed a great meal and a beer.

I had a good night's sleep and once back in the car I saw that I had covered 300 miles the previous day, meaning that I was well over halfway down the parkway and within easy striking distance of the Great Smoky Mountains National Park. Just a short drive along the parkway I came to the famous Linn Cove Viaduct. This sweeping piece of road is used to advertise the parkway and, apart from being an engineering marvel, it was also a great place to stop. There was a lovely trail which meandered around the rock face, and at one point it took you right underneath the viaduct itself. There was also a signpost telling me that I was now at an altitude of 4,154 ft, and looking up at the summit of Grandfather Mountain, whose peak was at 5,939 ft. It was early in the morning and there was nobody else around. At the small visitor centre I was surprised to read that the viaduct was the last piece in the parkway's jigsaw, and that the parkway was not one complete roadway until 1987. It was also fascinating to learn that the giant 'S' shaped road bend around Grandfather Mountain was constructed top-down, by crane, rather than from the ground up.

I spent the rest of the day on the final section of the parkway, stopping first at Linville Falls, which were impressive, particularly when viewed from the platform just off the marked trail. My next stop was Craggy Gardens. From the small visitor centre you could access several trails. I took the Craggy Pinnacle Trail, which, although not much more than a mile there and back, provided some spectacular views across North Carolina. I came off the parkway at the town of Asheville, because my camera was playing up. The very helpful camera store was able to sort me out. While they did that I took the opportunity to have lunch across the road. Soon afterwards I was back on the parkway with a fully working camera and I spent the afternoon pleasantly driving along the final section. At several points I got some spectacular views across the Pisgah National Forest, my photographs of which were enhanced, not only by having a fully working camera again, but also by the ever changing combination of clouds and sun.

I was also really lucky to get some great shots across the mountains and hills at the pull off which signposted the highest point on the parkway

(6,053 ft.). Not long after this I started descending towards the southern end of the parkway, but I didn't need to go all the way because I began to see signs pointing to the right (west) to the Great Smoky Mountains National Park. It was now early evening and I needed to look for some accommodation, so I stopped at the Oconaluftee Visitor Center to take stock and look at my maps.

The Linn Cove viaduct on the Blue Ridge Parkway, North Carolina

I drove into the town of Cherokee, which I later discovered was in the centre of the Cherokee Indian Reservation, and borders the national park. I drove up and down for a while before pulling into an unassuming chain-motel. It turned out to be a good choice. The room was big and clean, and I enjoyed a great Native American vegetarian meal just up the road. Although I was tired I took my maps to the restaurant because I needed to get oriented. After a beer and a good look at those maps I felt relaxed again. I could now see that I was, indeed, inside the Cherokee Reservation. I was surprised because there didn't seem to be any of the entry signs I had come across before when approaching a reservation. I assumed, because I was inside a reservation, that, technically, I wasn't inside the boundaries of the national park. I confess that I'm still not exactly sure what the relationship between the park and the reservation is, suffice it to say that I was exactly where I needed to be in order to start fully enjoying my surroundings the following morning.

The Smokies

Although I have stood in awe at the top of the south rim of the Grand Canyon, Arizona; looked down from Tunnel View at the Yosemite Valley, California; and looked across from Artist Point towards the Grand Canyon of the Yellowstone, Wyoming, I had always wanted to experience being on top of Old Smoky. I remember listening to Burl Ives (1951) singing the song of the same name when I was a child, and although I didn't even know what it meant at the time, this was probably what started my desire. No surprise then that this song was on a loop in my head when I got up the next morning. Well, it was for some of the time, because I also found myself singing *Three Wheels on my Wagon* (1963) – another childhood memory song – probably because of the mention of Cherokees in the lyrics.

It was another misty morning as I drove back along the road. I stopped first to take a photo at the official entrance to the park, and then stopped again at the Oconaluftee Visitor Center. I then drove up Highway 441 – following The Oconaluftee River – towards the path which would take me up to Clingmans Dome, where I would finally be on top of Old Smoky – assuming, of course that this is the spot to which the folk song refers.

The Great Smoky Mountains National Park was officially designated in 1934, but the work to preserve this vast area of forest and mountains was well underway up to ten years before. The story behind the establishment of the park reads like a textbook for how a lot of the national parks were established. The work was largely the result of two men, Horace Kephart and George Masa, who began tirelessly mapping the area, as well as promoting its recreational possibilities. They were also instrumental in creating the Appalachian Trail (which runs through the middle of the park). These efforts came to the attention of President Roosevelt (FDR), who began the legislation to get it designated, but not before a battle ensued, between the commercial interests of the logging companies – who may well have stripped the place bare if left to it – and those who donated their money to buy up the land. Half of the money needed came from these donations, but J.D. Rockefeller Jr – who donated money to many of the parks – stumped up $5 million dollars to make up the other half. Whereas halting logging companies is unlikely to cause real hardship, this cannot be said of the displaced Appalachians and remaining Cherokees who called the Smokies their home.

The Smoky Mountains, Great Smoky Mountains National Park, Tennessee

The only way this could be justified, I suppose, was on the utilitarian principle of the greatest good to the greatest number. I guess most of the displaced people ended up elsewhere in Appalachia, or on the Indian reservation in the case of the Cherokees. It should not be forgotten that one hundred years before, many Cherokees were forcibly removed from their homelands and made to walk to Oklahoma, on what became known as The Trail Of Tears – a dark chapter in American history.

Once again, we see politics and economics intertwining in complex ways in the establishment of a national park. The Great Smoky Mountains National Park also has other parts to its story. In the end, President Roosevelt did have to divert some federal funds to the cause, which was tricky in the Great Depression, but also unique to this park, because although federal funds were often required to maintain a park after its designation, here was a case where a park got some funding in order to get it established in the first place. It is also noteworthy that the park, although very accessible, is free to enter. This is because the road network through the park was already in place at its designation, and it was deemed too difficult – politically – to charge people to travel on these existing through routes. Perhaps this is one of the reasons why it is the most popular of the national parks.

One road which didn't exist was the road connecting Shenandoah National Park with the Great Smoky Mountains National Park (the one had driven on the previous day), but even this courted controversy because moves to build what became the Blue Ridge Parkway coincided with increased disquiet from 'wilderness' groups, who argued that the motor car was slowly but steadily contributing to the destruction of the natural environment. Herein also lies that great contradiction at the heart of American society throughout the 20th Century; that the personal freedom afforded to people by the internal combustion engine ended up being double-edged. On top of that there had always been a battle in the national park movement itself – from John Muir onwards – between those who thought the movement was over-protective and those who thought it wasn't protective enough.

I followed the signposts to Clingmans Dome (6,643 ft), then followed a few other cars into the designated parking area. I joined the small groups of hikers who were beginning the short (half-mile) journey to the top. It was early in the morning and I was surprised by how many people were already milling around. Given that this is probably the most walked path in the whole of the national park system, perhaps these people were just trying to beat the crowds. The path was steep, but not strenuous, and before long I could see the strange-looking observation tower, which would provide the 360 degree view of the mountains. The observation tower sits right on the border of North Carolina and Tennessee, and is also on the path of the Appalachian Trail, which follows the state border all the way through the park. I don't know whose idea it was to built such an odd looking structure, but I'm sure its sweeping wide path and large platform at the top were designed with the number of visitors in mind rather than by appeal to

A Slice of Americana Pie

A critical appreciation of: Airstream Trailers

The name Wally Byam might not trip off the tongues of many Americans, but he was the man who designed one of the great American icons of the 20th Century – the Airstream trailer. Known as the 'land yacht' by many of its owners, and as a 'silver bullet' by many others, the one thing you should never call it is a 'caravan' – only uninitiated Europeans would commit this sacrilege. Like the VW camper van it has become synonymous with the American great outdoors but for this icon we are talking *thoroughbred* Americana.

Airstreams can be found everywhere, including sitting abandoned on farm property, but also on people's driveways in pristine condition. In popular culture you will find a large Airstream in the TV yard of *The Sons of Anarchy* motorcycle club; in the film *What's Eating Gilbert Grape* (1993), where Gilbert's brother waits expectantly for the annual visit of an Airstream trailer club; and old footage of the first moon landing shows the three gallant astronauts from Apollo 11 quarantined in an Airstream after returning to Earth (that particular trailer can now be found in the National Air and Space Museum, Washington DC).

Wally Byam had two things in mind when he designed the Airstream. First, he wanted to utilise the technology he was familiar with from aircraft design. One has only to think of those American Flying Fortresses from the Second World War to understand that connection. Second, he was determined to offer the ordinary American family an opportunity to experience travel – cheaply, in comfort, and in style. No one doubts that he admirably achieved all of these things, and more. The design was pretty much iconic from the start, so much so that a 1963 Bambi Airstream had its own installation at the Museum of Modern Art, in New York, in 2007. Richard Riegel, the President of the Thor company from whom that particular Airstream was bought, said at the time: "Airstream is recognized worldwide as a metaphor for wanderlust, adventure and freedom and as an ideal of the American family experience."

The Bambi was the smallest of the Airstream trailers, measuring 17ft in length. Not only did it look perfectly formed from the outside, its interior managed to comfortably fit a dining area, a kitchen area, a full bathroom suite, and a fold-out double bed. But Airstreams were available in many lengths, including some that were over twice the size of the Bambi. But, no matter what the length, they all looked perfectly formed as they glided along the road behind any number of American cars in the 1950s and 1960s. They were all built in one of two factories, one on the outskirts of LA (until 1968, when it was flattened to make way for the new Interstate 5) and the other in Jackson, Ohio (which still exists).

Byam did not just design the Airstream, he was also keen to promote its exotic travel possibilities, organising many Airstream expeditions across the world, and bringing owners together at club meetings. The large red numbers seen on the front and rear of many trailers are often mistaken for factory registration numbers; actually, they were Wally Byam club registration numbers, which owners could join on an optional basis.

Byam had been experimenting with trailer design from the 1920s but it's the mass-produced ones from the post war period that he is mostly remembered for. The basic design hardly changed right up to 1969. After this date, Byam retired from the company, and the classic era of the Airstream ended. In the 1970s they became slightly wider, and boxier in shape, but they were still undeniably Airstream trailers. They are still being manufactured today, and the modern ones retain the essence of the original Airstreams – including beautifully designed interiors, and polished aluminium shells.

Various books and websites claim that the vast majority of Airstreams ever built are still serviceable and many have become the pride and joy of their owners, who spend many an hour searching for original parts and other items of authentic Americana to place inside their Airstreams. One of the main reasons why so many have survived is due to their build quality. On the inside, pretty much every part is a quality item; you only need to take a quick look at the door and window mechanisms to see this. The underside is a solid steel structure, perfectly complemented by the light-weight aluminium shell.

That aluminium shell receives a huge amount of attention, with websites and videos dedicated to demonstrating how to polish it to achieve a mirror like appearance. The shell also helps to date the Airstream. The early models had a large number of small riveted aluminium panels, before techniques to shape larger panels were perfected. Keen enthusiasts will also be able to date the models based on cursory glances at the exterior light lenses (teardrop lenses were on the earlier models), and from the general configuration of exterior lights and Airstream signs.

I own a 1968 Bambi, which was renamed the Caravel for its last years of manufacture. It was imported from Georgia around 2007 by the Silver Bullet company located in the Midlands of the UK, where I bought it. They made it UK street legal, and I then set about making it authentically a 1960s trailer by hunting out various Americana accessories. Each time I visited an American flea market I would look for toasters, radios, and coffee makers from the period, along with coasters, posters, and other interior fittings. The owner of the UK company also told me that Robert Plant, from Led Zeppelin, dropped by once to reminisce about Airstreams, having been housed in them while on American tours, and he had a cup of tea in my Caravel. I also know that my Airstream appeared in the video of *Start of Something* (2008) by the post-Darkness band Stone Gods. Airstreams often appear in nostalgia-oriented advertisements and videos, including the video which accompanied the song *Yah Mo B There* (1983), by James Ingram and Michael McDonald.

any aesthetic sensibilities. Regardless, I was eager to reach the top and take in a view I had thought about since childhood.

Unfortunately, the misty morning hadn't cleared in the way it had done on previous mornings and I found myself looking out on an eerie landscape, but I was in the Smokies, after all. I guessed that I was probably more likely to experience *this* scene than the 100-mile view that some of the blurb had promised me. I also read that the name 'Smoky' comes from the Cherokee word 'schaconage', meaning the place of blue smoke, which perfectly describes the effect and colour of the mist which hangs in the valleys. But then, just as I was about to give up and return to the car, I saw a little hint of blue sky, and then some more. It never completely cleared but it was enough for me to be able to look out over the vast canopy of trees, for a few miles at least.

After returning to the car I made my way further north on Highway 441. Up to this point on the road trip I had been in the States of Virginia and North Carolina, but I was now crossing into Tennessee. The park straddles North Carolina and Tennessee, roughly 50-50. The road had followed the path of the Little Pigeon River, all the way to the large Sugarlands Visitor Center, where I bought lunch and a small collection of souvenirs, including stickers, a cap and a tee-shirt, all advertising the park. As I drank a coffee I looked at a map of the trailheads in the park. I read that there are 800 listed trails throughout the Smokies. I thought that hiking a modest two or three might do me. What I really wanted to do was just head out on foot and see where it took me. I could see from the map that I was now close to the northern edge of the park, where I felt sure there would be plenty of places to stay that night. This meant I had a good four hours or so before I needed to head out of the park. There were several short trails around the visitor centre itself, but I fancied the more ambitious Alum Bluff Trail.

I went back down Highway 441 until I saw the Alum Bluff trailhead sign and parked up. The wooden sign told me that I was 1.4 miles from Arch Rock, 2.3 miles from Alum Cave Bluffs and 5 miles from Mt. Le Conte. It's not unusual in this area to see signs to Mt Katahdin – nearly 2,000 miles away – because those on the AT will want to know (or perhaps not) how far away they are from the northern finish in Maine. Even the short ten miles to the top of the local mountain and back was probably not on for me, but up to the bluffs and back seemed doable in the time. The hike turned out to be fantastic, covering lots of different ground and gradients. The first part followed the creek, and then up some stone steps through Arch Rock. The gradient then picked up, until I eventually found myself scrambling around the bluffs. I had meet several people on the trail, but I was now all alone at this point. Although I felt fit enough, there clearly wasn't enough time to climb to the top of Mt. Le Conte (6,593 ft), so I made my way back, arriving at the car around three hours after I'd left it.

It was now time to find some accommodation, but I was totally unprepared for what followed in the next hour or so. Having listened to Dolly Parton on the TV and radio speak with pride about her Tennessee home, with its welcoming, old-school charm, I was really looking forward to finding some of it, and some log cabin accommodation to go with it. I assumed I would find this in places like Gatlinburg and Pigeon Forge, which had been described to me as bustling. I headed up to Pigeon Forge because Gatlinburg was not the kind of bustling I was expecting, But I then found Pigeon Forge to be even worse. It was awash with people drinking beer, howling, and/or wandering around in gaudy cowboy outfits. I think I may be exaggerating a bit to make my point, which is: that I'd spend the day in the most glorious of natural spaces, only to find myself now in one of the most artificial spaces I'd encountered for some time. That said, after the initial shock, I quickly began to enjoy it, seeing it for what it was. When people ask me what I like about the United States, I often reply by saying that I enjoy its contradictions, or perhaps better, how it is able to reconcile its contradictions and just live with them. Here, I thought, was a good example. But it wasn't helping me find accommodation, and I really did want something that at least resembled a log cabin, even an artificial one. Time was getting on, but, knowing that I was so close to Dollywood, I couldn't resist first driving up to the entrance to take some photos [see Dolly Parton Slice of Americana Pie].

Looking at the map I could see that it was possible to loop back down to the national park on Highway 321, avoiding Gatlinburg altogether. Surely along that road there might be a sign advertising log cabins for rent? Well, I didn't see any, but just at the point where I thought I may have to bite the bullet, buy a cowboy hat, and check into a chain-motel back in Pigeon Forge, I found myself driving through what appeared to be a non-descript little place called Townsend. I drove up the road and back down again, and then, just before one of the national park entrance signs, I saw a another sign – a magical sign – advertising cabins for rent – or perhaps it was a mirage? I pulled over, and the welcoming receptionist told me that he had one room left for one night. I said I'd like to stay for two nights, which he said would be possible but it would mean changing rooms because my room had been pre-booked by someone else the next night. I immediately said yes, because it was now beginning to get dark and I was tired and hungry. Just for a moment I wondered if the change of room was going to cost me more, but no, I got both nights for a very reasonable price.

I instantly loved the room, which wasn't actually a log cabin, just a row of connected rooms laid out like those in the film *Psycho* (1960), but the room was all wood-clad and there were rocking chairs outside. After being turned upside down by the previous two hours, I had finally landed on my feet, and I quickly realised that this little town, all laid out along the highway, did have everything you might need, including a restaurant right next door. Before I went for dinner I wandered around within the rambling grounds, and found that it backed onto the river. It was lovely wandering along the river bank as the sun set, after which I enjoyed a great dinner in the restaurant, which had some live gospel music.

The next morning I went back to the restaurant for breakfast, packed up my things because of the room change, and then headed back into the park. It was a misty morning again and it was great driving slowly around the bends, with the window open, listening to the birds. I was heading for Cades Cove which was only around twelve miles from Townsend, but it took nearly an hour to get there, partly because I was driving slowly, but also because it was nice to stop a few times and just to take it all in. I had read that it was possible to hire a bike and cycle around Cades Cove on a circular roadway (11 miles). When I arrived at the adjacent campground, they directed towards the bike hire centre. I stopped for a few minutes to watch the cars and trailers pulling up in order to check in for camping. It was a hive of activity, and it made me wish I was towing an Airstream trailer. I decided to wander into the large campground itself, and I saw a vast array of recreational vehicles

(RVs) with families sitting outside enjoying breakfast. I loved the whole scene; indeed, I was beginning to love the national park. Looking at some of the old trailers, and watching the kids running around, it made me think about the generations of families who would have come here over the last sixty or so years. It all felt like a live Americana show [see Airstream Trailers Slice of Americana Pie].

I went into the bike hire centre, looking forward to being on a bike again. Unfortunately, I was told that I would not be able to hire a bike because my footwear was inappropriate. I was wearing shorts and sandals, and, because of good old health and safety regulations, open-toed footwear was prohibited. Luckily, all my luggage was in the trunk of the car because it had been too early to check into my new room, so within a few minutes I was in my training shoes. After ticking a string of indemnity boxes on a bike rental form, I was then on my way, following the signposts to the loop road. At first I was a little disappointed, because I could see that I was going to be joined by a steady stream of cars. But I soon became fascinated by the number of families and friends who had set up their picnic furniture in the back of their pick-ups, and who were enjoying the ride from this vantage point. After a while I started looking forward to being overtaken to see what the next pick-up truck might look like [see Pick Up Trucks Slice of Americana Pie]

The next two hours were fantastic. The road was pretty flat, the air was fresh, and the scenery alternated between dense woodland and views across beautiful meadows. The muted colours in the mist produced some great photographs, before, slowly, the sun began to break through. Every now and then I came across preserved cabins, with helpful information posted outside, about the lives of the people who would have occupied them. The highlight though was seeing a big black bear up a tree enjoying a snack. It's not uncommon to see black bears in the Smokies. Had I stumbled across it on my own I'm sure I would have been more than a little concerned, mainly because of the size of it, but I was comforted by the crowd of people who were gathering ahead, and I stuck close to them as I tried to get my photographs. After that wonderful encounter, the visitor centre half way round provided the opportunity to have a coffee and pick up a sandwich for the road. I ate that sandwich after dropping off the bike. There was a lovely path

A Slice of Americana Pie

A critical appreciation of: Dolly Parton (1946-)

If Americana could be embodied in a person, it just might be Dolly Parton. She is all-American in so many ways. First and foremost, she writes and performs songs steeped in American folk traditions and went on to help define the contemporary American country music scene. She also comes from East Tennessee, which provided her with a childhood built around log cabins, one room school houses, and the centrality of the local church in the community. Her manufactured persona as an artist manages to meld images of Mom's Apple Pie with glamorous Hollywood star, which has a concrete manifestation in her own theme park, Dollywood.

Dolly Parton was born and raised in Sevier County, in a tiny rural community near the Pigeon River and the Smoky Mountains of East Tennessee. She often speaks of how being one of 12 children living in a poor rural community shaped her character and gave her the inspiration for many of her songs, including, famously, *Coat of Many Colours* (1971) and *My Tennessee Mountain Home* (1972). She found her voice early and began writing her own songs, inspired not by radio and TV (because there were none at home in her early childhood) but by the songs she heard her relatives singing, and by the local church. By the age of ten a die was cast, because after several trips to nearby Knoxville, she was snapped up by the local country radio station and began making regular appearances.

Dolly Parton is closely related to the themes of this book. Her childhood home borders the Great Smoky Mountains National Park, which was established in 1934, and Country music stations are synonymous with American road travel. I cannot remember the last time I couldn't find at least a couple of country stations on the car radio when travelling in the USA (and not just in The South). Dolly Parton herself has also been instrumental in helping to define the music genre known as Americana – a roots music drawing on Bluegrass, and epitomised by simple rhythms, acoustic instrumentation, three-part harmonies, and lyrics which focus on feelings of loss and longing. This style of music was popularised by performers like Bill Monroe and Ralph Stanley, but Dolly's albums *The Grass is Blue* and *Little Sparrow* were significant in its revival. Earlier, the songs and sessions which made up the *Trio* albums (alongside Emmy Lou Harris and Linda Ronstadt) also helped to sustain more traditional country music styles alongside its more electrified contemporary variants.

Country music is huge in the United States, but within a music business built around classification by genre. Because of this it has its own scene – with its own charts, its own radio stations, and heated debates about the extent to which country artists who appear in the mainstream charts – so-called crossover artists – have sold out. A flavour of this issue runs through the TV series *Nashville*, which centres on the fractious relationship between a traditional Dolly Parton-type artist and an up and coming Taylor Swift-type (although insiders say that the actual inspirations were Faith Hill and Carrie Underwood). What is interesting about Dolly Parton herself is how much she has managed to negotiate her way through the country music scene such that labels like 'old country' and 'new country' don't stick very well on her.

Although she often speaks about her childhood desire to escape from her surroundings – which offered young women only the prospect of marriage, children and domesticity – she has also been central to celebrating the dignity in family values, simple pleasures, and hard work. East Tennessee is synonymous with these values, and the Great Smoky Mountains National Park also seems to exude them. It is a national park as much characterised by these values as its natural surroundings, and Dolly Parton has surely played her part in this, consciously or unconsciously. That said, the contrast between the serenity and beauty of the park compared with the commercialism of Dollywood – which is literally just up the road – could not be greater. Dolly Parton just seems to be able to reconcile the contradiction, so much so, that it is not uncommon for families to visit the park and Dollywood on the same trip. In this regard as well, Dolly Parton strikes me as deeply American – in being able to successfully contain, manage, and even celebrate this contradiction.

Dollywood was opened in 1986, on the site of an existing small theme park, but now covers around 150 acres, located just outside the town of Pigeon Forge. Driving through that town after having spent time in the Great Smoky Mountains National Park can be disorienting. Strangers may need to prepare themselves for its loud, tacky, touristy vibe. The town is like an airlock room on a spaceship, which prepares you for transfer from one atmosphere – The Smokies – to another – Dollywood. That airlock is necessary for someone like me, but the locals seem to be able to accept it as perfectly normal. In his biography, Stephen Miller states that although Dollywood attracts over two million visitors per year, the majority come from within 400 miles. What they get is a mixture of traditional theme park alongside a celebration of Southern Americana, including a mock-up of that log cabin home of Dolly Parton's childhood.

Dolly Parton is larger than life and known for her quick wit. When asked about the dumb blonde association she replied by saying that she wasn't dumb and wasn't blonde. When asked about how long it takes to do her hair before a show, she said she didn't know because she's never in the room at the time. Much more significantly, I remember watching her on British TV being asked about her desire to hold back the ageing process, to which she replied that Micky Mouse doesn't age so why should she. This struck me as deeply significant because Dolly Parton is very much an image; one steeped in Americana, and one which appears to resonate with many Americans.

Like so many manufactured images we are sometimes left wondering whether there is anything behind the image. Jean Baudrillard argued that this typifies a post-modern society – where the search for the real becomes pointless, as we accommodate to living in a world of simulacra – where the artificial image becomes reality (Baudrillard, 1983). Disneyland was his archetypal example of this, but Dolly Parton must come close, although with one significant difference: there is a real Dolly Parton behind the image. Both Dolly Partons strike me as deeply American, and very Americana. And long may they reign.

near the campground which followed a stream and it was great to sit amongst the trees for a while.

After lunch I took the car onto the loop road because I had seen a number of cars at the Abrams Falls trailhead, and this looked like it would be a good hike for the afternoon. It was a five-mile round trip to the falls and well worth the effort. It started off pretty flat, but then I found myself climbing up some decent gradients before finally coming back down to the wide river and then the falls. It was a hot afternoon and there were plenty of people jumping in the water around the falls. Given the number of people at the falls the trail itself wasn't that busy with people. At one point a small group had gathered because there was a family of black bears – a mother and two cubs – off to one side, but a fair distance away. All in all, it was quite a hike, particularly in the heat, and I was glad when I finally got back to the car.

A black bear enjoying a snack in Great Smoky Mountains National Park, Tennessee

It was now late afternoon so I drove back to my accommodation, in order to check-in to my new room. It was upstairs in another block. The room was nice, but not wood-clad so didn't have quite the same cabin appeal. Still, I was pleased to have found such a great little place so close to the park.

After a shower I sat at the fire pit in the middle of the grounds, and chatted with some people who explained that their extended family always met up here once a year. This cemented the view I was forming of the Smokies, that it really was a brilliant place to chill out. I'm sure this fire-pit scene is much more what Dolly Parton has in her mind when she sings about having had some Tennessee homesick blues; surely not downtown Pigeon Forge? [see Dolly Parton Slice of Americana Pie]. Dinner was accompanied by live bluegrass music, after which I strolled along the road and had an ice-cream at a very busy old-school, authentic, ice-cream parlour. It was a great way to finish a great day in the Smokies, and I knew already that I was going to miss the place.

Keeping it Country

After breakfast the following morning I was on the road again, heading west towards Nashville, Tennessee. I didn't want to follow my same path back up the Blue Ridge Parkway, so I created a loop back to DC which would include a night in Nashville. It felt like the right thing to do, not just because I'd never been to Nashville before, but also because there's a long tradition of the music and the spirit of the Great Smoky Mountains being captured on record in the studios of Nashville. This would have included a very young Dolly Parton, who was writing and performing songs before she was even a teenager [see Dolly Parton Slice of Americana Pie].

It was a straightforward route to Nashville, which was around 200 miles away. I followed Highway 321 all the way until I hit the interstate (I-40) going west. The highway was great, and kept producing its own slices of Americana pie, including a drive-in movie theatre, a drive-in diner, automotive junk yards, and a great collection of classic American cars, all lined up by the side of the road. It was Sunday morning and at one point I saw a string of cars disappearing down a side road, following signs to a flea market, so I tagged along, and ended up having a great time looking at rows and rows of secondhand American household products. I love these places, even more so when there's the prospect of finding some car memorabilia, and period things for my Airstream trailer back in the UK.

I stopped at a service area on the I-40 for a coffee and lunch. The picnic area outside gave me a great view of the freeway and the vehicles coming and going in the service area. I love the way that Americans take to the road, with those huge RVs and cars towing boats. At one point I saw an RV towing a car and a boat. It was a great way to while away some time, but I did need to get to Nashville, so I then steamed along the interstate and arrived downtown Nashville around 2pm. From the freeway the city looked huge, but once off the freeway I could see that the centre was easily navigable. I didn't want to drive downtown so I parked up in a parking lot ($10) off Broadway at the end away from the action. It took me around ten minutes of walking to reach the Country Music Hall of Fame, where I picked up a brochure which told me about tours of the Ryman Auditorium. There was no way I was going to miss that opportunity, so I asked the help desk about tickets. It turned out the Ryman was only five minutes away, so I headed straight there, to join the 3.20 backstage tour.

The Ryman Auditorium is the home of country music, and is often referred to as the Mother Church of Country Music. It was originally the Union Gospel Tabernacle, and named after the person who commissioned it. It shot to fame when it began housing the Grand Ole Opry, an AM country radio programme, which, because of the powerful antennae, was listened to by countless Americans across numerous states. Because people wanted to see the show, not just listen to it, the Ryman proved to be the perfect venue, and it was used from 1943 until 1974, when the Grand Ole Opry moved across town to a new huge purpose built complex. Like many famous venues, the exterior of The Ryman acts as something of a disguise for what lies inside. Once inside it was fantastic to be backstage and then to be able to look up at the church windows from the stage itself. No wonder so many musicians love playing there, because the amphitheatre of seats produces a wonderful intimacy, and the acoustics are legendary. Backstage was actually very small, but it was fantastic to hear the guide telling tales about who had played there, and there were photographs and posters everywhere. A great exhibit included two outfits worn on stage by Johnny Cash and June Carter. Their music and love story was portrayed on screen by Joaquin Phoenix and Reese Wetherspoon, in the film *Walk the Line* (2005).

After visiting the Ryman gift shop – where I bought far too much stuff – I wandered further downtown, past all the bars which were alive with music and people kitted out in cowboy boots and hats. I really enjoyed looking through the vinyl records in the various music stores and looking at the cowboy boots for sale in the shoe shops. I was surprised by how small the downtown area actually was, but there was a lot of action in that square mile or so. I wandered down to the river front, by the Cumberland River, which runs through the city, and then made my way back to the car.

It was now early evening and I needed somewhere to stay overnight. The helpful person back at the Country Music Hall of Fame had told me that there were a lot of cheaper motels over in the area where the Grand Ole Opry is now located (in Opryland – of course), which was to the east of the Cumberland River. I wanted to see this area anyway, so I drove over there, which took about twenty minutes. I settled on what looked like a nice inn, which was on the appropriately named Music Valley Drive. I got a great room for a good price. From there I could walk around the large music complex. The area had a pristine feel, very different from the honky-tonk feel of the downtown area. It was time for dinner, and very close to the inn was a great restaurant which had an open-mic evening. The people who walked on stage and sang or played were all fantastic, perhaps not surprising for such a musical city.

The next morning, it was time to head back to DC. Before I headed off, I drove down Music Row, where all the country music recording studios are located. It was great seeing all the studio signs, but not worth stopping because I knew I wouldn't be able to go inside of any them. It was time to get moving anyway because I was due in St Louis in two days time to do some student recruitment work, and I was currently 600 miles or so from DC, where my flight was booked from. My only regret about my swift exit from Nashville was that I didn't get a chance to visit the Bluebird Cafe, another famous country music venue, which often featured in the TV series *Nashville*.

With an extra day or two tagged onto this road trip a straightforward detour north from Nashville would have enabled a visit to Mammoth Cave National Park. This detour would involve travelling around 100 miles north on I-65 into the state of Kentucky. The park preserves over

400 miles of cave network – believed to be the largest in the world – but also protects the forest above ground. After a guided tour of the caves you could then drop back down on I-40 heading south-east, in order to join the I-81 heading north-east, and then pull over, once exhausted, or as the sun goes down. With more time I would certainly have done this.

Return to DC

I quickly settled into freeway mode, with country music playing on the radio. I motored back along I-40 until I hit I-81, heading east, and I made it to Salem, Virginia, that evening, where I hopped off the freeway and booked into a reasonably priced chain-motel. I had covered a good 400 miles since leaving Nashville, which had taken the best part of the day (around eight hours, with stops), but it did mean that I would be able to relax a bit the next day.

With an extra day added, it would be possible to make a quick visit to the newest of the national parks (designated in 2020): New River Gorge National Park and Reserve. To do this you need to travel north (left) from I-81 onto I-77. If, like me, you were travelling east on I-81, from Nashville, you might consider looking for a motel around the I-81/I-77 intersection (near Wytheville). The following morning you would then only be around 80 miles from the park, which should take less than 90 minutes. New River Gorge is in the Appalachian Mountains, and has steep sides and river rapids, so if you are into climbing and/or river rafting it might be worth a longer stay. Otherwise, later the same day, just drop back south, to meet the I-80 going east (left).

After my stop-off at Salem, I continued north-east on I-81 until I hit I-66 where I turned right (east) to get back to DC, via Front Royal, where I had begun this adventure. I stopped there again for a coffee and started to think about where I might stay in the DC area. I like downtown DC and I was thinking about the diners and restaurants there, but as I was driving along I-66 I saw a sign pointing to Manassas, and I made an instant decision to follow it. What was on my mind was whether this was the Manassas that Stephen Stills had named his band after, when Crosby, Stills Nash and Young began to implode in the early seventies. As I drove into town my mind took me back to a record shop in Croydon, south London, where I used to comb the stacks of LPs when I was a teenager. I distinctly remember looking at the cover of an album where the band were lined up on the platform of a railway station, called Manassas. They look ridiculously cool, but I was in to Bowie and Pink Floyd at the time, so didn't buy a copy.

I followed the signs to Manassas railway station, but was disappointed because this surely couldn't be the place. But I went on the platform anyway, and then realised that this *was* the place, all except the Manassas hanging sign. When I checked on the internet later that evening, I discovered that all the hanging signs had been removed by the authorities because people kept stealing them. On my way into town I had clocked some motels by the side of the road, so I headed back there, but not before stopping off at a secondhand record shop to look for a vinyl copy of that Manassas album. I didn't find one, but made a point of searching for one back in the UK. I'm pleased to report that I am now, finally, the proud owner a scratch-free copy, bought at a record fair in Brighton. There were several chain-motels on the road out of town and I chose one close to a Mexican restaurant. I had a lovely meal and beer there, sitting outside in the warm evening air.

The next morning I packed up ready for my flight to St Louis, but because it didn't leave until early afternoon, I had time on the way to the airport to stop off at the Air and Space Museum. I wanted to go there because I knew that some of the Apollo moon landing craft were there, but what I really enjoyed seeing was the Airstream trailer that the three Apollo 11 astronauts were quarantined in when they came back from the moon [see Airstream Trailers Slice of Americana Pie]. The museum also houses an Air France Concorde and the infamous Enola Gay, the American plane which dropped the atomic bomb on Hiroshima, Japan, at the end of the Second World War. The plane's name was also used as the title of the anti-war song by Orchestral Manoeuvres in the Dark (1980).

Conclusion

The Great Smoky Mountains National Park is the most visited of all the national parks – some ten million people visit each year – and I'm really glad I finally got to be one of them. I soon came under its spell, which seems to be as much to do with the warmth of the people as the beauty of the natural surroundings. Getting there was also an absolute delight, because both the Skyline Drive (through Shenandoah) and the Blue Ridge Parkway, take you right across the crest of the Blue Ridge Mountains. There was definitely something mesmerising about those blue-coloured mountains and those misty valleys.

This trip was also a joyous musical journey, from Appalachian hillbilly and bluegrass music, heard regularly in the Smokies, through to the electrified violin and slide guitar more commonly heard in Nashville. Many of the roads were lined with wonderful slices of Americana, reminding visitors of times past, and times which many Americans, it would appear, would like to return to.

If you are able to extend your trip by a few days, it's also worth spending some time in Washington DC, either at the beginning or end of the trip. If nothing else, it's a really pleasant walk around the various memorials, which branch off from the famous Lincoln Memorial (which is administered by the National Parks Service). It was on the steps of this memorial in 1963 that Martin Luther King Jr. delivered his immortal *I Have a Dream* speech, the most famous part of which was to dream "that my four little children will one day live in a nation where they will not be judged by the color of their skin, but by the content of their character" (King, 1963).

Six things to do in Washington DC – which are free or relatively cheap

Washington DC is the capital city of the United States. Technically, it doesn't sit in a state, but in its own District of Columbia (hence DC). It should not be confused with Washington State, which lies in the far north-west of the country. It is around 225 miles from New York City, which makes combining a visit to both cities an interesting proposition – both cities have a very different feel. Regular trains and buses operate between the two cities (some of the buses are very cheap). It is relatively straightforward to get your bearings in Washington DC, and most of the federal government buildings are located in one area – which you can easily walk around. And the downtown area is easy to walk around. The further you venture from the downtown area the more likely you are to need a hire car, but there are regular buses and trains going between some of the main sites. Here are some things to do which will not break the bank and which include some of the paths less trodden.

1 Georgetown

Catch the bus to Georgetown from downtown DC – regular route, many buses – and spend the morning or afternoon browsing the shops and old streets. Walk to the famous University – at the far west end – and then head back to find Prospect Street NW and 36th Street to see the steps that were used in the film *The Exorcist* (1973). At the bottom is M Street, the main route back through Georgetown, where you can get the bus back to DC.

2 Ford's Theater

The theatre is in downtown Washington DC on 10th Street. This is where President Lincoln was shot in 1865. He survived the shot and was taken across the street (to Petersen House) but died there the following morning. You can take a tour of the theatre and the Petersen house, which includes the story of Lincoln's life and artefacts. It's run by the National Park Service (small fee; book in advance).

3 The top of the Washington Monument

Order a ticket (not expensive) on-line and at the allocated time ascend the Washington Monument, by elevator, for the best view of the city. The Monument is the tallest obelisk in the world, and from the top you can see how the whole area was laid out, including the famous Reflecting Pool and the Lincoln Monument. You will also be able to look down on the White House and the security guards on the roof.

4 Bike along the River Potomac

Hire a bike and head out past the White House, the Lincoln Monument, and then across Arlington Memorial Bridge. From there, turn left, under the bridge, and on to the Mt Vernon path that follows the river south, through Lady Bird Johnson Park (see The Texas White House Slice of Americana Pie). Keep an eye to the right in order to catch glimpses of the Pentagon. Continue down to the town of Alexandria for lunch, where you can decide whether to continue on to Mt Vernon (the estate of George Washington) or just head back if you've had enough.

5 Arlington Cemetery

Take a walk, catch a bus, or take a train to Arlington Cemetery, across the Potomac River from the centre of DC. The cemetery is huge, with the tomb of the unknown soldier near the centre. It's a military cemetery, but it was decided that President Kennedy should be buried here after his body was returned from Dallas Texas, where he was shot in November 1963. The plot also now includes his wife Jackie, and two of their children, alongside an eternal flame.

6 The Historic Triangle of Colonial Virginia

Best done in a hire car. Drive south out of Washington DC on I-395, then I-95, towards Richmond, Virginia, to visit Jamestown, Williamsburg and/or Yorktown. Jamestown was the first permanent English settlement, and Williamsburg has been reconstructed as a living museum, with detailed attention paid to early white American life and its artefacts. The three towns are now linked by a 23-mile scenic parkway, which can be entered via Highway 64, from Richmond. Williamsburg is 150 miles from DC so all-day planning would be essential.

Chapter 10

The American South West and The Grand Canyon

National Parks: Death Valley, Zion, Bryce Canyon, Great Basin, Capitol Reef, Grand Canyon, Petrified Forest, Joshua Tree
Other notable sites: Monument Valley, Historic Route 66

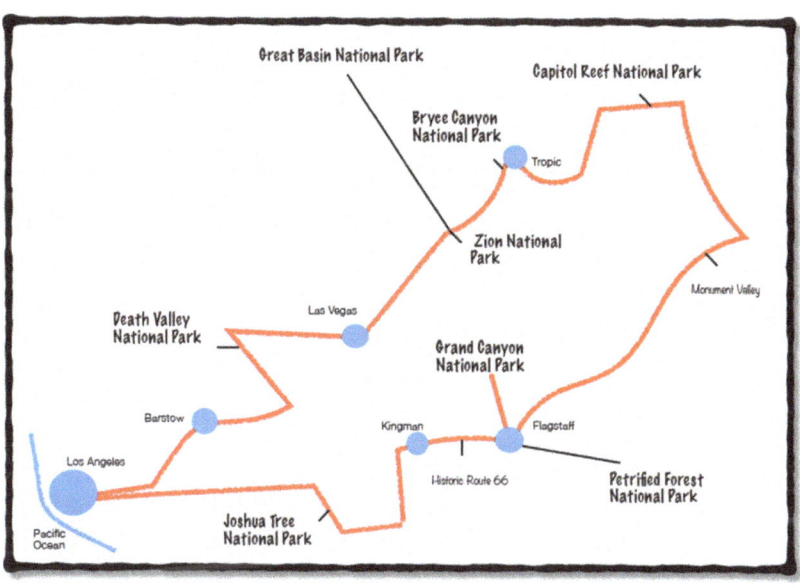

This chapter was composed while singing:
Take it Easy, as performed by The Eagles (1972) and
(Get your kicks on) Route 66, as performed by Chuck Berry (1961)

Introduction

I undertook this trip at the beginning of September 2012. My dates were dictated by the need to be in Chicago in mid-September for some work. The weather in the south western part of the country is usually very warm, so pretty much any time of the year would work for this trip. The basic idea was to head out into the desert from Los Angeles, loop around southern Utah, then return along Route 66 back into Los Angeles. You could head straight out into the desert from Los Angeles Airport (LAX), but on this occasion I decided to spend the night in Los Angeles County in order to visit some famous LA landmarks.

Arrival and orientation in Los Angeles

Cheap accommodation in Los Angeles is not easy to find, so it's worth doing a little internet homework before you leave home. If you just want somewhere to get your head down for the night you will find most of the usual motel chains around the airport.

It's a straightforward route out of the airport, towards the interstate freeway – I-405. This is the main north/south freeway through LA, but it's notoriously slow, particularly at peak times. The car rental company will normally provide you with some straightforward instructions out of the airport, which involves heading north on South Sepulveda Boulevard until you hit the freeway.

On this occasion I drove north from the airport towards Santa Monica. I decided to avoid the I-405 and turned left from South Sepulveda Boulevard onto Lincoln Boulevard (signposted as Highway 1). This road took me straight into Santa Monica, and although not a freeway, it could well be quicker than the I-405 route. It was mid-afternoon and I was keen to get down by the beach as soon as possible, so I tried a few cheap-looking motels on Lincoln Boulevard. The one I plumped for turned out to be rather shabby. I stuck with it because at least the bed was clean; it was very convenient; and it was cheap for LA. That said, while walking towards Santa Monica Pier, I did wish that I had at least checked out the prices of some of the better-looking motels I was now walking past.

Santa Monica Pier is a good place to get your bearings and to check out some of the famous LA beach scene. The pier is also the official finish of Route 66 [see Route 66 Slice of Americana Pie]. The sun was shining, and the LA vibe helped me to stay awake after the long flight from Heathrow. A block or so away from the pier I decided to hire a bike for a few hours, and I was soon on my way along the coastal path heading south towards Venice Beach – home of the hip – and then on to Marina Del Ray – home of the rich. Venice Beach is also where you will find the famous Gold's Outdoor Gym (right on the beach) – which features in many shots of LA. After taking a photo of the mural of Jim Morrison (lead singer of The Doors), who lived here in the mid-sixties, I headed off to the canals (hence the name Venice) before returning along the coastal path back to Santa Monica.

After returning the bike I headed back to Santa Monica Pier for dinner, and then walked back to my motel. I intended to be up early the next morning, so rather than dwelling on my shabby surroundings, I brushed my teeth, checked that the bed *was* actually clean, and then promptly fell asleep, but not before I tried to close the curtains; as if to confirm my poor choice of room, the one curtain moved easily back and forth along the rail but never quite covered the whole window.

I left my motel at 6am the next morning and returned to Venice Beach in the car, looking for a classic American diner. I didn't find anywhere particularly classic but after coffee and toast I was now awake and looking forward to exploring more of the area before heading east into the desert. I headed north-east on Venice Boulevard, through Culver City, and then turned left (north) onto La Cienega Boulevard, (crossing under the interstate – I-10). This took me towards Beverley Hills and West Hollywood. I continued to the northern end of La Cienega Boulevard and then turned right (east) onto Sunset Boulevard. This part of Sunset Boulevard is the section commonly referred to as The Sunset Strip. If you turn left at this point you will be close to four famous music venues – The Viper Room, The Whisky-a-Go-Go, The Roxy Theatre – and a little further south – on Santa Monica Boulevard – The Troubadour. I drove in the opposite direction because I was heading towards Laurel Canyon Boulevard, which winds north from Sunset Boulevard. This canyon was made famous in the late-sixties when it became the home of many singer-songwriters and is often credited as the place where soft/country rock was born. Many of these musicians would try out their new songs at The Troubadour, before recording them [see Laurel Canyon Slice of Americana Pie].

It was a beautiful Californian morning as I drove up Laurel Canyon, and I had a very pleasant coffee and bagel at The Country Store, which is half way up. The store has some fascinating photos on display of previous residents in the canyon. I then continued up the canyon until I hit the junction with Mulholland Drive, where I turned right (east). Mulholland Drive winds its way along the top of the Hollywood Hills, which is where you will find the famous Hollywood sign. Before heading towards the sign I stopped off at the signposted turnoff – Universal City Overlook – to take a photo of the Hollywood studios, down in the valley below (on the opposite side to the Sunset Strip).

It's possible to hike up to the Hollywood sign, and the quickest way to do this is to continue along Mulholland Drive until you hit Highway 101, but instead of getting on the highway you can turn right (south) to follow the adjacent road, South Highland Avenue, until you hit Hollywood Boulevard. This will take you past another famous music venue, the Hollywood Bowl. When you hit Hollywood Boulevard it's worth breaking the journey and parking up (relatively easy on a side street) for a walk west along to the Chinese Theater, to see the hands of celebrities in the paving slabs, and then down a block to see the 'stars' in the paving slabs – signposted as the 'Hollywood Walk of Fame' – which celebrates achievements in the Arts. If you walk east towards Vine Street you will be able to see (looking north) the famous Capitol Records building (where Frank Sinatra recorded a lot of his songs), and you will also be close to the junction of 'Sunset and Vine' – mentioned in the Bowie *Cracked Actor* song (1973) – and the junction of 'Hollywood and Vine' – which was converted to *Heartattack and Vine* by Tom Waits (1980).

Back in the car, I continued east along Hollywood Boulevard until I hit North Gower Street, where I turned left (north) until I hit Franklin Ave, where I turned right (east) and then first left (north) onto Beachwood Drive, which took me to the signposted path to the Hollywood sign. It's a great little hike up to the sign, where you feel like you have left the hustle and bustle of Los Angeles and entered the backcountry, even though you have only travelled a few miles from 'the strip'. The sign has changed over the years. It was first erected in 1923 as a property development advertisement to entice people to move to the area, and originally read 'Hollywoodland'.

The first time I visited the sign I remember it being a bit tatty. Now it is very pristine and it has clearly been strengthened. It's also now a protected space, but you can still get close enough to take some nice photos, and the paths around the sign are well worth exploring. But, it looks like local residents have got increasingly annoyed about visitors parking up near their houses and then hiking up to the sign. If you find yourself getting annoyed by 'no parking' signs or blocked access, you can always park up at Griffith Observatory (see below) and access the sign from there, but it's more of a hike.

It was still only midday by the time I returned to the car, so, once back on Franklin Avenue, I decided to take the signposted road up to the Griffith Observatory, from where you can get some great views of downtown Los Angeles. You can also see the statue of James Dean, which celebrates his performance in the cult film *Rebel without a Cause* (1955), which used the observatory for some of the scenes. I then drove back (south) down the road until I hit Sunset Boulevard again. I turned left (east) on the Boulevard and followed the road all the way into downtown Los Angeles. I parked in a small parking lot (for a few dollars) and found my way to the historic centre of Los Angeles, where the city was founded in 1773. There'a a commemorative plaque which marks the spot.

Downtown LA is certainly worth exploring and can be done on foot. Immediately around the plaque is a very pleasant Spanish-inspired square, with a mixture of food stalls and arty shops. A little further along is the main train station – Union Station – from where the cross-country trains arrive and depart. To the north is Chinatown, and to the west is City Hall and the headquarters of the LAPD (which features in countless films and TV series). I walked west along 1st Street towards the Disney Concert Hall, and took some photos of this iconic post-modern building, designed by Frank Geary. The sun was shining off the brushed metal shapes which make up the exterior of the building. I spent some time outside trying to work out how the whole thing hangs together. But, as with many of these buildings, I found interior a little bland, by comparison.

I made my way back to the car, happy that I'd had my fill of LA, and ready to get out of town, and head off into the desert. I bought a sandwich back at the historic centre, and after checking my map, I could see that I was just a few quick turns from the San Bernardino Freeway (I-10) heading east. I was relieved to be on the freeway. I checked to make sure that I had turned turned east, not west, and then relaxed into the drive, knowing that this road would lead me directly out of Los Angeles County.

Death Valley

I drove out of Los Angeles on I-10 (east) until I hit I-15 (going north). This would take me to Barstow, which I thought would be a good place to stop before heading off into Death Valley early the next morning. I drove for just over 100 miles, which took me around two hours and then had a very pleasant night in a chain-motel just off the freeway.

I continued north on I-15 early the next morning. As I drove off, the temperature gauge in the car was registering 70 degrees Fahrenheit. After driving for around an hour I turned off the interstate onto Highway 127, going north. The temperature gauge had now risen to 90 degrees. Another hour later I found myself in the little settlement of Shoshone, with the temperature gauge now having gone over the 100 degree mark. I stopped off at a small gas station and store because I was intrigued by who would live here. The two people inside were great, and it was clear that both of them were just getting on with their lives, which made my questions about their choice of habitat seem rather foolish. I bought some souvenirs and wished them well. A little way further along the road I turned left onto Highway 178 and made my way into Death Valley National Park.

Death Valley was not designated a national park until 1994, but it had been afforded federal protection before then as a National Monument. I was not surprised to read that the hottest temperature on the planet had been recorded in Death Valley (134F), but I was surprised to read that it was the largest American national park (outside Alaska), covering over 3 million acres (making it bigger than Yellowstone). Somewhat surprisingly, given that it is part of the Mohave Desert, it also has a number of distinct landmark features, including colourful wild flowers, Ubehebe Crater, and the large hotel complex known as Scotty's Castle.

As I made my way down into the Valley I had to resist the temptation to keep stopping to take it all in. I was not sure whether to keep the windows of the car open or shut. I wanted to experience the warm gentle wind, but I was also aware that if I didn't let the car's air conditioning unit do its job I would soon be roasting hot. My first proper stop was at Badwater Basin, famous for being the lowest point in the United States. The signpost in front of me proudly displayed the fact that I was now 282 feet below sea level. I couldn't resist walking out onto the salt flats for a few minutes. Back in the car it wasn't long before I stopped again, this time to take a short hike into a canyon – following Gower Gulch loop. I then drove further north until I hit the Furnace Creek Visitor Center. As I pulled into the parking lot the temperature gauge in the car was now registering 120F.

At the visitor centre I paid my park entrance fee and then made my way towards the food and drink area. I love the United States: just a few minutes ago I had been in one of the wildest places on the continent, and now here I was confronted with yet another vast array of commodities. This included a huge wall of fridges, neatly housing every imaginable drink, but, as it turned out, all containing sugar or a sugar substitute. I plumped for plain water, taking a few bottles for good measure, and then made my way to a shaded terrace for a sandwich lunch.

I checked my map and could see that I wasn't far from Mesquite Flat Sand Dunes, so I decided to make that my next stop. I had a great time clambering over the sand dunes before preparing myself for the journey out of the park towards Las Vegas, where I planned to stop for the night. When I got back to the car I opened the trunk to retrieve a better sun hat from my luggage, only to find that I had made a serious rookie error. Before I left the motel that morning I thought that it would be a good idea to put all my possessions in the trunk so they wouldn't roast on the back seat, only to find that they had actually roasted in the trunk. This was confirmed when I realised that the small stream at the bottom of my toilet bag was a mixture of deodorant and shower gel, which had merged to become one hot liquid. My toothpaste had also lost its usual firm consistency. I put everything on the back seat in the hope that all the liquids might at least harden a little before I got to Las Vegas.

A Slice of Americana Pie

A critical appreciation of: Laurel Canyon

Laurel Canyon Boulevard runs up into the hills north of Sunset Boulevard in Los Angeles. This is where the giant Hollywood sign sits (although a few miles further east). As you continue up you will eventually hit Mulholland Drive, which runs along the top of the hills. This road has been the home to many Hollywood superstars, and is the setting for David Lynch's dark mystery of the same name (2001). After crossing Mulholland Drive the road descends towards the San Fernando Valley, Burbank, and the Universal Studios – where those superstars have plied their trade. Had you turned left before you hit Mulholland Drive, onto either Kirkwood Drive or Lookout Mountain Avenue you would have found yourself amongst the homes (past and present) of another group of artists – a string of successful American singer-songwriters.

The collection of small roads and dead-ends to the west of Laurel Canyon Boulevard had long been the home for radical artists and counter cultural figures, but in the late-sixties it became particularly significant in the music scene. Frank Zappa was a long-term resident and he seems to neatly encapsulate this transition. Joni Mitchell was referring to the area in her song and album of the same name: *The Ladies of the Canyon* (1971*)*. Joni Mitchell's house here was also the inspiration for Graham Nash's tune *Our House* (1970). She was one of the many to make the journey from East Coast to West Coast – which included James Taylor and Carole King – to contribute to an emerging laid-back sound, whose variations became known as Country Rock, Folk Rock, and Electric Folk.

A lot of that soft rock sound was pretty much in place by the time that Joni Mitchell had arrived – from the Greenwich Village, New York, folk scene. The Byrds were the first band to have a recognised hit with a form of electrified folk music, when they recorded Bob Dylan's *Mr Tambourine Man* in 1965. It is a matter of conjecture whether Dylan would have had a better reception for his own electric sound, had he too moved to LA at that point. Instead, he chose to settle in Upstate New York [see Woodstock Slice of Americana Pie].

The Byrds were a guitar band, but session musicians were used for the initial recordings, with the band employed as singers. Those session musicians were used on numerous LA based recordings, including on hits by The Mamas and Papas and The Beach Boys. They were coined the Wrecking Crew by session drummer Hal Blaine, and included bassist Carol Kaye, guitarist Tommy Tedesco, pianist Leon Russell, and even guitarist Glen Campbell, before he became known as a singer in his own right. Hal Blaine is probably the most famous pop drummer ever – having played drums on countless hits – even though his name does not trip off the tongue.

The Mamas and Papas' big hit *California Dreamin'* (1965) was written by John and Michelle Phillips and spoke of the desire to make the journey west to escape the cold winters of New York. It neatly encapsulated the scene, as east coast musicians continued to join their indigenous counterparts, like David Crosby and Jackson Browne. And, as with so many of the Wrecking Crew hits, the recording included the band's voices alongside the session musicians. This was also famously the case with the TV manufactured band The Monkees, two of whom were accomplished musicians (Mike Nesmith and Peter Tork), but the recording studio only wanted the voices of Mickey Dolenz and Davy Jones. However, by the time of their biggest hit – *Daydream Believer* (1967) – The Monkees had wrestled control over the musicianship.

Back in Laurel Canyon, most musicians appeared pretty relaxed about the recording business and would make the short journey down the hill to the recording studios whenever required to do so. Studio time was expensive so why not employ experienced session musicians who could perform on demand and in just one or two takes? In reality, the Wrecking Crew probably only demonstrated just how much a lot of popular music is highly manufactured and packaged anyway.

Joni Mitchell's house in the canyon is famous for several reasons. She lived next door to the communal home of Canned Heat – before the house burnt down. It was also here that Joni Mitchell introduced Graham Nash to David Crosby and Stephen Stills. Nash had recently moved in with Mitchell, after leaving Manchester, England, and his band The Hollies. The book about the Laurel Canyon scene by Barney Hoskyns (2005) says that some people think the encounter happened at Cass Elliot's place, but I am taking my information from Nash's autobiography (2013). Does it matter? As the old saying goes: 'if you can remember the sixties, you probably weren't there'. Many Laurel Canyon stories are probably a mixture of folklore and loose recollections, which seems to fit this Americana story, fuelled as it was by drugs and hedonism. Some of that spirit is captured in the fictitious film, *Laurel Canyon* (2002).

Stephen Stills was one of the first east coast-based musicians to move across to LA, where another famous recollection was documented – his chance reunion with Neil Young on Sunset Strip – who was driving a hearse with Ontario, Canada, license plates. They formed the band Buffalo Springfield, and many of their songs were written in and around Laurel Canyon, before personal tensions took hold, and the introverted Neil Young opted to go it alone, although he joined Crosby, Stills and Nash on and off.

Also significant in Laurel Canyon folklore were Jim Morrison and The Eagles. Jim Morrison lived for a while just by the Laurel Canyon Country Store, which was a hub for the growing community of artists and musicians. His view of the comings and goings around the Store was the inspiration for The Doors hit single *Love Street* (1968). He also wrote *LA Woman* (1971), the pulsating road tune, which was a little paradoxical given that he seemed to walk everywhere. Around the same time a young Jackson Browne moved into Laurel Canyon, to be followed a few years later by both Glen Frey and Don Henley. One of their first collaborations was the now famous road tune *Take it Easy* (1972). So the story goes, the song was completed by Glen Frey after he was introduced to the bulk of the tune by Jackson Browne. Both Browne and The Eagles went on to record it. Many Eagles songs were were inspired by life in Laurel Canyon.

The Country Store at 2108 Laurel Canyon Boulevard is still a going concern and is a great place to grab a coffee and think about how much the surrounding area has contributed to the soft rock music scene and its laid-back culture, and how easy it is to turn to that music as you contemplate a drive to work on a damp and dreary day… *California Dreamin'* indeed.

I made my way back towards Furnace Creek, but this time stayed on Highway 190 (going east) and then made my way towards Death Valley Junction, where Highway 190 hits highway 127. It was now decision time, because the quickest way to Las Vegas would have been to continue north on the 127 until I hit I-95 going east, but there was a very helpful sign in the road enticing me to take Highway 160 (going east) – through the town of Pahrump.

The road less trodden was more appealing, as was the sound of Pahrump on my lips. Perhaps the sign had been put there by the Pahrump tourist office. I'm really glad that I took that route because the road was a delight. It was fast, mainly because there were hardly any other cars, and the desert countryside was fascinating, all the way to the outskirts of Las Vegas.

Road junction in Death Valley, Death Valley National Park, California

What must it have been like at the first planning meeting for the city of Las Vegas? I know, (says one person) let's create a huge urban complex right in the middle of the desert, and, (says another person) let's have a bunch of casinos in luxury hotels, each one recreating mock versions of famous world landmarks. That's bonkers, says a third person. 'Let's do it', says the chair of the meeting. So, we now have

Las Vegas; a bizarre, all-American, modern city – or perhaps better, a post-modern city – a mixture of styles and cultural references, all sitting within its own hyper-reality (Baudrillard, 1983).

As I entered the city, along I-15, which takes you right onto the Las Vegas Strip – the main thoroughfare through the downtown area – I remembered the first time I visited many years before, when I found the place not so much tacky, as rather seedy. But, and as if to confirm that the city does inhabit its own post-modern world, the town planners agreed that The Strip *had* become seedy, but rather than clean it up, they just moved it and created a new one a few miles down the road. What does it matter though, if the whole place is an artifice anyway?

I was in a reflective mood, contemplating the incongruity of being here but also being so very close to some of the most spectacular wilderness in the whole of the United States. I needed to find somewhere to stay but I decided to avoid the flashy hotels (so as not to get sucked into a Las Vegas vibe), even though I knew that some of them do offer cheap rooms – in the hope that you will spend what you have just saved on the room-rate in their casinos. Instead, I pulled off The Strip when I saw a chain-motel sign, and – just for a moment – it looked like I had re-entered a normal American reality again, because, just fifty yards from The Strip, here was the most bog-standard motel, and I instantly loved it. I booked in for the night. The room was large and I spent a few minutes outside leaning on the railings, feeling the warm desert air, before taking a walk along The Strip. I was looking forward to being alone in this most social of cities, but not before I was approached by a woman as I crossed the parking lot. I assumed she was a prostitute, because she seemed to be far more interested in me than she should have been, so I quickly ushered her away. A few minutes later it crossed my mind that she may have just been a fellow traveller, and that I'd been rude and abrupt with her, but by that time I was wandering down the Las Vegas Strip.

I really enjoyed my visit to the Eiffel Tower, the Statue of Liberty, and the Venice canals, and after an enjoyable Mexican meal I made my back down The Strip on the opposite side of the road until I reached my motel.

The next morning I was up at 6am eating breakfast in a diner, which was on The Strip just by my motel. I couldn't work out whether my fellow diners had just got up or hadn't yet gone to bed. As I stared out of the window at New York's Chrysler Building, I realised that this city could well be considered to be America's best idea – by a few people, at least.

Zion and Bryce Canyons

Not long after breakfast I was heading east on I-15, in the direction Zion National Park. As I was leaving Las Vegas I drove under one of those giant gantries that straddle the freeway, with road signs directing me to: Salt Lake City; Phoenix; and Reno (if I went in the opposite direction). I ploughed on up I-15, out of the State of Nevada, crossing into Arizona, and then into Utah. The interstate was fast and direct and all I had to remember was to turn east on Highway 9 in order to get to Zion. That road was clearly signposted, and within three hours (around 150 miles) I was at the visitor centre in Zion National Park. My watch said 10.00am, but the visitor centre clock told me it was 11.00. I had lost an hour because I'd crossed into the Mountain Time Zone. I was annoyed with myself for not remembering this, but I soon forgot about the time after getting some orientation advice from one of the rangers. I grabbed a sandwich to-go, and then jumped on the free shuttle bus, which took me down into the canyon.

Zion National Park was designated in 1919. For the previous ten years it had been afforded federal protection as Makuntuweap National Monument – a native American word meaning 'straight canyon'. When it became a fully fledged national park, the NPS renamed it Zion, in deference to the Mormons who had set up farming communities in and around the canyon. Zion: a spiritual sanctuary, or New Jerusalem. Its most striking feature is the vivid colour of the sandstone canyon walls, which rise over 2,000 ft from the Virgin River, which continues to shape the canyon. It is often said to be Yosemite in colour.

I was a little surprised by the amount of traffic going up and down the road which follows the canyon; an unfortunate similarity with Yosemite. Something in me wanted to shout out: 'why not take a hike to get down into the canyon?' That said, the shuttle bus does stop at a number of places, from which extensive hikes could be taken. The canyon featured in some of the scenes in the film *Butch Cassidy and the Sundance Kid* (1969) – a road movie without tarmac, and with real horses rather than steel ones.

I got off the bus at Zion Lodge, crossed the river, and then followed the marked trail to Emerald Pools. The hike was not strenuous and not particularly busy, enabling me to amble along in quiet, reflective mood. I ate my lunch at the Pools, and then walked further north along the Virgin Rim trail, until I came to the footbridge which took me back over the river to Grotto, where there was a bus stop, which would take me back to the visitor centre. This had been a great hike. It was easy-going, which was welcome because it was a hot day, and it only took me around an hour and a half to experience this majestic canyon.

With more time I would certainly have visited Kalob Canyons – a separate part of the park, which was added in 1956, and is located to the north-west of Zion Canyon. This would have involved another car journey, back to I-15, and then north to the Kalob Canyons Visitor Center. Instead, I looked around the gift shop back at Zion Canyon Visitor Center, and then returned to my car. I then made my way down into the canyon again, but this time turned right onto the 'Zion – Mt Carmel Highway' (Highway 9). This road would take me in the direction of Bryce Canyon, which the ranger in the gift shop told me was only 86 miles east of Zion.

With a couple of days added to this road trip it would be possible to get to another national park, Great Basin, Nevada (but on the border with Utah). Doing this would mean that you could also include that trip to Kalob Canyons (up I-15). From there you could then continue up I-15 to Cedar City, and then switch to Highways 130 and 21, heading north-west. It's around 200 miles from Zion to Great Basin, but its remote location is likely to mean that you would have to come back down the same route again, and possibly stay overnight in Cedar City before heading to Bryce Canyon the next morning. Or you could venture up to the park by heading north from Las Vegas (around 300 miles) and then come back down to Zion and Bryce Canyon. Great Basin National Park was designated in 1986 and although it sits in the Grand Basin Desert, the park also includes Lehman Caves and the Wheeler Peak (over 13,000 ft up) scenic drive. Unfortunately, this would have been too far for me on this trip.

The road between Zion and Bryce Canyon was wonderful, including a mile-long tunnel, which was blasted in the late 1920s. The bright red sandstone rocks continued to make a spectacular backdrop, before they gave way to a string of chequerboard grey rocks – where thin grooves had been cut into the rock faces. It was mid-afternoon and I was keen to get to Bryce, but it was difficult not to keep stopping to take photos. After Highway 9 finished, I needed to turn left (north) to follow Highway 89, and then right (east onto Highway 12). A few miles along was a signposted righthand turn to the park, along Highway 63. I finally arrived at one of the official entrance signs two hours after leaving Zion, around 4pm. I was concerned that I was arriving a little late, but the ranger at the entrance booth assured me that the 18-mile road that winds through the park was easily drivable before sunset, and that early evening was a great time to be visiting the park. The sun was shining and I was looking forward to this next mini-adventure.

Evening vista of hoodoos, Bryce Canyon National Park, Utah

I was not prepared for just how spectacular the next four hours were going to be. I stopped at the first string of major pull off points – Sunrise Point, Sunset Point, Inspiration Point, and Bryce Point. The stop offs were all within what is called The Bryce Amphi-theater. It is difficult to describe the other worldly landscape I was witnessing. My ever-helpful park brochure told me I was looking at 'hoodoos' – pillars of rock formed by erosion. But no dictionary definition could have done justice to the sublime nature of it all. For a start, the sheer number of hoodoos was breathtaking, as was the view towards the horizon; only the earth's curvature was stopping you looking even further.

Bryce Canyon became a national park in 1928. It was named after one of its earliest white inhabitants – Ebenezer Bryce. Before then, generations of Native Americans had occupied the plateau on which the hoodoo ranges sit. My brochure told me that the Pauite Indians called the hoodoos 'Legend People' – who had been turned to stone by coyotes. As with so much of the landscape of the USA, the scale of Nature's work is almost beyond belief. In this area, tectonic plate movement in the earth's crust, combined with relentless freezing and thawing of water, had produced a mesmerising result. I tried to photograph everything, but in the full knowledge that my efforts would inevitably be an insult to what was actually in front of my eyes.

I drove all the way to the end of the road, to Rainbow Point and Yovimpa Point, stopping off to take a hike around Black Birch Canyon. The wooden post there told me that I was 8,750ft up, but that knowledge seemed insignificant given the scale of everything.

I was completely alone in my thoughts, helped by the fact that there were no other cars or people around. It felt like I had the park to myself, but it was now beginning to get dark. I hadn't thought much about where I was going to stay that night, but I was sure that there would be some motels back on highway 12 (which I planned to follow east the next day). For the time being I wanted to extend my stay as long as possible, and just when I thought the evening couldn't give me anymore, I saw a full moon rising over the canyon.

After leaving the canyon and making my way north to rejoin Highway 12 (going east) I finally pulled into an inn, at the small town of Tropic. The inn was right on the main street and I was pleased that I could eat dinner close-by. Not long after dinner I was fast asleep, after an exhausting, but amazing day, in Utah.

Capitol Reef and Monument Valley

I was up at 6am the next morning, contemplating the day ahead. This was going to be a driving day. My next planned stop was the Grand Canyon and I could have just headed south and probably arrived there early afternoon, but I wanted to see more of Utah, so I extended my loop to include Monument Valley. This meant that I would be covering around 500 miles in one day – much more than I would normally drive – but I did have a good twelve hours in which to complete my loop. If this sounds daunting, you could easily stop overnight around half way (perhaps at the small town of Mexican Hat, which appeared to have a couple of places to lodge). As it turned out, this Utah loop was so exhilarating that any thoughts of driving fatigue were quickly quashed every time I looked out at the landscape. In all my years of driving in the US, this day was definitely one of the best.

After leaving Tropic, I continued east on Highway 12, which eventually turns north to hit Highway 24. This road was an absolute delight to drive. The road twisted around red sandstone rock formations, and the morning air felt warm and fresh. I drove past a camp site full of Airstream trailers, which you could rent. With the benefit of hindsight I would probably have stayed here – although I don't know how easy it would have been to book a night in an Airstream without prior notice. I did stop at the entrance to pick up a brochure though [see Airstream Trailers Slice of Americana Pie].

When I hit Highway 24 I turned right (east), and soon found myself at the entrance to Capitol Reef National Park, formally designated in 1971. I hadn't planned a visit to this park, but it was such a beautiful morning that I couldn't resist stopping to at least take some photographs. Again, with hindsight, I would probably have engineered more time to fully explore this area. The official entrance sign is right on Highway 24, and the entrance booth just a short way off the highway, to the right. It's geological structure comprises a 100 mile north-south water-fold pocket – formed by tectonic plate movement, which created a warp in the earth's crust. Fantastic views can be had by following the eight-mile scenic drive, and there are also many trailheads from which hikes can be taken.

I continued east on Highway 24, until it hit Highway 95 at the town of Hankville, where I turned right (south). The landscape became more expansive, including huge sand plains, and, increasingly, I started seeing examples of those wonderful red towers of sandstone rock – the ones seen in all the Western movies. I crossed the Colorado River, which introduced a new vista, as you looked into the distance at its meandering path through the rocks.

A little further down the road I saw a right turn, signposted as Highway 261 – an un-gravelled road down to the town of Mexican Hat. I paused, wondering whether this meant that I needed to be in a four-wheel drive vehicle, but the pull was irresistible, so I ploughed on down the road. What a road it turned out to be. The next hour was an amazing switchback ride, across the Ceda Mesa. The road is named 'The Moki Dugway Scenic Backway', where Moki refers to the ancient Pueblo people who lived here for centuries, and dugway refers – literally – to how the road was dugout of the mountainside. Driving slowing down the switchbacks provided me with the most stunning views of the expansive valley below. This was yet another example of how the vastness of the landscape just takes your breath away. My only concerns were whether the road would narrow and become rocky, and what I would do if I met a large vehicle coming the other way? I needn't have worried because the road stayed pretty much the same all the way, and I didn't see any other cars. Perhaps nobody else would have been so foolish to take this route, but I concluded that this simply couldn't be the case because the road must be well known, and is surely a 'must-do'.

At the end of Highway 261, I turned right (south) onto Highway 163, heading towards the small town of Mexican Hat. As I approached the town I realised how it got its name because to the side of the road there was a rock formation which looked exactly like someone had placed a sombrero on top of a pyramid. This was a good place for lunch and I stopped at a great diner just by the side of the road. I had covered 275 miles since leaving Tropic, which had taken me around seven hours (including several stops). After lunch I continued along Highway 261, which had begun heading west. I was now over halfway round my Utah loop and heading back towards The Grand Canyon, but not before I had driven through the famous Monument Valley, on the Utah-Arizona border.

Anyone who has seen a John Ford-directed Hollywood Western will also have seen Monument Valley because it is the backdrop to many scenes. But it is much more than a backdrop, acting in the films as an important motif, in referencing the vastness of the American Frontier. Except, of course, from the perspective of the Navajo, where it is not a frontier at all, simply the land of their forefathers. I'm not

A Slice of Americana Pie

A critical appreciation of: Route 66

If a road could ever embody a culture, it might just be Route 66. Even those who have never been anywhere near it probably know what is being invoked when it is referred to, and many will know the route, courtesy of the famous song of the same name, which tells us that it winds over 2,000 miles from Chicago to Los Angeles, through the towns of St Louis, Joplin, Oklahoma City, Amarillo, Gallup, Flagstaff, Winona, Kingman, Barstow, and San Bernardino – (*Get you Kicks on) Route 66* (1946).

In the song, the towns are in the right order if you are travelling west from Chicago to Los Angeles, except Winona, which is actually east of Flagstaff and therefore should come first, but the lyric works because we are told not to forgot it, which you would have done if you were already in Flagstaff. The song was written and performed by Bobby Troup but made famous by other performers. The performances also signify a popular cultural shift from jazz to rhythm and blues, to rock: Troup's own rendition (1946) alongside Nat King Cole's (1957), then onto Chuck Berry (1961), and then the Rolling Stones (1964), which all helped to give the tune (not just the lyrics) a hybrid resonance.

Route 66 probably has more ingredients to bake its own Americana pie than any other road-related artefact. It is par excellence nostalgic – conjuring up images of a past, somehow better, life, and is full of associations that are archetypically American, including diners and Burma Shave Signs [see Burma Shave Signs Slice of Americana Pie]. Perhaps the key ingredient though is a re-imagination and reconstruction of its own past life. In some respects, the reconstruction is a real phenomenon, with many towns along the route seeking to restore and rebuild some of the original structures – such as old-style filling stations – which had either been pulled down or left to wrack and ruin. Herein, once again, lies one of those intriguing aspects of American cultural life: how the relentless march of progress and celebration of the modern often results – some time later – in a desire to rediscover what was lost in the process.

One practical outcome from this rediscovery is that it is now easier to trace Route 66 – and actually get some kicks on it – rather than just becoming extremely frustrated about where you should turn next. The original route was a purposeful political decision made in the 1920s, to create a long-distance highway, but it took many years to completely pave the route, which in effect connected a series of existing trails. The route also coincided with the decision to number, rather than name highways, and there was quite a lot of debate at the time about which number it should be given.

It has been given several names over the years; famously, Main Street of America, and the Will Rogers Highway. In *The Grapes of Wrath* (1939) Steinbeck referred to it as the Mother Road. That book, although a novel, also explained why the road became significant for many people; because it was an important escape route from the 'Dust Bowl' and The Great Depression, as people travelled West in search of work and a new life in the 1930s [see Woody Guthrie Slice of Americana Pie].

Today, the official start is signposted in Chicago (on East Adams Street), as is the official finish at Santa Monica Pier, in Los Angeles county. The original route stopped in downtown Los Angeles, but – for tourist reasons alone – there is an obvious logic in now having the official finish at the edge of the Pacific Ocean. Indeed, sections of the whole of the official route have been modified in several places over the years, so if you want to trace the route, you will have to decide which version you want to follow. The good news though is that there are now several books and maps dedicated to the route, and although the majority of the original Route 66 signs are gone (either stolen, or because sections have been reclassified), a series of new brown signs have been erected on parts of the route, proudly announcing 'Historic Route 66'.

I first got some of my kicks on the route when I took a Greyhound Bus all the way from Chicago to Los Angeles, stopping off at the Grand Canyon. The bus naturally followed the interstates, (such as I-55 at the Chicago end, and I-40 at the Los Angeles end) but it did make stops at many of the places mentioned in the famous song. I have never driven the whole route in one go, but on several long-distance trips I have found myself on parts of it, and stopped at towns which now sell memorabilia and Americana artefacts associated with the route. Many people argue that the best part of the route – geographically – is through Arizona (including the Grand Canyon) and on to Los Angeles. Many parts of the route at the Chicago end travel through the corn fields of the Mid-West, where the towns and crossroads have become the main features.

For many years I undertook student recruitment trips around Community Colleges in the Mid-West which gave me the opportunity to explore some of the quirkier features at the Chicago end of the route, including a giant statue of a spaceman, The Gemini Giant, in Wilmington, Illinois. Much further along the route in Arizona, you also get the opportunity to stop off in Havasu and see London Bridge – which was bought by the property developer, Robert McCulloch, dismantled, and then reconstructed in the desert. The route also now includes three national parks – Gateway Arch, in St. Louis, and two in Arizona – the famous Grand Canyon, (on a detour from Flagstaff), and Petrified Forest, half way between Gallup, New Mexico and Winslow, Arizona – where you could search for that corner immortalised by The Eagles and Jackson Browne – *Take it Easy* (1972).

Although not on the official route, one popular short detour is to Cadillac Ranch – a string of 1950s Cadillacs all in a row, buried in the ground, with only their huge tail fins glistening in the Texan sunshine, just outside Amerillo. Bruce Springsteen penned the song inspired by the site (1981). It is actually an art instillation, purposely commissioned by the land owner, who at one point decided to move it – to distance it from the urban sprawl of Amarillo. This piece of art strikes me a great example of Americana itself, and deserves its place in Route 66 folklore, even if it's not technically on the route. Does that matter though, when we are primarily talking here about the manufacture of an imagined, mythical, past? In these respect, it just adds to the folklore.

a fan of the Western genre but even I felt I knew the place from the numerous times I must have seen this landscape on my TV over the years – for example, in *Stagecoach* (1939) and *The Searchers* (1956).

My drive that morning now appeared to be designed to prepare me for the most spectacular of red stone rock formations – known as buttes – which I could now see on either side of the road. Monument Valley is part of the Navajo Nation Reservation and you must pay a fee to drive through it. There are plenty of hikes you can undertake in the valley, but I was content to drive slowly through this magnificent landscape and to take some roadside photos. Although the rock formations are truly spectacular it was also great to get some shots of the road itself, with the heat haze as it rises above the tarmac.

Highway 163 cuts straight through Monument Valley so there was no need for any detours. Eventually, this highway hits Highway 160 (going west). Highway 160 then stops when it hits Highway 89 (going south) and this would be my road to Flagstaff, Arizona, where I planned to stop that night. Had it been earlier in the day I could have turned west off Highway 89 – on Highway 64 – and this would have taken me straight to the Grand Canyon. But I was happy to be heading to Flagstaff, knowing that I could head towards the Grand Canyon early the next morning.

Flagstaff is a large town and I knew there would be plenty of motels and places to eat. I plumped for an unassuming motel right on the old Route 66. I had driven round 200 miles since my lunch stop at Mexican Hat, which had taken me around four hours, including stops. After settling in, I strode into town and enjoyed a well-earned beer and dinner in one of the many eateries in town. The evening was warm and there was a nice buzz in town, with plenty of people wandering through the streets.

The Grand Canyon

The next morning I was up early and excited about my short journey up Highway 180 to meet Highway 64 going north straight to the Grand Canyon, but not before I wandered across the street to take a photo of the roadsigns which displayed Albuquerque to the left and

Phoenix to the right. I was standing on a corner which was part of the original Route 66 [see Route 66 Slice of Americana Pie], and I knew this would be my road for a lot of the next two days as I headed back to Los Angeles. I also began singing The Eagles tune *Take it Easy* (1972) probably because a few miles east from the corner where I was standing was that corner in Winslow, Arizona, made famous by the song.

Looking down towards the Colorado River,
Grand Canyon National Park, Arizona

It's around seventy-fives miles from Flagstaff to the official entrance to the Grand Canyon, which took me around ninety minutes. I had been to the Grand Canyon before so I knew pretty much what to expect, but I can't believe that anyone – no matter how many times they have visited – doesn't just stand still and gawp as they approach the south rim and look out on a truly wondrous sight. The scale is unbelievable, and you have to work hard to catch a glimpse of the Colorado River, which winds its way through the valley floor. The river is actually one mile down from the top, and the whole valley- that the river has helped to carve – is between 10 to 15 miles wide, depending on location.

Strange as it might sound today the Grand Canyon was once in danger of being blighted by over commercialisation. It was saved by President Theodore Roosevelt who used the Antiquities Act of 1906 to designate it a National Monument, which afforded it federal protection. Somewhat bizarrely, that Act was designed to enable a President to protect small areas of outstanding natural beauty, which could hardly be said of the Grand Canyon, whose size almost defies belief. In 1919 it became a fully fledged National Park, when the recently formed National Park Service began administering and monitoring it.

The canyon is fascinating, because its geological layers can be clearly seen. It looks like a textbook image as the different coloured rocks appear as a series of steps from the top to the bottom. The last time I visited I took a hike down into the valley, and there are guides available at the visitor centres to help plan such a venture. You should definitely take advice from the rangers if you plan to go down into the canyon. It's not something you should undertake lightly, and you certainly shouldn't contemplate getting to the bottom and back up again, in one day. This time I decided to hire a bike ($25) and set off west from the main visitor centre, eventually arriving at the Hermit's Rest, where I had a coffee at the snack bar. The Hermit's Rest was one of the original structures in the area before the NPS stopped further building works. After returning along Hermit Road, which was delightful, I then ventured a little way east, to the South Kaibab trailhead, and then back to the visitor centre. In total I had cycled around twenty-five miles. If this sounds a bit daunting, there are free jump on/off shuttle buses running along the top of the south rim.

I had an early sandwich lunch at the huge Grand Canyon Village complex, and then jumped back in the car to follow the south rim road east all the way to Desert View. Had I came up to the canyon the previous evening I would have entered at this point (on Highway 64 heading west) and this is a good option if you don't want to double up on the roads in and out of the park. The south rim road is actually Highway 64 which loops back down to Flagstaff. It's a 40-mile round trip from the main visitor centre to Desert View, and with more time I probably would have cycled this section as well. It's certainly worth exploring east and west of the main visitor centre – by car, bike or shuttle bus – if only to get away from the crowds. Venturing out towards Desert View will also enable you to get some of the best views across the canyon. It is possible to get to the north rim of the canyon, but this is a 200-mile car journey, which confirms the scale of the whole area.

Route 66

It was around 4pm when I decided to make way back down Highway 64 to join Interstate 40 (heading west). I-40 pretty much follows the path of the old Route 66 [see Route 66 Slice of Americana Pie] and just as the song says, I travelled from Flagstaff, Arizona, to Kingman, but not Winona (which is to the east of Flagstaff). I arrived in the small town of Kingman at 7pm, after having driven around 175 miles since leaving the Grand Canyon. I stayed in a relatively cheap chain-motel, which was right on the main road through town.

If you have the time (perhaps one more day) you could head back east along historic Route 66 (now I-40) from Flagstaff to visit Petrified Forest National Park. This is about 100 miles down the road, which would take a couple of hours. On the way, you could also stop off to find that corner in Winslow, Arizona, immortalised by The Eagles song (1972). Petrified Forest is aptly named because it contains trees and logs which, through earth-crust movements over 200 million years ago, were uprooted, submerged, and then re-deposited, to form a geological wonder of fossilised remains. The area achieved protected national monument status in 1906 and became a fully-fledged national park in 1962. The forest was also visited by national park pioneer John Muir [see John Muir slice of Americana].

You could also venture slightly north from the Petrified Desert and see another geological wonder, where different coloured layers of sandstone rock give the impression of a painted desert. With an extra day or two to spare you could visit the Petrified Forest and the Painted Desert before the Grand Canyon, by heading slightly back on yourself after coming through Monument Valley. To do this, you would need to turn back east (left) onto Highway 160, and then head south (right) when you hit Highway 191. This will take you to I-40, where you would need to turn west (right). The interstate will then take you straight to the park, and then onto Winslow and Flagstaff, Arizona, following the path of Historic Route 66.

I left Kingman early the next morning still on the highway that's the best. The sky was clear and the Arizona desert landscape was vast. Unfortunately, my road revelry was rudely interrupted by a highway patrol car which overtook me and then poodled along in front of me. I was nervous about overtaking it because it had just overtaken me, but before I could do anything I was pulled over and cautioned about driving too close to a police car. I wanted to call the officer out for being so petty but once he realised I was British he became very polite and asked me if I was aware that London Bridge was just up the road on the left. I thanked him and decided that this could be a nice breakfast stop, and would enable me to see something that many people in Britain considered a joke – that a crazy American had bought what he thought was Tower Bridge, only to discover that he had bought a rather boring alternative (in comparison). I don't know whether or not this was true, but, either way, his aim was to bring tourists to the little backwater town of Lake Havasu City. Clearly, his plan worked, because when I arrived the place was a little hive of tourist activity, with people – including me – enjoying a bizarre slice of London. The whole scene was rather surreal – London Bridge in the Arizona desert – and I really enjoyed it. But I needed to get moving so I didn't stay long.

Lake Havesu is on Highway 95 going south, so I continued along this lovely road until I hit Highway 62 (going west). I could see from my map that if I continued along this road until I hit Highway 177 going south, I would be able to enter Joshua Tree National Park from the south. That way, I could drive right through the park and exit on the road which would take me back to LA. Highway 177 south stops when it hits I-10, so I turned right (going west) on the interstate until I saw the Joshua Tree National Park sign. It was now mid-day and I was looking forward to my slow drive through the park's desert. I had driven around 200 miles since leaving Kingman.

Joshua Tree

Joshua Tree National Park was not designated until 1994, but it was a national monument before then. The eastern half is part of the

Colorado Desert and the western half is part of the Mojave Desert. The distinctive Joshua trees are scattered around the western part of the park; so named because early Mormon settlers thought the branches resembled the raised hands (in prayer) of the Old Testament figure, Joshua. They are actually tall yucca plants, and I made many stops to try to get some nice photos of them.

After getting some orientation from the rangers in the Cottonwood Visitor Center, I made my way down to Cottonwood Spring, which was just a short distance from the visitor centre. I then drove slowly northwest through the desert. The whole park is a remote and haunting place, and hardly surprising therefore that it is a well-known sojourn for many LA residents looking for solace and enlightenment. In the opposite direction (back towards Cottonwood Spring) was the place where the writer Claire Nelson lost her footing on some boulders and ended up spending four days on her back on the desert floor. She retells the story in her book *What I Learnt from Falling*, which was published while I was writing this chapter (Nelson, 2020). One thing I learnt from reading that book was the need to keep reminding myself to stick to well-trodden paths when on my own in remote places (and carry a knife, sunscreen, back-up phone charger unit, mirror, whistle, etc., etc.).

I turned left (west) towards the West Entrance station and then left again down towards the Keys View. From here, you could look across to the famous desert town of Palm Springs and the San Andreas fault, which is responsible for the earthquakes often felt in California, and which many people think will – one day – send California off into the Pacific Ocean. Proud Californians often joke that it will be the rest of the continent which will float off into the Atlantic Ocean.

Before heading off out of the park at the western entrance, I took the short loop hike to Barker Dam, a small reservoir and sanctuary for wildlife. I emerged from the park onto Highway 62 heading west towards LA, but not before I stopped off at the Harmony Motel. This was the motel that the band U2 used when they were making their album *The Joshua Tree*, and the album cover includes photos of the band in and around the motel. It was late afternoon and I was tempted to stay at the motel for the night. Had my flight out of LAX to Chicago the next morning been later in the day I certainly would have. The owner of the motel remembered the band taking over the motel, and to my surprise, room 4 – the room that Bono stayed in – was available for the night (for $65). I explained that I had a flight the next morning and that it would be too risky to expect the freeway into LA to be clear, so I thanked him for his time and headed off to LAX, by rejoining I-10.

It took me around two and a half hours to reach West Century Boulevard, where many motels serving the airport can be found. The airport (LAX) is clearly signposted as you approach LA. I was glad I hadn't taken the risk of staying at the Harmony Motel, and instead stayed in one of many chain-motels, just a quick drive from the airport. I had a pizza and a beer before packing my suitcase, ready for the next morning.

Conclusion

This had been a truly magical road trip. Not only had I visited a string of famous national parks, I had also driven on some fantastic roads, and experienced so much of what is wonderful about the big open spaces in this part of the United States. It's not so much a case of *if* you plan to motor towards the west, it has to be a case of *when*.

My only regrets were that I didn't spend more time hiking around Bryce Canyon, and Capitol Reef, but with just one to two more days tagged onto a ten-day road trip this would certainly be possible. Add another day, and a trip to Petrified Forest would also be doable.

Six things to do in Los Angeles – which are free or relatively cheap

Los Angeles is big, very big. It stretches over forty miles from north to south and around thirty miles from east to west. And that's just the *city* limits; not to be confused with LA County. It's not impossible to get around LA by public transport. Indeed, a massive project to restore some of the lost train routes is now well under way. But here is a city – particularly if time is tight – where a hire car will definitely come into its own. That said, it can pay huge dividends if you check the route maps between places, and you must check your watch. Rush hours can be an absolute nightmare, where you might find yourself stuck on a freeway and/or moving slower than someone walking. But the danger in coming off a freeway is you might then find yourself battling with an endless row of stop lights. My advice is not to expect to get to places at agreed times and just to go with the flow. Driving between the hours of ten in the morning and three in the afternoon are probably the best times – the afternoon rush hour starts early. Of course, part of the fun of being in LA is to be in a car; it's an essential part of the experience. But do keep an eye on that re-growth in public transport.

Here are a list of things to do in LA which will not break the bank, including some paths less trodden.

1 Santa Monica Pier and Venice Beach

If you are able, rent a bike near Santa Monica pier and cycle on the beach paths up to Venice Beach. You will pass the famous outdoor Gold's Gym, and a huge mural of Jim Morrison of The Doors (at 1811 Speedway). The band was formed here in the summer of 1965. The area also has a network of small canals (hence the name) and there are plenty of coffee shops along the route.

2 The beaches of south LA.

Best to do this in a hire car. Head south on I-405, and take Highway 39 south to Huntington Beach, then follow the coast down to Newport Beach, finishing off at Laguna Beach – the most spectacular of the beaches, and the setting for the TV series *The OC*. The roads will be busy so don't be in a hurry. If you have more time, include Long Beach, which houses the Queen Mary liner.

3 The Hollywood Hills

Best to do this in a hire car. Get yourself on Sunset Blvd (west end) and head up Laurel Canyon Blvd [see Laurel Canyon Slice of Americana Pie]. At the top turn right on Mulholland Drive and pull over at the Universal Studios overlook (signposted). Continue along (the internet will locate superstar addresses) until you hit the 101. Turn right on Cahuenga Blvd, which becomes Highland Ave. This will take you down to Hollywood Blvd (right where the stars in the sidewalk are) and Sunset Blvd (east end) a couple of blocks further south.

4 Historic Downtown Los Angeles

Locate the Union (railway) Station and you will be in the original historic centre of LA, with Chinatown to the north and Little Tokyo to the south. There is a plaque in the Old Plaza which commemorates the birth of the city. You can walk from here to the Frank Gehry designed Walt Disney Concert Hall (spectacular in the sunshine) along W 1st Street, and close by is the headquarters of the LAPD and City Hall – made famous through a string of films and TV series. Head for the Grand Central Market at 317 S Broadway for lunch.

5 Around Malibu

Best to do this in a hire car. Head along the Pacific Coast Highway (PCH) on the north side of LA. El Matador beach is spectacular (about 10 miles north of Malibu) and Zuma Beach is a famous surfing spot (and title of a Neil Young album). You can also visit the Getty Museum – with guided tours around the exhibits and the remodelled Roma villa. You pay to park in the grounds, which includes the entrance fee. It's signposted on the right as you head north out of Santa Monica, on the PCH.

6 The Griffith Observatory and The Hollywood Sign

Best to do this in a hire car (+ hike). Position yourself to the east of the 101 freeway on either Sunset or Hollywood Blvd. Turn north until you hit Franklin, then turn left and right for Canyon Drive. This will take you to a hiking path to the sign. Or turn right onto Franklin and then left up to the Griffith Observatory (signposted). You can hike to the sign from the observatory car park (about 3 miles). Look out for the statue of James Dean at the observatory – which is where some scenes from *Rebel Without a Cause* (1955) were filmed.

Chapter 11

The Delta Blues and the Sunshine State

National Parks: Hot Springs, Everglades, Biscayne, Dry Tortugas

Other notable sites: Highway 61

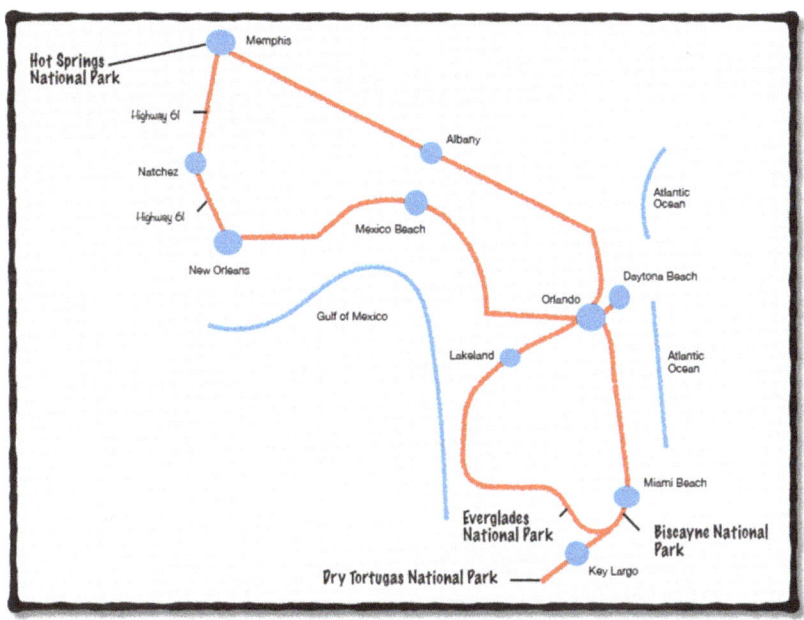

This chapter was composed while singing:

On the Road Again, as performed by Willie Nelson (1980) and

Graceland, as performed by Paul Simon (1986)

Introduction

This chapter recounts the story of one of the first long distance car trips I undertook in the USA and is different from the others which feature in this book. First, it is really two trips, combined as one, and second, it involved my family. Previous chapters have included a lot of references to periods of quiet contemplation on my part, but here is my example of a road trip involving some family fun, often at my expense.

Having spent several years before this road trip criss-crossing the USA on Greyhound buses, I was keen to get back in a car. And most of my previous long distance driving had been on the west coast, so here was a chance to try something a little different, and go to some places I'd never been before. My partner was also up for it, never having been to the USA. Our girls had long-harboured thoughts of experiencing some of the magic of Disney, and I harboured thoughts that they might also appreciate some of the wider culture of the country.

I was nervous though, that the girls might not enjoy a trip up Highway 61, so I hatched a plan to undertake a double loop starting each time from Orlando, Florida. My partner and I would head west to New Orleans, Louisiana, then up to Memphis, Tennessee, and then back to Orlando, through the states of Alabama and Georgia. We would then pick up the girls from Orlando Airport, and do another loop, this time around the state of Florida, including a trip to Disney World and the Everglades National Park.

Each loop took around ten days to complete, and could be undertaken separately, or combined into one three-week trip.

First Loop – Arrival in Orlando and across to New Orleans

My partner and I took a flight from London Gatwick to Orlando, via St. Louis. The stopover in St Louis was short and smooth, but given the ever growing attraction of Disney World there are now many more cheap and direct flights to Orlando, so a stopover should not be necessary. We arrived mid-afternoon and immediately made the 30-minute drive down to the town of Kissimmee and booked into a relatively cheap chain-motel. We were tired after the flights and decided to order in a Chinese take away from the menu left in the room. The menu included the unappetising option of a 'Poo Poo platter' – obviously something got lost in translation there. Our actual meal choices arrived quickly, directly to the room.

The next morning we headed north on the Florida Turnpike (small fee), then took Highway 44 to the west coast of Florida. We then took Highway 98 all the way round the Gulf Coast. We were heading to New Orleans, Louisiana, and made it halfway on the first day. The weather was gloriously hot and the coast road was a delight to drive. We stopped at the small town of Mexico Beach, and pulled into a beach-side motel, mainly because I loved its strap-line: 'The beach stops here and the fun begins'. We had driven around 400 miles, which had taken around nine hours, with stops. The lovely owner explained that all the mainstream rooms were taken, but we were welcome to take a look at a beachside garage conversion. The room was large and ramshackle in appearance, and we instantly said that we would take it. As the sun was going down we headed out onto the still hot, white, sandy beach, and then splashed around in the sea, which felt like warm bathwater.

The next morning we continued along Highway 98, until we reached the town of Mobile, Alabama. Knowing that we were eventually heading for Memphis, Tennessee, it was difficult to get *Stuck inside of Mobile with the Memphis Blues again* out of my head – thank you, Bob Dylan (1965). At this point we got onto the I-10, heading west, which took us directly into New Orleans. We arrived in New Orleans late afternoon after having driven around 350 miles, which had taken around seven hours, with stops. Knowing that New Orleans is a busy city, I had phoned ahead and booked two nights at a guesthouse. It turned out to be a great choice. It was not expensive, had great rooms, was in a great location, and had free parking. It was in the Historic Garden District just to the east of downtown.

After settling in, we headed downtown to Bourbon Street. The guesthouse was very close to a great old streetcar stop, which we couldn't resist a ride on. The night life was frenetic. We stopped off at a couple of bars, and enjoyed the street music and dancing. Yes, it was very touristy, but the buzz of the place was infectious. This was my one and only visit to New Orleans and with hindsight and the knowledge I gained from watching the HBO series *Treme*, I would certainly have been more adventurous and moved away from Bourbon Street. But, of course, the devastation caused by Hurricane Katrina in 2005, took a terrible toll on the city.

The next morning we wandered back into the downtown area, which seemed quite subdued after the previous evening, but things slowly came to life again, including the live street music. From my experience, only the island of Cuba competes with New Orleans when it comes to live music, which seems to emanate from every possible source. Perhaps because of that I went into several record shops, and bought more records than I intended, including some Cajun, Zydeco, Jazz and Blues. Although New Orleans is synonymous with traditional Jazz music and was the home to legendary producers like Allen Toussaint, and legendary performers like Dr John, its French roots are clearly evident in the Cajun music of performers like Eddie LeJeune, and the more upbeat Zydeco music of performers like Clifton Chenier. The word Cajun is a contraction of Acadian, referring to the original French settlers on the continent. It also provided the name for the national park in the north east of the USA (see chapter seven). Although both Cajun and Zydeco have influenced each other, the roots of Cajun lay with white performers and Zydeco with black Creole performers.

We stopped for coffee and hot beignets (French doughnuts) at the famous Café Du Monde in the French Market and listened to a street band, complete with upright bass and washboard. I bought some coffee and chicory in a large tin, which I still use to store my daily fix of caffeine. We spent the afternoon wandering around town and down by the Mississippi River, to see the obligatory steam boats and paddle boats, whose big wheels, it seems, really do keep slowly turning, as made famous in the song *Proud Mary* (1969), by Creedence Clearwater Revival. We had dinner at Mulate's Restaurant in town, where we had a great time listening to The Mamou Playboys, and watching the locals dancing as we ate.

Highway 61 visited

We were up early the next morning in preparation for heading up Highway 61. We were going to Graceland – home of The King – in Memphis, Tennessee, just as the song required us – Paul Simon, *Graceland* (1986). We began by enjoying a great breakfast in the outdoor quad at our guesthouse. Breakfast was included in the price, which confirmed that this had been a great choice of accommodation.

After packing up the car, we headed west on I-10 and after an hour or so's driving, we stopped at Baton Rouge for a wander and a coffee. It was mid-morning and there wasn't much of a buzz at that time, so we got back in the car, headed north out of town, and looked for our first sighting of a Highway 61 sign. Once we had picked up the highway, we headed north, hoping to get as far as we could that day, but not before stopping at every opportunity to take photos and to rummage in roadside junk yards. Paul Simon sung about how the Mississippi Delta had been shining, like a metal guitar from the National company. For us it appeared to be the plastic coverings on the crops which were providing this effect.

We arrived at the town of Natchez on the Mississippi River in the early evening. We stayed at an old, traditional motel, right by The Natchez Trace Parkway. For some, that motel might have been described as a little run down, but, for us, it had authenticity. The room was clean, and we had a good night's sleep, after a short trip into the downtown area for dinner. The next morning we continued heading north on the Natchez Trace Parkway, which turned out to be a beautiful drive through green and pleasant pastures. Natchez Trace was an ancient Native American route across the states of Mississippi, Alabama, and Tennessee, eventually arriving in Nashville, Tennessee (444 miles away from where we were). The Parkway runs adjacent to Highway 61, and we rejoined the highway at the point where the 'Old Trace' started heading further east.

We were now heading into the heart of the area immortalised by Blues singer-songwriters [see Highway 61 Slice of Americana Pie]. This includes Muddy Waters, who was born in Rolling Fork, which we passed through mid-morning. We stopped for lunch and some map orientation at the small town Leland, after having been on the road for around four hours, covering around 150 miles. The next couple of hours were surreal. I was looking at my map on the hood of the hire car when we were approached by three young black males, who were interested in why two white people had stopped in town. One of them asked if I was from the media (assuming, I suppose, that because we were off the usual tourist trails, we must be journalists, or the like). I explained that I was following the route of Highway 61 and that I was interested in the roots of Blues music. He then asked if I would like to meet his grandfather, who, it turned out was none

A Slice of Americana Pie

A critical appreciation of: Highway 61

Whereas the Lincoln Highway [see Lincoln Highway Slice of Americana Pie] dissects the United States from East to West, Highway 61 dissects from South to North. It roughly follows the path of the Mississippi River, and is referred to as The Great River Road because of that – up from New Orleans, through the Mississippi Delta, on to Memphis, Tennessee, and eventually finishing in Wyoming, Minnesota, although it originally went through Duluth, Minnesota, and up onto the Canadian border. The original route was commissioned in 1926 as part of the national highway initiative began in 1921, but it wasn't completed, and certainly not paved, until the 1940s. That original route from the Gulf of Mexico to the Canadian border was around 1,700 miles long.

Like Route 66 [see Route 66 Slice of Americana Pie] it is steeped in Americana folklore, as well as being historically significant. Just as Route 66 took migrants west to the promised land of California, Highway 61 took migrants north towards the industrial and urban centres of St Louis and Chicago. But the highway south of Memphis is the section for which it is most famous. This area is the symbolic home of the Blues, and the folk and roots music from which it came, and Highway 61 has become entwined with this music. The significance of the Mississippi Delta to the development of the Blues is beautifully explored in the book by William Ferris (1978).

The blues: a state of melancholy. In musical form it captures the experiences of the black slave, migrant, and labourer. In the 20th Century it became associated with the itinerant, solitary, rural, black, male, guitar player, but Bessie Smith sang the Blues in urban settings. Like a lot of music of black origin, its deeper roots appear to lie in the rhythmic chants of the slave ship rowers, and the call and response to the work gang leader who set the pace of work, and also the sound of the tools which hammered out a beat.

If the Blues needed a mailing address it would probably be a house in one of the towns in the Mississippi Delta, perhaps Clarksdale or Leland. Some of its most famous sons come from this area – including B B King, Howlin' Wolf, and Muddy Waters – whose name perfectly describes the Mississippi River.

At the town of Clarksdale you will find the junction of Highway 61 and Highway 49 – said to be the place where Robert Johnson sold his soul to the devil, in exchange for mastery of the Blues. Regardless of whether or not anything actually happened at that crossroad, it has entered Americana folklore, along with a host of songs which refer either literally or metaphorically to it – in the sense of someone needing to make a significant decision or enter a Faustian pact.

The religious connotations of being at a crossroad in one's life has also made this junction on Highway 61 a form of antidote to the Road to Damascus, where choosing the devil – and particularly the devil's music – has befallen many a musical traveller. This was not lost on Bob Dylan, whose song *Highway 61 Revisited* (1965) and album of the same name, made numerous references to lost souls and potential saviours. The title itself is also symbolic, as we see Dylan dipping deep south down Highway 61, to rediscover the roots of his own music. Before settling in New York, his home was Duluth, Minnesota, through which the original highway ran, thus completing a string of connections.

Naturally, highways run in both directions, but Highway 61 almost dictates that you should undertake it from south to north, at least until you reach Memphis. Paul Simon's song *Graceland* (1986) bows to this logic when he sings of his desire to visit the home of Elvis Presley in Memphis, by travelling up through what he refers to as the cradle of the civil war. Like Dylan before, he is also symbolically rediscovering the roots of his own musical style. The song of the same name included the Everly Brothers as backing singers – whose musical style heavily influenced the sound of Simon and Garfunkel. The album was not without controversy though because he also travelled to South Africa to record with a number of black musicians – thereby breaking the international cultural boycott on apartheid at the time.

Highway 61 is very much a musical journey – charting a course through a range of hybrid forms of American music, and the transformation of the Blues, into Rhythm and Blues, and eventually Rock and Roll – and its appropriation by mainstream white Americans. Starting in the heart of New Orleans, around Bourbon Street, it is possible to listen first to some Jazz and Latin inspired music, then move on to Baton Rouge to dance along to some traditional Cajun or Zydeco, then on through Clarksdale, while listening to Robert Johnson in the car, then roll into Memphis and stroll along Beale Street, listening to the music drifting out from the (now very touristy) bars and clubs, before doffing your cap to the statue of W C Handy – the Father of the Blues – in the nearby square.

The next morning, you could then drive up the street a few blocks to 760 Union Street, to the Sun Studio, and see the white faces of Elvis Presley, Johnny Cash, Carl Perkins and Jerry Lee Lewis adorning the studio wall. The logo on Sun Studios records was bright yellow and featured a cockerel. Perhaps Dylan was making a surreal reference to this on the *Highway 61 Revisited* track, *Tombstone Blues* (1965) where he proudly proclaims that the sun isn't yellow, it's actually chicken. And, of course, Graceland itself – the home of Elvis Presley – is only a few miles from the studio.

Across town, to the south of the Sun Studio was the home of Memphis Soul, or Southern Soul, where many legendary soul singers recorded their hits at the Stax recording studios – 926 E McLemore Ave – including Otis Redding. The House Band there was the multi-racial Booker T and the MGs, which included guitarist Steve Cropper. They were the session musicians on many of the hits to have emerged from this label.

The journey described in the previous paragraphs is a distance of around 500 miles, which, for me, included detours and an overnight stop off in Natchez. On the way I also got to have my wonderful chance encounter with the grandson of the Blues singer James 'Son' Thomas.

other than James 'Son' Thomas, a legendary Bluesman, who lived just around the corner.

We followed the three guys around that corner, and there, as if it had been staged, we saw the man in his rocking chair on the porch of his cabin. He was a mine of information and a total delight to talk to. He showed us around the cabin, where we admired his artwork, and he signed copies of one of his albums for us. I still proudly display his photograph on the wall of my house [see Highway 61 Slice of Americana Pie].

Road signage, travelling north on Highway 61, Mississippi

After lunch we headed further north along the highway. We stopped at the small town of Shaw and spoke with a guy who ran an automotive junk yard. We each bought used car license plates from him, which started my interest in owning a plate from each of the 50 states. That collection is now complete, which includes many very old plates, the majority of which were bought from the state in which they were originally registered. We then continued on, through the legendary crossroads in Clarksdale where the Blues singer Robert Johnson allegedly sold his soul to the devil in exchange for mastery of the blues [see Highway 61 Slice of Americana Pie]. We eventually arrived on the outskirts of Memphis, Tennessee, late afternoon, after having travelled around 150 miles since leaving Leland, which took around four hours, including stops.

Memphis Blues

I was keen to get wandering around downtown Memphis, so we started our search for a motel as soon as we arrived. We headed in the direction of Graceland, the home of Elvis Presley, which we were going to visit the next morning. We were on Elvis Presley Boulevard (what else would it be called?). At our first stop, the guy on the reception – after looking out the window towards my partner – asked me how many hours I wanted the room for. I stopped the conversation at that point, and we headed further down the road.

The next motel was one step up. Not a huge step, but I didn't want to waste any more time, so we took the room for two nights, which turned out to be just fine, if a little noisy at night, courtesy of the late-night merriment. The road up to Graceland has a large number of motels, catering to different tastes and budgets. Our motel was a bit shabby looking so I didn't even make a note of its name, but I do remember it advertising itself as having 'wall to wall carpet'. So there's one in the eye for those cheapskates down the road where the carpet didn't stretch to the skirting board.

After settling into our room, we we soon off to Beale Street, the home to many Blues music venues, including B.B. King's Blues Club. There was music playing in every bar, and the place was a hive of activity. I doffed my cap at the statue of W. C. Handy – the father of the Blues – which was in the small Handy Park, right on Beale Street. This scene (and its deeper significance for the writer) was captured on record when Marc Cohn sang *Walking in Memphis* (1991). Unfortunately for us, the whole area had the feel of a tourist trap, which, from all accounts, appears to have got worse over the years. It seems to be a very American way of doing things: first, have places grow organically; second, stand by and watch as they go to wrack and ruin; and then, third, rebuild them as theme park versions of the original. That said, once we relaxed into the vibe, we enjoyed the experience. We bought tickets (very cheap) to the Memphis Music and Heritage Festival. Unfortunately, we had an argument about extortionately priced beer at the event. I wanted to get some cheap beer at the supermarket before we went in because I guessed this was reason the tickets were so cheap. I was right, but instead of being magnanimous, I kept saying it at every opportunity. Because of this the evening finished rather abruptly – on the fun side, anyway.

The next morning we had breakfast in a diner close to the entrance to Graceland. The scene was bizarre, and not what I was expecting at all. The whole of the road up to Elvis Presley's former home had become a mass of cheap motels, which gave way to diners and gift shops, and surely nothing like it had been before Elvis decided to live there. And although the gates to Graceland were huge, the mansion itself wasn't anywhere near as big as I had imagined. To cap it off Jacky was hung over from the previous night's drinking of extortionately priced beer, and spent most of the tour of Graceland in a delicate state. For me, I found the tour fascinating, particularly the Jungle Room, where Elvis spent a lot of his time while at home. Our guide was full of interesting information about the live and times of Elvis, including the story about how he fired a gun at his TV screen. We finished the tour by respectfully trailing past his grave.

The legendary Sun Studio, 710 Union Avenue, Memphis, Tennessee

We then drove up to the Sun Studio on Union Street, where we had another tour. This time the tour was much shorter, because the studio was tiny, which heightened the sense that magic had been conjured up from within its walls, under the guidance of maverick producer, Sam

Phillips. All of Elvis' early hits were recorded here, with his backing musicians, all finding their place on the small floor space. The studio also proudly displayed a poster of the, so-called, 'million dollar quartet' – a photograph of Elvis Presley, Johnny Cash, Carl Perkins and Jerry Lee Lewis, at a jam session in the studio in 1956 [see Highway 61 Slice of Americana Pie]. We finished the tour by having a coffee in the Sun Studio cafe, after which we bought some souvenirs, which were irresistible because most of them featured the famous yellow cockerel logo, which appeared on all the 7-inch singles that the studio produced.

We then drove across town to the Lorraine Motel on Mulberry Street, where Civil Rights leader, Martin Luther King Jr, was assassinated on April 4th, 1968. Bono sings about that shot which rang out, on the U2 song *Pride (in the name of love)* (1984), and in the same year as the assassination, Dion (1968) had sung in honour of Dr King, Abraham Lincoln, President John Kennedy and his brother Bobby, who were all assassinated – Bobby Kennedy just a couple of months after King.

The Lorraine Motel still stands, frozen in time, and now houses the National Civil Rights Museum. The motel has a chequered history, having transferred from being an all white establishment, to become a welcoming place for black travellers and musicians, and was listed in *The Green Book* in the 1950s and 1960s – an essential travel guide for black travellers in a divided society. In 1982 it was almost demolished before it was bought by a group of local black leaders. When we visited the site the museum had only just opened, and across the road from the entrance I was handed a photocopied sheet which explained why Jacqueline Smith was camping on the sidewalk. She had been the front desk manager at the motel for fifteen years, and along with many others associated with Martin Luther King, she felt his legacy was not being best served by a museum which had the feel of a Disney attraction. Smith was adamant that the motel should have been put on the National Register of Historic Places and used to serve the poor. In respect for her protest, we did not visit the museum.

Across the South

We were now at the halfway point in our road trip and it was time to start heading back east towards Orlando to pick up our girls. If you were feeling particularly intrepid you could venture out west from Memphis for around 200 miles on I-40 (a fast interstate) to visit Hot Springs National Park, in Arkansas, which was designated in 1921. As

A Slice of Americana Pie

A critical appreciation of: Chuck Berry (1926-2017)

Chuck Berry played the kind of raunchy rhythm and blues music which helped establish rock 'n' roll as a distinct genre, and he wrote songs for teenagers before American youth was even recognised as having a culture. For ten years (from 1955-1965) he produced a string of singles for the Chess record label in Chicago, including tunes as diverse as *Rock and Roll Music* (1957), *Memphis, Tennessee* (1959), and *Promised Land* (1964). And many of these recordings were instrumental in developing a distinct British popular music sound, which then made its way back to the USA.

Born in St Louis, Chuck Berry would have heard Blues music throughout his early life. His influences were wider however, and included Country music and particularly white Hillbilly music. This mix helped him stand out from the musical crowd and complicates the story of how his contemporary Elvis Presley raided black music to make it palatable for white folk, because there was Berry raiding white music and playing it to mainly black folk. In effect, Berry was a crossover artist before the term became popular.

Berry had good reason to be annoyed about how numerous white artists (including British bands like The Beatles and The Rolling Stones) carved out more successful careers than the black musicians upon whom their success was based. He was a shrewd operator though when it came to the business side of his career, and followed the money whenever he could. One of his early lessons was probably the writing credit for his first hit *Maybellene* (1955), which went, in part, to the DJ Alan Freed, as a form of payola (payment for radio play). At least it got him on the radio. The tune was actually based on an existing one *Ida Red* (1938), performed by Bob Wills and his Texas Playboys – which confirms Berry's influences.

When Berry spoke of his major influences – Lonnie Johnson, Charlie Christian, T Bone Walker, Carl Hogan and Louis Jordan – we can see how his innovative style was actually an amalgamation of much of what had come before. This was very apparent in the opening guitar section of the Louis Jordan tune *Ain't That Just Like a Woman* (1946) (played by Carl Hogan) which is identical to the opening guitar section on *Johnny B Goode* (1958). Although his 'duck walk' was probably uniquely his, the pointed guitar stance appears to come from T Bone Walker.

Claims of plagiarism and issues of song ownership continued throughout Berry's career. He wanted *fair dos*. But the issues highlighted just how difficult it is to draw a hard line between influence and stealing. Popular music, at heart, has a simple structure, so how could one cord sequence completely differentiate itself from another, and if catchy lyrics and guitar riffs enter the subconscious, how would it be possible to definitively argue that someone had deliberately copied someone else? Both Bob Dylan and Keith Richards have argued that there is an unhelpful cul-de-sac here, but when the lyrics from a famous Beatles tune – *Come Together* (1969), credited to Lennon-McCartney – appear to be a direct lift from Berry's *You Can't Catch Me* (1956), perhaps that line had been crossed? Lennon was a huge Berry fan (as were The Beatles in general), and he made amends with his *Rock 'n' Roll* covers album, so that the original writers and publishers could claim royalties.

A lot of the copying of Berry's tunes and lyrics were more likely homage than stealing, as in Marc Bolan's outro to *Get it On* (1971), where he muses about the fact he is still thinking, in the style of Berry's *Little Queenie* (1959), and Bruce Springsteen gives his own nod to *You Can't Catch Me,* referring to the New Jersey Turnpike in the wee hours of the morning, just as Berry had done in *Open All Night* (1982). Some cases are trickier, for example, when the Beach Boys lifted the whole tune of *Sweet little Sixteen* (1958) for *Surfin' USA* (1963). Brian Wilson agreed to co-credit Berry a few years later. And where does that leave Fleetwood Mac's *Albatross* (1968), which does sound very similar to Berry's *Deep Feeling* (1965); inspired by, perhaps?

On the other hand, how lucky was Berry in having Johnnie Johnson as his unassuming piano player on his early hits? In John Collis' (2002) biography of Berry it would appear that he was very lucky. For, without Johnson's right hand perfectly following Berry's guitar, and his left hand banging out the distinctive rock 'n' roll back beat, could Chuck Berry have become the king of a genre? In reality, it was probably never a monarchy. Johnson saw himself as a jobbing piano player, who just wanted to be paid for performing, and didn't demand writing credits, at least not until nearly fifty years later, when nothing came of it.

When *Maybellene* hit the airwaves in 1955 it was hugely successful and set Berry off on a series of tours and demands for more hits. He duly delivered. Many of the follow up tunes spoke to a growing youth culture – particularly young males – presenting them with the glorious possibilities of aspiring to car ownership, driving fast, and chasing women, including *School Days* (1958) and *No Particular Place to Go* (1960).

Roll Over Beethoven (1956) was a perfect rock 'n' roll anthem, which the Beatles covered in 1964; ditto for *Rock and Roll Music*. And *Brown Eyed Handsome Man* (1956) was a big post-humous hit for Buddy Holly in 1963. That tune had a wonderfully subversive quality, hidden in the title, and to some extent by the Holly cover, because, the lyrics appear to speak of the attractiveness of the black male (Berry himself?) to the white female. At the time, this would have been too much for polite society to discuss. Buddy Holly accompanied Berry on some of the 1950s tours – before his tragic death in 1959 – and had similar musical influences, confirming that rhythm and blues and rock 'n' roll have hybrid musical roots.

Chuck Berry's music was rock 'n' roll and so was his personal life. He went to jail three times, for armed robbery, transporting an underage girl across a state line, and tax evasion, and was later accused of assault, drug possession and installing hidden cameras in toilets. Was he guilty on all counts? I don't know. Was he harassed by the police? I don't know. Those who knew him speak of how difficult he could be, including in and around the stage. Keith Richard once famously said that he wouldn't warm to him if he was cremated next to him, but John Lennon said that if you wanted to give rock 'n' roll another name you might call it Chuck Berry.

Enigmatic, innovative, and hugely influential, Chuck Berry was a large slice of Americana pie – but maybe with a bitter taste for some, if we include his personal life.

the name implies the park protects the thermal water emerging from the sandstone rocks at the foot of Hot Springs Mountain. The park is located in downtown Hot Springs, which was the childhood hometown of President Bill Clinton. The park is free but you pay to bathe. Given that you would be on a fast interstate there and back, you could make this a day trip and arrive back in Memphis the same evening.

Hot Springs would have been too much of a stretch for us, so the next morning we headed south east out of Memphis, and pretty much stuck to this trajectory all the way back to the east coast, at Jacksonville, in north-east Florida. Our main thoroughfare for the day would be I-22. However, in order to complete our Elvis tour, we stopped first at the town of Tupelo, where Elvis was born, and took a photo of his childhood home. Our quick stop was around 100 miles from Memphis. We then continued on, through the large urban area around Birmingham, Alabama, until we hit the town of Montgomery, Alabama, where we stopped for lunch. We had driven around 200 miles since leaving Tupelo, which had taken around three and a half hours. We were in the heart of The South, and at the location of several significant flash-points in the fight for civil rights in the USA.

> **Critical Cultural Comment – Alabama and the Fight for Civil Rights**
>
> In Montgomery, Alabama, in December 1955, Rosa Parks, a black bus passenger, and local activist, famously refused to give up her seat to a white passenger, as ordered by the bus driver. This sparked a year long bus boycott, which culminated in the Supreme Court ruling that segregated buses were unconstitutional. These events were celebrated in the song *Sister Rosa Parks*, by The Neville Brothers (1989). Montgomery now houses the beautiful granite engraved memorial, which immortalises those who died in the struggle for civil rights in the US.
>
> Fifty miles west of Montgomery is the town of Selma, where, in 1965, peaceful civil rights protesters (including Martin Luther King Jr) were attacked by the police as they attempted to march to the state capitol building in Montgomery. They were protesting about the right to register to vote, which was being denied to many black people, even after the Civil Rights legislation of 1964 – which formally outlawed segregation. On the third and final attempt to march, it is estimated that around 25,000 people finally made it to Montgomery, which resulted in

the Voting Rights Act, passed by President Johnson [see The Texas White House Slice of Americana Pie]. The road between the two towns is now known as the 'Voting Rights Trail', and the whole series of events is portrayed in the film *Selma* (2015). Some of the hypocrisy and prejudice of the time was also captured in P.J. Sloan's tune *Eve of Destruction* (1965), sung by Barry McGuire.

Martin Luther King Jr and Malcolm X led competing visions for black liberation and equality in the 1960s. King preached a message of future racial unity, while Malcolm X remained distrustful of white power and preached a more separatist message. But, not far from Montgomery and Selma was Muscle Shoals, Alabama, a place where black and white musicians were already united by a universal language of popular music. At the Fame Studios in the town, the white producer Rick Hall, along with the white house band (affectionately known as The Swampers), were busy throughout the sixties recording hits with legendary black singers, like Wilson Picket and Aretha Franklin. At the end of the decade the session musicians formed their own Muscle Shoals Sound Studio just down the road.

One of the big hits to emerge from the new studio was *Brown Sugar*, by the Rolling Stones, which helped cement the black and white hybrid nature of popular music. It is well known that Keith Richards (from the Stones) puts many of his guitar riffs down to listening to Chuck Berry in his youth, but equally, in *his* youth, Chuck Berry was busy listening to the white Hillbilly music of the southern states [see Chuck Berry Slice of Americana Pie].

We deliberately sought out one of the downtown diners which we knew had been segregated in the 1950s, in order to pay our own little tribute to those who fought for civil rights. After lunch we headed back to the car with the intention of getting as far as we could that day. We continued heading south-east, on Highway 82, and we eventually pulled over and stopped at a chain-motel, in Albany, Georgia. We had covered around 350 miles since leaving Tupelo, which had taken around eight hours, including our stops along the way.

With more time, and with the benefit of hindsight, I would certainly have made a detour up to Muscle Shoals, on the Tennessee River to pay another little tribute to the legendary music studios located in this small town. The town is on The Natchez Trace Parkway, a couple of hours north east of Tupelo. Strange as it might sound, particularly given the explosion of popular music talent in the 1960s, it is highly likely that a large percentage of all the hits on the Billboard 100 charts throughout this period featured instrumentation from just three groups of session musicians – The Wrecking Crew, based in LA [see Laurel Canyon Slice of Americana Pie]; The Memphis Group (The MGs), based in Memphis, Tennessee, at Stax Records; and The Swampers, based in Muscle Shoals. This included the instrumentation for *Good Vibrations* by The Beach Boys (1966), (Sittin' on the) *Dock of the Bay*, by Otis Redding (1967), and *Respect* by Aretha Franklin (1967).

The next day we needed to get back to the airport in Orlando by mid-afternoon to pick up our girls. We continued along Highway 82, until we hit highway 23 at the town of Waycross, still in Georgia. This took us straight down to Jacksonville, Florida. We then followed the coast south along I-95, and then inland on I-4, which took us straight to the airport, which was well signposted. We had covered 350 miles, since leaving Albany, which took us around seven hours. We arrived in good time to meet the girls. They had flown across from London, Gatwick, as unaccompanied minors, but they were still escorted onto the plane in the UK, and then escorted off the plane in the US (for a small additional fee). Naturally, it was fantastic to see them, all kitted out in tee-shirts and baseball caps. We drove from the airport back to the chain-motel in Kissimmee, the one we had stayed in the previous week.

Second Loop – Around the Sunshine State

The next morning we headed off to a local all-you-can eat restaurant. I thought this would be a good opportunity for the girls to experience some good 'ole American portion distortion. Perhaps they were a little jet-lagged, because their reaction to the abundance of food was not what I was expecting: 'You mean we can take whatever we want?' Even after telling them 'yes', their faces indicated that I must be winding them up, and surely someone was going to tell them off. The result was that they didn't eat as much as I was expecting.

We returned to the car, where I delivered a fatherly lecture to everyone, about not messing with the windows and door locks. An employee at the car hire place had warned me about the possibility of locking the keys in the car. After which our Florida adventure began in earnest.

Our first stop was Daytona Beach, a small town, and home to the famous Daytona 500 (the annual motor racing event). It has a famous strip of wide, white sand, replete with everything that American beach culture has to offer, including the possibility of driving on the beach, because of the firmness of the sand. I thought the girls would enjoy the buzz, and it would be a good chance for all of us to relax for a couple of days. We drove north from Kissimmee, along I-4, back to the coast road where we had turned off for the airport the previous day. This only took an hour, and before long we had settled into a beach-side motel, on Atlantic Avenue. We booked in for three nights. I assumed that the girls would spend the majority of their time on the beach, but instead they spent almost all of their time in the motel pool. So much so that our eldest ended up with an ear infection, which we had to treat with antibiotics. It was actually me that ended up on the beach, which I enjoyed. The area around the motel had its share of shops and eating places, and altogether the two days we spent there were a nice combination of recuperation for the grown-ups and acclimatisation for the girls.

On the third morning we set off down the coast on Highway 1 and then I-95, heading towards Miami Beach. It was gloriously hot and the air conditioning in the car was full on. We drove around 300 miles, and the trip took us around six hours to complete, including stops. Miami Beach sits on a peninsula, out in the sea, and is connected to the city of Miami by a series of bridges. We arrived late afternoon and booked into, what looked like, an affordable motel, which had free parking. It turned out to be good-value for the area. We then walked along Ocean Drive, past all the glorious Art Deco hotels, which were so well maintained that it looked like we were on a movie set for a film from fifty years ago. Some of the hotels had perfectly restored classic cars and motor bikes proudly sitting out front and it was great fun trying to get some perfect photos. I couldn't even imagine what it might cost to stay in one of those hotels. Luckily, our motel wasn't that much further up the road. The weather remained hot and balmy all evening and into the night.

The Keys and the Everglades

Miami Beach was a quick stop-over on our way south to the foot of Florida and the long strip of small islands, known as keys – hence the name 'Florida Keys'. As soon as we left the motel we looked for the Highway 1 signs, and then spent the whole of the day on this highway, which stretches all the way down to the last key, Key West. After about an hour's driving, we found ourselves driving out into the sea, towards one of the most famous of the keys, Key Largo – famous in no small part due to the film of the same name, starring Humphrey Bogart and Lauren Bacall (1948).

To say that the next two hours were spectacular would be an understatement. We appeared to be driving on the sea; we were actually on a series of road bridges, which connected the small islands (the keys) all the way to Key West. The longest bridge was seven miles long, either side of which the colour aquamarine found its most perfect variant in the water. There were also small puffy white clouds in the azure-coloured sky. The whole scene had a surreal quality. By the time we arrived at Key West we had driven around 100 miles since leaving Key Largo.

We wandered around Key West, which contained the usual mix of restaurants, bars and tourist shops. We had a family photograph taken at the southern-most point in the United States, where we found ourselves surrounded by pelicans, both real and plastic. At this point we were also less than 100 miles from the island of Cuba, which was due south. Hardly surprising therefore that Cuba has a long history of connection with the United States, including its large casino-resort hotels, apparently funded by American mobsters in the 1950s; the infamous Cuban missile crisis and failed American Bay of Pigs invasion following the Cuban Revolution of 1959; the long-running embargo and suspension of diplomatic relations, which was finally overturned by President Obama in 2015; and the detention centre at Guantanamo Bay, which is on Cuban land, leased to the USA. Less controversially, the author Ernest Hemingway had a home in Key West in the 1930s (which we visited) before he moved to Cuba in 1939, where he stayed for the next 20 years.

Late afternoon, we made our way back up the Keys and looked for somewhere to stay in Key Largo. We were fortunate to stumble on a great motel. The sign advertised 'Bay Front Cottages', and we were soon settling into a very large and very comfortable suite. We booked for two nights, mainly because it was inexpensive. It was only the next morning when we realised what a great place it really was, because just a short walk along a jetty we found ourselves able to swing our legs in the beautiful, warm, and calm sea. Then, within just a few minutes, we started to see shadows beneath the surface of the water. It turned out that the shadows were manatees, which the owner explained were friendly, harmless, and loved being fed. We went to the local store to get some supplies – for us, and the manatees – and before long we were back amongst a small crowd of these beautiful sea creatures. Our youngest was trepidatious to begin with, but before long she was in the water with them and feeding them from her hands. It was a lovely way to spend an hour.

On leaving the motel, we retraced our path back up Highway 1 until we came to Highway 9336, where we turned left to follow the signs to the Everglades National Park. The journey had taken less than an hour from our motel. Everglades National Park is unlike most of the other parks in not being known for spectacular vistas and geological wonders. It is essentially a huge swamp, or wetland if you are being kind, and if developers had been left to it, it would probably have been cleared years ago. Developers did clear large swathes of the wetlands before what was left finally became protected by the National Parks Service in 1947. This was largely due to the tireless efforts of a former developer, Ernest Coe, and a journalist, Marjory Stoneman Douglas, who drew attention to the unique eco-system which supports a vast array of wildlife, including over 300 species of birds.

After getting some orientation and advice at the visitor centre, we stopped off at a place where we could view alligators and crocodiles from a safe distance. We were educated on the difference between them: essentially, the snout of an alligator is more U-shaped, and the snout of a crocodile is more V-shaped. Not that I was that keen on getting a close up view of the difference. We also learnt that crocodiles were – of the two – more dangerous. The most fascinating fact though, was that it was only in the Florida Everglades where both creatures live side-by-side. We then drove to Tram Road, and climbed to the top of the observation tower to get a 360 degree view of the wetlands. Although the tower is less than 50ft above ground you get a great view, because the whole area is almost completely flat.

The highlight of the visit was the chance to go on an airboat – those boats with the huge fans on the back. We joined a small group of other visitors, and once on board, our driver told us about how these boats were a way of life for those who live in the area. The boats enable high speed travel across the rivers of grass, which make up the Everglades, but our driver explained that this would be a leisurely glide. Soon into the trip I found my family stressfully raising their feet from the floor because they were afraid of the spiders they had seen in the bottom of the boat. I told them not to be so stupid; that spiders were harmless; and I plonked my sandalled feet firmly on the floor to reinforce my point. They ignored me and kept their knees close to their faces for the whole of the trip.

Resting alligator in the Everglades National Park, Florida

For me, at least, it had been an exhilarating ride on the airboat. However, I now look back on it with mixed views. Clearly, our driver and guide was a mine of information about the Everglades and the people who inhabit the area, but I am now aware that environmental groups have been campaigning for years, arguing that these airboats disturb the wetlands in detrimental ways, and because of that a long-running battle to ban the boats has ensued. At the time I was unaware of any such battle. After returning to the car, we drove back to our motel for a well-earned evening meal, and reflection on what a great day it had been. I had thought that we would come back from the Everglades bitten to death by mosquitos, but we weren't suffering. Perhaps we were lucky, or perhaps they appear in larger numbers later in the season than July.

The Magic of Disney

The girls were now keen to get to Disney World. Truth be told, I think they had been keen since they stepped off the plane, and all I'd been doing was enforcing a pre-entry cultural education they could quite easily have done without. So, after packing up and thanking the motel owners for a lovely time, we headed north once more, on Highway 1, but this time with the aim of driving up the west coast of Florida. Had I been on my own this would have been the point where I would have paused to explore the possibility of visiting two other national parks in the area – Biscayne and Dry Tortugas. Both Parks require more than the usual planning because they are off the mainland.

Biscayne National Park, designated in 1980, is at the north end of the Florida Keys and can be accessed from the town of Homestead – on Highway 1 – from where you can catch a free shuttle bus to the visitor centre. The park itself is largely underwater, because what is being protected is a coral reef. I'm scarred of water so I'm not sure I would have taken the opportunity to go scuba diving, but the possibility was there. Dry Tortugas National Park, designated in 1992, lies at the other end of the Keys and needs to be accessed by plane or five-hour round-trip boat journey (both of which appear to be costly). This park also protects water based wildlife, based around seven small keys, one of which houses a military base. – Fort Jefferson. The park's name refers to the fact that the fort has no freshwater (hence Dry) and uses the Spanish word for turtles (Tortugas). Once again, snorkelling around the coral is surely a must-do, but probably not for me. To reiterate, both parks appear to need some considerable planning to fully appreciate them.

When Highway 1 hit Highway 41 we turned left (west) and drove through Big Cypress National Preserve, another large area of swamp land which is protected by the National Parks Service. It might easily have become part of an extended Everglades National Park had things played out differently. When we hit the coast, we headed north on Highway 41 to Fort Myers where we stopped for lunch. We then followed Highway 17 northward to Lakeland. From here we could easily access Disney World, so we checked into an unassuming, and cheap, motel for three nights. I took it for granted that had we got too close to Disney World for our accommodation the prices would be much higher. Since leaving Key West that morning we had covered around 300 miles, which had taken us around six hours, including stops.

After everyone had taken their luggage up to the room, I stayed behind at the car to clear out the rubbish we had been collecting over the previous few days. Job done, I shut all the doors and the trunk, and only then checked my pocket for the keys. Looking through the driver's door window, I could see I had left them on the front seat, and we were now locked out of the car. I wasn't sure what was worse, the fact that we were locked out of the car, or the fact that I now had to explain to everyone that it was me who had locked us out, and after repeated reminders that this was not to happen. I slowly made my way up the exterior staircase to the room, with my tail firmly between legs, and as I entered the room I casually mentioned the fact that I had locked us all out of the car. Everyone looked glum, but as soon as I left to have another go at getting in the car, I heard pent-up roars of laughter coming from the room.

Too embarrassed to return to the room, and after endless attempts at pulling hard on the door handles, I asked the person at reception what I might do. The receptionist calmly phoned the local locksmith, and within the hour he showed up and soon had me back in the car. I thanked him profusely, but not for his bill, which cost nearly as much as the three nights at the motel, completely obliterating the cost saving from staying a fair distance from Disney World. I then spent the rest of the evening stewing in my pot of stupidity, and hoping that everyone would just go to sleep. The Florida Keys now had a new and unfortunate meaning for me.

The next morning the sun was shining and we were all looking forward to visiting Disney World. We were about 45 minutes away from the entrance to the large complex, which involved us travelling north east on I-4, until we saw the signs. Although everything was clearly signposted it took a while before we were firmly ensconced in our parking space. Disney World continues to grow. It was huge when we visited, but now includes many more attractions and facilities. Not that it hasn't had its setbacks, which the Disney Corporation appears to take on the chin, and then simply moves on. Although many people still refer to it as Disney World, its official title is now Walt Disney World Resort.

I'm never quite sure what Americans mean when they add 'world' to anything, as in 'New York's world famous pizza restaurant', because from my experience, it's normally only people who live in the immediate area that have ever heard of it. And what exactly is a Baseball *World* Series, where nobody else in the world appears to compete in it, or, in many cases, is even that interested in it (with the exception of the Japanese and the Canadians). Of course, this cannot be said of Disney, because here is a corporation which *is* world famous, but in this case 'world' may simply refer to the world of Disney, which, if the magic is to be believed, is not a reference to *this* world, but another world altogether.

Critical Cultural Comment – The World of Walt Disney

The original Disneyland was opened by Walt Disney in Anaheim, in Los Angeles County, in 1955. Disney appeared to regret that he had not bought up more land, because he lost the opportunity to fully exploit food and lodging possibilities. He also felt that those that had grown up around the park were somewhat tacky. For that reason he started buying up large amounts of land in Orlando, Florida, which eventually became Disney World when officially opened in 1971. Walt died in 1966 so never witnessed the opening, but his brother (and business partner), Roy, *was* there, (along with Mickey Mouse). Unfortunately he died later the same year, so neither brother was able to witness its success. The site was not only able to accommodate Disney run hotels, but also provided the opportunity to move beyond a simple replication of the original Disneyland. This included an EPCOT Center – an experimental prototype community of tomorrow. Disney envisaged this as a real community of scientists and engineers, but eventually it just became another theme park, but with more educational content than the Magical Kingdom – the name for the main theme park.

Apart from the many theme park rides, including Space Mountain and the Pirates of the Caribbean, one of the most intriguing features of both Disneyland and Disney World is Main Street USA, which is what visitors first encounter after they pass through the entrance gates at both parks. The street is, essentially, a string of merchandising stores, but from an architectural point of view, they reproduce what Disney considered to be a model for the perfect American town. The street is most likely an idealised version of his childhood memories, and speaks volumes about Disney's desire to create a sanitised and safe space. In the process he thereby contributed hugely to an Americana myth – that reminiscences about the past are always of better times, which are in need of resurrection.

Before Disneyland, American theme parks had a much more edgy – even ill repute – feel, typified by Coney Island in Queen's, New York City [see Six things to do in New York]. This reputation was turned completely on its head by Walt Disney and his team, whose vision was as much about creating a 'Mom's apple pie' version of American society, as well as providing an opportunity to enter a magical kingdom.

The sanitised/safe idea was taken to its logical extreme in the construction of the town of Celebration (just down the road from the Orlando resort) which provided Americans with a chance to actually live in an idealised version of 'small town America', replete with white picket fences, manicured lawns, and a perfectly clean town square. Back in California, a further experiment in sanitised experiences was undertaken when the corporation opened California Adventure in 2001, which offered the prospect of visiting artificial reconstructions of California, located in the real California (if you can call anything in California real).

No wonder that the French philosopher Jean Baudrillard was able to find in Disneyland a perfect way to explore the dimensions of a post-modern existence, resting on the idea of simulacra – copies of reality which can no longer be traced back to an original reality, and ones which people have become comfortable inhabiting. Here, again, is a post-modern trick, because the artifice of Disneyland implies that what is outside of it must therefore be real. In actuality, this disguises the giant artifice of American society at large (Baudrillard, 1983).

I had visited Disneyland, in California, several times before, but I was as excited as the girls to be entering Disney World, Florida, although perhaps for some different reasons.

Once you pass through the entrance gates, you arrive on Main street USA which is architecturally significant in being scaled in such a way that it naturally leads the eye towards the fantasy castle at the end of the street. The castle image features on all Disney advertising, and at the beginning of Disney films. Somebody told me that the castles in Disneyland and Disney World are actually different, but I'm not nerdy enough to know in what ways. From the fantasy castle you are then directed out to the various 'lands', where all the rides can be found.

We all had a great time on the rides, spent additional money in the stores, and enjoyed all-American diner food. There was a vast accumulation of Disney commodities for sale, and I enjoyed the enthusiastic chatter on the drive back to the motel, where we were accompanied by a small collection of Disney characters, including Donald Duck with a soft beak. It had been a great day.

On the second day we returned to the complex, but this time to visit Universal Studios, which is next door to Disney World, but a separate business concern. Unfortunately, I found myself increasingly dragging one of my legs around the Studios' attractions. As I looked down I saw that the problem leg was now nearly twice the size of the other one, and realised that I probably needed to visit a medical centre. Naturally, I was relieved when I finally entered the door of the plush-looking place, but I was not at all ready to do battle with the gatekeeper on the reception, who was adamant that I would not be speaking with a doctor until I deposited a major credit card on the desk in front of her. Clearly, my sarcastic comments about not wishing to buy anything were lost on her, probably because she was used to viewing medicine as a commodity like any other.

When I did get to see a doctor, he explained that my problem was the work of a brown recluse, a small poisonous spider, and that I would need a large dose of antibiotics to counteract its effects. He also explained that it was a good job I came in when I did. I was now at the point of too much information, and I was keen to get to a local chemist (drug store) in order to take the required medicine. It cost me a small fortune, but I was fully expectant that my insurance cover would take care of it all when I was back in the UK (which it did). Luckily, the bite was on my left leg, which meant I could still drive the automatic car. My only restriction was the inability of that leg to properly tap out the beat of the songs on the car radio.

R n R

I was now feeling tired and weary and in need of some rest. I think the children were disappointed that we wouldn't be spending at least one more day in Disney World, but they didn't say anything, and anyway, they soon perked up when I announced that I thought Daytona Beach might be a good place to recuperate at the end of our Florida adventure. This option would also cut short their cultural education programme, meaning that we were now all truly on holiday. We returned to our motel in Lakeland for the final night before heading back to Daytona Beach the following morning. But not before my family had put the final nail in my coffin of humiliation. They were absolutely sure that my spider bite had occurred in the airboat in the Everglades. What small amount of authority I had previously earned was now completely in tatters. I had locked us out of the car, after repeatedly saying that this was not to happen, and I had been bitten by a poisonous spider, after firmly announcing that spiders were harmless. Acutely aware that I had been twice hoisted by my own petard, I vowed to chill out and not deliver anymore life lessons; well, not for the next few days anyway.

The next morning, we retraced our path up the I-4, an interstate we were becoming very familiar with, and then checked into a different motel on Atlantic Avenue in Daytona Beach, for three final nights. The motel advertised itself as: 'Directly on the World's Most Famous Beach', which made me wonder what people on Bondi Beach or the Copacabana might say to that. It had only taken us a couple of hours to get to Daytona Beach, after which I put my leg up, and the girls dived into the new motel pool. I spent the following day relaxing in the sunshine, while the others went off exploring in the car. On the final evening we packed up everything and the next morning we made our way back down the I-4 for the final time to catch our flight home to the UK. I allowed a couple of hours to get the airport and return our hire car, which turned out to be about right.

Conclusion

This had been an adventure and a half. It had actually been two adventures, both of which were very different, and could easily have been undertaken separately. The trip up Highway 61 was as much a magical musical history tour as a road trip. The tour of Florida was surreal, particularly the trip down to the end of the Florida Keys. And the trip to Disney World had been hyper-real (Baudrillard, 1983), particularly in pointing to how much of American society is a form of artifice. That, for me, though is one of the main reasons why the country remains fascinating.

The trip also enabled a visit to one of the most intriguing national parks – Everglades – which was the culmination of a concerted effort to preserve wildlife, rather than a spectacular landscape, and in the face of some very aggressive commercial interests. But it could be argued that this has been a recurring theme throughout the history of the whole national park movement; indeed, the history of the United States itself, as graphically portrayed in the TV series *Yellowstone* (2018).

Chapter 12

Conclusion: Re-creating in the American Great Outdoors

America's Best Idea?

Are the national parks "America's best idea"? It's a good shout.

Many of the parks were contentious from the start: their advocates were often confused about their understanding of conservation, and the efforts to establish them were often mired in politics. Even the 'best idea' quote has turned out to be a little contentious. Dayton and Burns (2009) tell us that it is attributable to the writer and historian Wallace Stegner, but he doesn't ever seem to have used those exact words. And if he did use that phrase, it was more than likely he was referencing the *British* Ambassador to the US at the time – Lord James Bryce (MacEachern, 2011).

Controversies aside, there can be little doubt that all the parks are uniquely spectacular, brilliantly run, and wonderful places to visit, and if you have a hire car (even if you don't) and some money (not a huge amount) it's possible to have so much more than a holiday by visiting them.

Recreating in the USA

Americans love to turn nouns into verbs – for example, 'to party' instead of to have a party – which never sounds quite right to my English ears, but I do like turning the noun 'recreation' into its verb, because of the inference that people might actually be re-creating themselves. I think this notion fits perfectly with a trip to a national park, where there is a distinct possibility – if you are open to it – that you will return a different person. It also offers a deeper meaning to the notion of heading out on the road in a 'recreation vehicle' (an RV): less a literal metal object on wheels, and more a metaphorical vehicle for re-creation.

I conceived this book with this notion of re-creation in mind, and thank you Zinta, my American friend, who gave me the idea when I heard her refer to some 'recreating cyclists', as they rode along the shoreline of Lake Michigan, one Sunday morning. That got me thinking about some of the deeper inferences behind the notion of re-creation and how they relate to the themes of this book.

Being in the American Great Outdoors

The slices of Americana pie which appear throughout the book are my examples of things which could be viewed as uniquely American in some way. The concept also seems to address something deeper, a yearning perhaps, to escape from everyday life, along with the desire to recover something which has been lost. Being on the road and experiencing the American great outdoors is a tried and trusted means to satisfy some of this yearning. That yearning is not uniquely American, but the USA – because of its expansive geography and somewhat rootless modern outlook – has certainly helped to capture the essence of this sensibility.

This sensibility runs deep in American society, which seems to have cultivated an ingrained need for exploration, rooted perhaps in the idea of forging character from a Frontier mentality (Turner, 1893). But an important part also seems to come from John Muir's rallying call not to lose touch with our own past and that sense of exaltation which comes from directly experiencing Nature (which has become lost for so many who now inhabit urban-industrial – and post-industrial – landscapes). A third part can also be gleaned from Jack Kerouac's notion of 'beat' – and how the weariness engendered by having to conform to stifling social conventions is at one and the same time the impetus to get on the road in search of beatification – a blissful salvation.

Exploration, Exaltation, Salvation.

Is it ridiculous to expect this kind of liberation to be experienced in a ten-day road trip around some of the American national parks? Probably, particularly when you consider how long the journeys were for the wagon trains which took the European settlers out west; the number of years that John Muir spent in the wilderness in order to comprehend its wonder; and the number of times that Jack Kerouac criss-crossed the US in his quest to comfort his restless soul. *But, forearmed with some of this knowledge, I think it is possible to at least glimpse at some of these glorious possibilities.* If all else fails at least you will have spent some time in some fantastic places.

Every American road trip I have undertaken has produced those moments where I have been stopped dead in my tracks: not because of the traffic, but because the pause button has been pushed inside me. No need for any intellectualising at these points; best just to let your mind wander and wonder. I now view these pauses as my gateways into the contemplation of glorious possibilities. They help me to let let go of all the things which normally occupy my mind, including the mental chatter associated with them, and push me gently towards re-tuning into something altogether different and deeper.

Pure on the road Americana, Alabama

More, More, More…

If you've never experienced the American great outdoors, I hope this book has inspired you to do so. If you've already visited an American national park, I hope this book will encourage you to visit more. If you've been on a long road trip in the US, I hope this book will inspire you to dig deeper into the opportunities they present. And if this book has sparked an interest in Americana, I hope it doesn't result in your partners and friends becoming increasingly concerned about the number of artefacts which keep appearing around your home.

As for me, I am now planning my next trip, possibly to Glacier National Park, to include a visit to Grand Teton, and a return to Yellowstone….and then, just possibly, there's Alaska…

"*The mountains are calling and I must go…*"

(John Muir, in a letter to his sister, 1873).

Happy Re-creating!

Afterword

While I have been putting this book together talk of climate crisis has escalated and now features routinely on TV and radio news. I joined the Friends of the Earth movement when I was at school; stopped eating meat in my twenties; and have always travelled by foot, bike or train whenever I could. Because of all that, my love of classic cars; my unfettered wanderlust; and the number of times I have been on long-haul flights (mostly for work), strikes me, increasingly, as somewhat contradictory. I don't beat myself up about this though, partly because I can't remember a time when I wasn't thinking about what I could do to protect the environment, but also because I think it's part of the human condition to be ambivalent about things, and it's easy to be compromised, sometimes unwittingly.

Ambivalence and compromise often come from ignorance (or a desire to put one's head in the sand), which we can correct by educating ourselves. But how do we know we have the full facts? The internet is awash with contrasting information and conspiracy theories, and the notion of fake news has become a byword for things we don't like the sound of. Clearly, navigating our way around this information overload is not easy and the algorithms that social media companies use often results in us sitting in our own echo chambers, confirming what we already believe rather than giving us access to alternative perspectives. Personally, I've always thought that governments and big business have vested interests in persuading individuals to see *themselves* as the problem, because that way it absolves them of responsibility for doing anything. At the end of the day, yes, we can all recycle plastic, but why are so many of our products wrapped in plastic in the first place? But I'm happy to accept that I might be wrong about this.

It's not all bad news though. For example, I was listening to an interview on the radio with the authors of the book *The Future We Choose: Surviving the Climate Crisis* (Figueres and Rivett-Carnac, 2020), where it was mentioned that the Chinese are close to producing electric cars for around £8,000. Okay, they might be doing this for economic reasons rather than strictly environmental ones, but the effect is that many more people might now be able to consider buying an electric car, rather than it just being the preserve of the rich. On that note, I remember a great episode of the cartoon *South Park*, where instead of Southern California smog alerts (which were a feature on many radio stations when I lived near LA), the San Francisco Bay Area was now giving out *smug* alerts, which were alerting people to the number of rich people living there who could afford to buy hybrid cars. But the good news, according to Figueres and Rivett-Carnac, is that we might just be reaching a tipping point where carbon neutral environments are a very real possibility for everyone.

This is also very good news for the themes which are at the heart of this book. The expansion in the use of the internal combustion engine coincided almost exactly with the growth in the national park movement in the United States. Given the desire to preserve 'wilderness' – with or without its inverted commas – this would appear to be one of the biggest contradictions that we all have to face if we visit a national park in a 'traditional' car. But I always come back from a visit to a national park with an enhanced understanding of conservation, environmentalism, and my relationship with the world around me, and because of that, the contradiction then becomes more of a compromise, with some benefits, not just costs. I suspect it will not be long before the roads in and out of the national parks will be full of much greener modes of transport.

If we get this right there is every possibility that people will continue to visit national parks, and once there, not just receive information about conserving the parks, but also more information about how best to arrive at, and then, explore the parks. Maybe, by hiring electric cars at park entrances, or even hydro/steam-based cars, and/ or getting on electric bikes. And while sitting on that long-haul flight, that should give us plenty of time to think about how we might offset our heavy carbon footprint, while we wait for airline companies to come up with their own alternative fuel-based solutions.

I love the thought that everyone returning from a visit to a national park might take on renewed commitments to act in positive ways to ensure we don't lose what is precious to us. We might then also help to keep alive the legacy of people like John Muir, who was as much concerned about what we lose if we have no relationship with the natural world, as what we gain when we do reconnect with it. In reality, we inter-act with the natural world, rather than just observe it, but we don't need to destroy it through our interactions. We can all at least try to tread lightly. And perhaps spend some time reflecting on just how much our lives are now spent obeying artificial linear clock-time, rather than observing the cyclical rhythms of nature, and the effects this may be having on our general well-being.

Strangely (perhaps), all this alternative thinking and action might also actually increase people's interest in a lot of the Americana which features in this book, because, as it becomes more of historical interest, it might also promote new ways to conserve a lot of it – as heritage.

Note on Musical Journeys

One the benefits of modern technology – from the Sony walkman, through the iPod, to the modern phone – is that, whatever way we continue to get on the road, we should still be able to enjoy our own musical journeys. The songs which have featured throughout this book have become my own themed playlist, but, naturally, they represent my own taste and are born of the associations that my mind made as I drove around. I'd love to hear of other people's 'on the road' playlists.

Final Note

If you have any questions or comments about this book, or comments about your own road trips around the national parks and beyond, I'd be delighted to hear from you. You can contact me at:

johnleaauthor@gmail.com.

Road Trips Juke Box and Song Credits

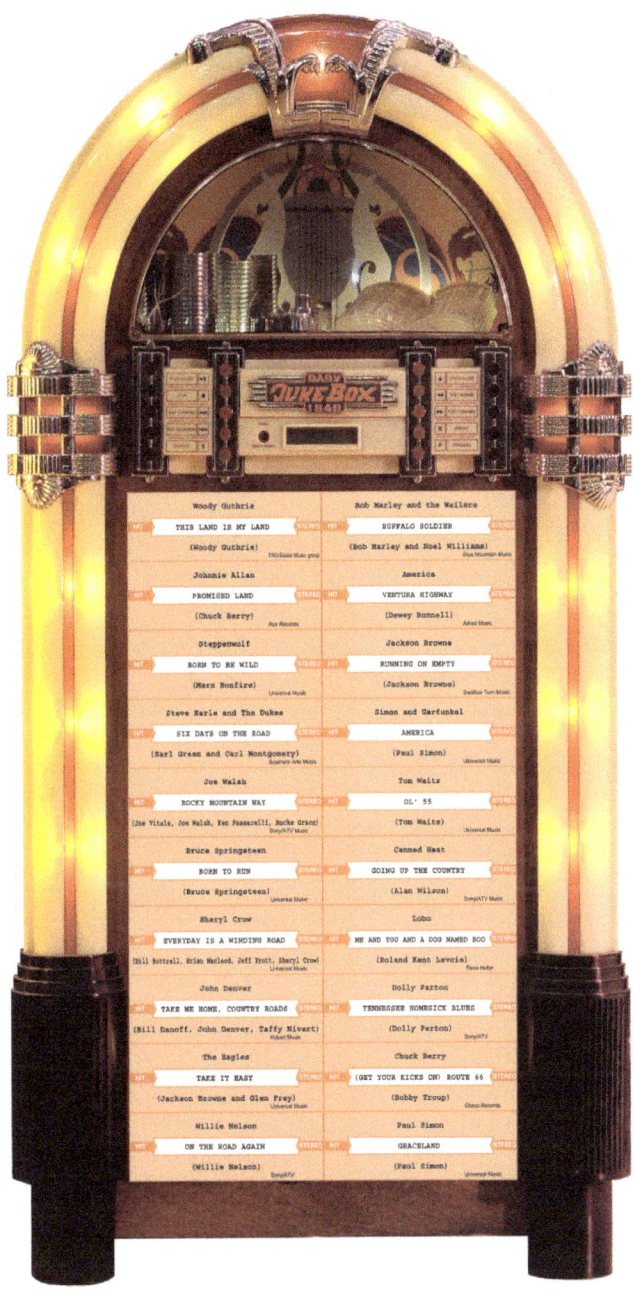

Artist	Song	Writer(s)	Publisher
Woody Guthrie	THIS LAND IS MY LAND	(Woody Guthrie)	TRO-Essex Music group
Bob Marley and the Wailers	BUFFALO SOLDIER	(Bob Marley and Noel Williams)	Blue Mountain Music
Johnnie Allan	PROMISED LAND	(Chuck Berry)	Arc Records
America	VENTURA HIGHWAY	(Dewey Bunnell)	Arlost Music
Steppenwolf	BORN TO BE WILD	(Mars Bonfire)	Universal Music
Jackson Browne	RUNNING ON EMPTY	(Jackson Browne)	Swallow Turn Music
Steve Earle and The Dukes	SIX DAYS ON THE ROAD	(Earl Green and Carl Montgomery)	Southern Arts Music
Simon and Garfunkel	AMERICA	(Paul Simon)	Universal Music
Joe Walsh	ROCKY MOUNTAIN WAY	(Joe Vitale, Joe Walsh, Ken Passarelli, Rocke Grace)	Sony/ATV Music
Tom Waits	OL' 55	(Tom Waits)	Universal Music
Bruce Springsteen	BORN TO RUN	(Bruce Springsteen)	Universal Music
Canned Heat	GOING UP THE COUNTRY	(Alan Wilson)	Sony/ATV Music
Sheryl Crow	EVERYDAY IS A WINDING ROAD	(Bill Bottrell, Brian Macleod, Jeff Trott, Sheryl Crow)	Universal Music
Lobo	ME AND YOU AND A DOG NAMED BOO	(Roland Kent Lavoie)	Famo Music
John Denver	TAKE ME HOME, COUNTRY ROADS	(Bill Danoff, John Denver, Taffy Nivert)	Reber Music
Dolly Parton	TENNESSEE HOMESICK BLUES	(Dolly Parton)	Sony/ATV
The Eagles	TAKE IT EASY	(Jackson Browne and Glen Frey)	Universal Music
Chuck Berry	(GET YOUR KICKS ON) ROUTE 66	(Bobby Troup)	Chess Records
Willie Nelson	ON THE ROAD AGAIN	(Willie Nelson)	Sony/ATV
Paul Simon	GRACELAND	(Paul Simon)	Universal Music

Book and Article References

Anderson, J. and Anderson, N. (2016) *59 Illustrated National Parks.* Nashville, TN: Anderson Design Group.

Barr, N. (1993) *Track of the Cat*, New York: G.P Putnam's Sons.

Baudrillard, J. (1983) *Simulacra and Simulation,* Ann Arbor, MN: University of Michigan Press.

Baudrillard, J. (1989) *America,* London: Verso.

Becker, H. (1963) *Outsiders: studies in the sociology of deviance.* New York: Free Press.

Berger, P., Berger, B., and Kellner, H. (1974) *The Homeless Mind: modernization and consciousness.* London: Viking.

Brown, D. (1970) *Bury my Heart at Wounded Knee.* New York: Holt, Rinehart & Winston.

Bryson, B. (1998) *A Walk in the Woods: Rediscovering America on the Appalachian Trail.* New York: Doubleday.

Collis, J. (2002) *Chuck Berry: the biography.* London: Aurum Press.

Colwell, M. (2014) *John Muir: the Scotsman who saved America's wild places.* Oxford: Lion.

Dayton, N. and Burns, K. (2009). *National Parks: America's best idea.* New York: Alfred A. Knopf.

Ferris, W. (1978) *Blues from the Delta.* New York: Da Capo Press.

Firestone, S. (1970) *The Dialectic of Sex: the case for feminist revolution.* New York: William Morrow

Friedan, B. (1963) *The Feminine Mystique.* New York: W.W. Norton and Co.

Goddard, S. (1996) *Getting There: The Epic Struggle Between Road and Rail in the American Century,* Chicago, IL: University of Chicago Press.

Guthrie, W. (1943) *Bound for Glory.* New York: E P Dutton and Co.

Hamilton, E. L. (2018) Beautiful Story: The couple in the iconic Woodstock photo are still together. *The Vintage News.* [Available at:

https://www.thevintagenews.com/2018/06/12/woodstock-couple/ accessed 16.03.20].

Hoskyns, B. (2006) *Hotel California: Singer-songwriters and cocaine cowboys in the LA canyons 1967-1976.* London: Harper Perennial.

Kerouac, J. (1957) *On the Road.* New York: Viking Press.

Kerouac, J. (1958) *The Dharma Bums.* New York: Viking Press.

Kerouac, J. (1965) *Desolation Angels.* New York: Coward McCann.

Kesey, K. (1962) *One flew over the cuckoo's nest.* New York: Viking Press.

King, M.L.Jr. (1963) *I Have a Dream.*
[Available at: https://www.archives.gov/files/press/exhibits/dream-speech.pdf accessed 16.03.20]

Krakauer, J. (1996) *Into the Wild.* New York: Villard.

MacEachern, A. (2011) Who had "America's best Idea"? Blog post: NiCHE [Available at: https://niche-canada.org/2011/10/23/who-had-americas-best-idea/ accessed 16.03.20].

Marx, K. (1867) *Capital, Vol 1.* London: Lawrence and Wishart.

Miller, S. (2015) *Smart Blonde Dolly Parton: a biography.* London: Omnibus Press

Mills, C.W. (1956) *The Power Elite.* New York: Oxford University Press.

Morrison, T. (1987) *Beloved.* New York: Alfred A. Knopf.

Muir, J. (1901) *Our National Parks.* New York: Houghton Mifflin.

Nash, G. (2013) *Wild Tales.* New York: Crown Archetype.

Nelson, C. (2020) *Things I Learned From Falling.* London: Aster.

Penn, R. (2011) *It's All About the Bike: the pursuit of happiness on two wheels.* London: Penguin.

Pirsig, R. (1974) *Zen and the art of motorcycle maintenance.* London: Black Swan.

Post, R. (2006) *Urban Mass Transit: The Life Story of a Technology,* Westport, CT: Greenwood.

Pynchon, T. (1997) *Mason & Dixon.* New York: Henry Holt.

Ralson, A. (2011) *127 Hours: Between a Rock and a Hard Place.* London: Simon and Schuster

Ritzer, G. (2000) *The McDonaldization of Society: New Century Edition.* London: Sage.

Spence, M. D. (1999) *Dispossessing the Wilderness: Indian removal and the making of the National Parks.* New York: Oxford University Press.

Strayed, C. (2012) *Wild: from lost to found on the Pacific Crest Trail.* New York: Knopf.

Steinbeck, J. (1939) *The Grapes of Wrath.* New York: Viking Press.

Turner, F. J. (1893) *The Significance of the Frontier in American History.* Reproduced as chapter one of The Project Gutenburg ebook (2007) of *The Frontier in American History* (1921)*:* [Available at: http://www.gutenberg.org/files/22994/22994-h/22994-h.htm accessed 16.03.20].

Turner, S. (1996) *Jack Kerouac: Angelheaded hipster.* New York: Viking Penguin.

Twain, M. (1884) *Adventures of Huckleberry Finn.* London: Chatto and Windus.

Waller, R. J. (1993) *The Bridges of Madison County: a novel.* London: Mandarin Paperbacks.

Weber, M. (1904) *The protestant ethic and the spirit of capitalism.* London: Allen & Unwin.

Wolf, G. (1981) *Who Censored Roger Rabbit?* New York: St. Martin's Press.

Young, N. (2012) *Waging Heavy Peace.* New York: Blue Rider Press.

Film references: [Title (Year) Director. Film Distributor.]

127 Hours (2010) Danny Boyle. Fox Searchlight Pictures.

Across 110th Street (1972) Barry Shear. United Artists.

A Walk in the Woods (2015) Ken Kwapis. Broad Green Pictures.

Brazil (1985) Terry Gilliam. 20th Century Fox.

Bullitt (1968) Peter Yates. Warner Bros.- Seven Arts.

Butch Cassidy and The Sundance Kid (1969) George Roy Hill. 20th Century Fox.

Dead Man (1995) Jim Jarmusch. Miramar

Deliverance (1972) John Boorman. Warner Bros.

Dirty Harry (1971) Don Siegel. Warner Bros.

Easy Rider (1969) Dennis Hopper. Columbia Pictures.

Giant (1956) George Stevens. Warner Bros.

Grand Torino (2008) Clint Eastwood. Warner Bros.

Green Book (2018) Peter Farrelly. Universal Pictures.

Hyde Park on Hudson (2012) Roger Michell. Focus features.

Into The Wild (2007) Sean Pean. Paramount Vantage.

Key Largo (1948) John Houston. Warner Bros.

Laurel Canyon (2002) Lisa Cholodenko. Sony Pictures.

Le Mans (1971) Lee H. Katzin. National General Pictures.

Little Miss Sunshine (2006) Jonathan Dayton and Valerie Faris.

Marathon Man (1976) John Schlesinger. Paramount Pictures.

Milk (2008) Gus Van Sant. Focus features.

Mulholland Drive (2001) David Lynch. Universal Pictures.

North by Northwest (1959) Alfred Hitchcock. Metro-Goldwyn-Mayer.

On Any Sunday (1971) Bruce Brown. Cinema 5.

On Golden Pond (1981) Mark Rydell. Universal Pictures.

On the Road (2012) Walter Salles. IFC films.

One Flew Over the Cuckoo's Nest (1975) Milos Forman. United Artists.

Paris, Texas (1984) Wim Wenders. 20th Century Fox.

Planes, Trains and Automobiles (1987) John Hughes. Paramount Pictures.

Psycho (1960) Alfred Hitchcock. Paramount Pictures.

Raging Bull (1980) Martin Scorsese. United Artists.

Rear Window (1954) Alfred Hitchcock. Paramount Pictures.

Rebel Without a Cause (1955) Nicholas Ray. Warner Bros.

Rope (1948) Alfred Hitchcock. Warner Bros.

Selma (2015) Ava DuVernay. Paramount Pictures.

Shadow of a Doubt (1943) Alfred Hitchcock. Universal Pictures.

Sideways (2004) Alexander Payne. Fox Searchlight Pictures.

Stagecoach (1939) John Ford. United Artists.

Straight Story (1999) David Lynch. Buena Vista Pictures.

Taking Woodstock (2009) Ang Lee. Focus Features.

Terminator 2: Judgment Day (1991) James Cameron. TriStar Pictures.

The Birds (1963) Alfred Hitchcock. Universal Pictures

The Bridges of Madison County (1995) Clint Eastwood. Warner Bros.

The Exorcist (1973) William Friedkin. Warner Bros.

The Great Escape (1963) John Sturges. United Artists.

The Hateful Eight (2015) Quentin Tarantino. The Weinstein Company.

The Man Who Knew Too Much (1956) Alfred Hitchcock. Paramount Pictures

The Searchers (1956) John Ford. Warner Bros.

The Wild One (1953) Laszlo Benedek. Columbia Pictures.

The Wrong Man (1956) Alfred Hitchcock. Warner Bros.

Thelma and Louise (1991) Ridley Scott. Metro-Goldwyn-Meyer.

Three Billboards outside Ebbing, Missouri (2017) Martin McDonagh. Fox Searchlight.

Twister (1996) Jan de Bont. Warner Bros.

Vanishing Point (1971) Richard C. Sarafian. 20th Century Fox.

Vertigo (1958) Alfred Hitchcock. Paramount Pictures.

Walk the Line (2005) James Mangold. Fox 2000 Pictures.

What's Eating Gilbert Grape (1993) Lasse Hallstrom. Paramount Pictures.

Who Framed Roger Rabbit? (1988) Robert Zemeckis and Richard Williams. Buena Vista.

Wild (2014) Jean-Marc Vallee. Fox Searchlight Pictures.

Wild at Heart (1990) David Lynch. The Samuel Goldwyn Company.

Woodstock (1970) Michael Wadleigh. Warner Bros.

Straight Story (1999) David Lynch. Buena Vista Pictures.

Song References: [Title (Year) Performer(s). (Writer(s). Publishers.]

59th Street Bridge Song (Feelin' Groovy) (1966) Simon and Garfunkel. (Paul Simon). Universal Music.

Abraham, Martin and John (1968) Dion. (Richard Holler) BMG.

Across 110th Street (1972) Bobby Womack. (Bobby Womack and J. J. Johnson) BMG.

Ain't That Just Like a Woman (they'll do it every time) (1946) Louis Jordan. (Louis Jordan) Universal Music.

Alabama (1972) Neil Young (Neil Young). Wixen Music.

Albatross (1968) Fleetwood Mac. (Peter Green) Sony Music.

America. (1968) Simon and Garfunkel. (Paul Simon) Universal Music.

Anchorage (1988) Michelle Shocked. (Michelle Shocked) Michelle Shocked.

Badlands (1978) Bruce Springsteen (Bruce Springsteen). Universal Music.

Big Sur (2003) The Thrills (Alanis Morissette and Guy Sigsworth) Concord Music.

Big Yellow Taxi (1971) Joni Mitchell. (Joni Mitchell) Sony/ATV.

Born to be Wild (1968) Steppenwolf. (Mars Bonfire) Universal Music.

Born to Run (1975) Bruce Springsteen. (Bruce Springsteen) Universal Music.

Bridge Over Troubled Water (1970) Simon and Garfunkel. (Paul Simon) Universal Music.

Brown Eyed Handsome Man (1956) Chuck Berry. (Chuck Berry) Dualtone Music Group.

Brown Eyed Handsome Man (1963) Buddy Holly. (Chuck Berry) BMG Music.

Brown Sugar (1971) The Rolling Stones. (Jagger and Richards) Abkco.

Buffalo Soldier (1983) Bob Marley and the Wailers. (Bob Marley and Noel Williams) Blue Mountain Music.

Burma Shave Sign (1992) Tom Waits. (Tom Waits) Universal Music.

Cadillac Ranch (1981) Bruce Springsteen. (Bruce Springsteen) Universal Music.

California Dreamin' (1965) The Mamas and the Papas. (John Phillips and Michelle Phillips). Universal Music.

California Here I Come (1992) Sophie B. Hawkins. (Sophie B. Hawkins) Sony/ATV.

California Soul (1968) The Fifth Dimension. (Ashford and Simpson) Sony/ATV.

Coat of Many Colours (1971) Dolly Parton. (Dolly Parton) Velvet Apple Music.

Come Together (1969) The Beatles. (Lennon and McCartney). Sony/ATV.

Cracked Actor (1973) David Bowie. (David Bowie) Sony/ATV.

Deep Feeling (1965) Chuck Berry. (Chuck Berry) Dualtone Music Group.

Do Re Mi (1940) Woody Guthrie. (Woody Guthrie) Woody Guthrie Publications

Enola Gay (1980) Orchestral Manoeuvres in the Dark (Andy McCluskey) BMG.

Eve of Destruction (1965) Barry MacGuire (P.F. Sloan) Universal Music.

Everyday is a Winding Road (1996) Sheryl Crow. (Bill Bottrell, Brian Macleod, Jeff Trott, Sheryl Crow) Universal Music.

Freedom (1969) Richie Havens. (Michael James Hucknell). Sony/ATV.

Get it On (1971) T. Rex. (Marc Bolan) Westminster Music Ltd.

(Get your kicks on) Route 66 (1946) Bobby Troup (Bobby Troup) Consul Music Group.

(Get your kicks on) Route 66 (1957) The Nat King Cole Trio (Bobby Troup) Edwin H. Morris and Co. Inc.

(Get your kicks on) Route 66 (1961) Chuck Berry. (Bobby Troup) Chess Records.

(Get your kicks on) Route 66 (1964) The Rolling Stones (Bobby Troup) Abkco.

Going up the Country (1968) Canned Heat. (Alan Wilson) Sony/ATV Music.

Good Vibrations (1966) The Beach Boys. (Brian Wilson) Universal Music.

Graceland (1986) Paul Simon. (Paul Simon) Universal Music.

He's Gonna Step On You Again (1971) John Kongos. (John Kongos and Christos Dimetriou) Bucks Music Group.

Heartattack and Vine (1980) Tom Waits. (Tom Waits) Universal Music.

Hey Jack Kerouac (1987) 10,000 Maniacs (Natalie Merchant and Robert Buck) Big Deal Music.

Highway 61 Revisited (1965) Bob Dylan. (Bob Dylan) Sony/ATV.

Ida Red (1938) Bob Willis and his Texas Playboys. (trad) Unichappell Music Inc

Johnny B Goode (1958) Chuck Berry. (Chuck Berry) Dualtone Music Group.

Jungleland (1975) Bruce Springsteen. Bruce Springsteen. Universal Music.

LA Woman (1971) The Doors. (Jim Morrison) Morrison Estate, Ray Manzarek, John Densmore and Robby Krieger.

Ladies of the Canyon (1971) Joni Mitchell. (Joni Mitchell) Universal Music.

Little Queenie (1959) Chuck Berry. (Chuck Berry) Dualtone Music Group.

Love Street (1968) The Doors. (Jim Morrison) Morrison Estate, Ray Manzarek, John Densmore and Robby Krieger.

Maybellene (1955) Chuck Berry (Chuck Berry) Dualtone Music Group.

Me and You and a Dog named Boo (1971) Lobo. (Roland Kent Lavoie) Reno Holler.

Memphis, Tennessee (1959) Chuck Berry. (Chuck Berry) Dualtone Music Group.

Mendocino County Line (1992) Willie Nelson and Lee Ann Womack. (Matt Serletic and Bernie Taupin) Universal Music.

Mr Tambourine Man (1965) The Byrds. (Bob Dylan) Audiam.

My Tennessee Mountain Home (1972) Dolly Parton. (Dolly Parton) Sony/ATV.

New York, New York (so good they named it twice) (1978) Gerard Kenny. (Gerard Kenny) Chappell Music.

No Particular Place to Go (1960) Chuck Berry. (Chuck Berry) Dualtone Music Group.

Ol' 55. Tom Waits. (1973) (Tom Waits) Universal Music.

Ol' Man River (1927) Paul Robeson. (Jerome Kern and Oscar Hammerstein II).

On the Road Again (1980) Willie Nelson. (Willie Nelson) Sony/ATV Music.

On Top of Old Smoky (1951) Burl Ives. (Trad) Universal Music.

Open All Night (1982) Bruce Springsteen. (Bruce Springsteen) Universal Music.

Our House (1970) Crosby, Stills and Nash. (Graham Nash) Sony/ATV.

Pretty Boy Floyd (1945) Woody Guthrie. (Woody Guthrie. Woody Guthrie Publications.

Pride (in the name of love) (1984) U2. (Adam Clayton, Paul Hewson, David Evans, Laurence Mullen) Polygram Int. Music Publishing.

Promised Land (1964) Chuck Berry. (Chuck Berry) Dualtone Music Group.

Promised Land (1983) Johnnie Allan. (Chuck Berry) Ace Records.

Proud Mary (1969) Creedence Clearwater Revival. John Fogerty. The Bicycle Music Company.

Respect (1967) Aretha Franklin. (Otis Redding) Universal Music.

Roadrunner (1976) Jonathan Richman and The Modern Lovers. (Jonathan Richman) Sony/ATV.

Road Runner (1960) Bo Diddley. (E. McDaniel) Arc Music.

Rock and Roll Music (1957) Chuck Berry. (Chuck Berry) Dualtone Music Group.

Rock and Roll Music (1964) The Beatles. (Chuck Berry) Northern Songs.

Rockaway Beach (1977) The Ramones (Douglas Colvin / Jeff Hyman / John Cummings / Thomas Erdelyi) Warner Chappell Music.

Rocky Mountain High (1972) John Denver. (John Denver, Mike Taylor) Warner Chappell Music.

Rocky Mountain Way (1973) Joe Walsh. (Joe Vitale, Joe Walsh, Ken Passarelli, Rocke Grace) Sony/ATV Music.

Roll Over Beethoven (1956) Chuck Berry. (Chuck Berry) Dualtone Music Group.

Roll Over Beethoven (1964) The Beatles. (Chuck Berry). Northern Songs..

Running on Empty (1977) Jackson Browne. (Jackson Browne) Swallow Turn Music.

Sailing to Philadelphia (2000) Marc Knopfler. (Marc Knopfler). Universal Music.

San Franciscan Nights (1967) Eric Burdon and The Animals. (Barrie Jenkins, Danny McCulloch, Eric Burdon, Johnny Weider, Vic Briggs) Warner Chappell Music, Inc.

San Francisco (wear some flowers in your hair) (1967) Scott Mackenzie. (John Phillips) Trousdale Music

School Days (1958) Chuck Berry. (Chuck Berry) Dualtone Music Group.

Sister Rosa Parks (1989) The Neville Brothers (Charles Moore, Cyril Garrett Neville, Cyril Garrett Neville Jr., Daryl Johnson, Jason Neville, Liryca Neville) Universal Music.

(Sittin' on) The Dock of the Bay (1968) Otis Redding. (Steve Cropper and Otis Redding) Warner Chappell Music, Inc, Universal Music Publishing Group.

Six Days on the Road (1987) Steve Earle and The Dukes. (Earl Green and Carl Montgomery) Southern Arts Music.

Song to Woody (1962) Bob Dylan. (Bob Dylan) Sony/ATV

Southern Man (1970) Neil Young (Neil Young). Wixen Music.

Start of Something (2008) Stone Gods. (Edwin James Graham, Daniel Francis Hawkins, Richard Benjamin Edwards) Hawkland Music Ltd.

Step On (1990) The Happy Mondays. (John Kongos and Christos Dimetriou) Universal Music.

Stuck Inside of Mobile with the Memphis Blues Again (1966) Bob Dylan. (Bob Dylan) Sony/ATV.

Surfin' USA (1963) The Beach Boys. (Brian Wilson and Chuck Berry). Universal Music.

Sweet Home Alabama (1974) Lynryd Skynyrd. (Ronnie Van Zant, Gary Robert Rossington, Edward C. King). Universal Music.

Sweet little Sixteen (1958) Chuck Berry. (Chuck Berry) Dualtone Music Group.

Take it Easy (1972) The Eagles (Jackson Browne and Glen Frey) Universal Music.

Take me Home, Country Roads (1971) John Denver. (Bill Danoff, John Denver, Taffy Nivert) Kobart Music.

Tamalpais High (At About 3) (1971) David Crosby. (David Crosby) BMG Music.

Tennessee Homesick Blues (1984) Dolly Parton. (Dolly Parton) Sony/ATV.

The Trail of the Lonesome Pine (1937) Laurel and Hardy (Ballard Mac Donald and Harry Carroll) Shapiro, Bernstein & Co.

The WASP (Jim Morrison, Ray Manzarek, John Densmore and Robby Krieger) The Morrison Estate.

Morrison Estate, Ray Manzarek, John Densmore and Robby Krieger.

This Land is my Land (1940) Woody Guthrie. (Woody Guthrie) TRO-Essex Music Group.

Three Wheels on my Wagon (1963) The New Christy Minstrels. (Burt Bacharach and Bob Hilliard) Warner Chappell Music.

Tombstone Blues (1965) Bob Dylan. (Bob Dylan) Sony/ATV.

Ventura Highway (1972) America. (Dewey Bunnell) Alfred Music.

Walking in Memphis (1991) Marc Cohn. (Marc Cohn) Sony/ATV.

Woodstock (1970) Joni Mitchell. (Joni Mitchell) Sony/ATV.

Yah Mo B There (1983) James Ingram and Michael McDonald. (James Ingram, Michael McDonald, Rod Temperton, Quincy Jones) Warner Bros.

You Can't Catch Me (1956) Chuck Berry. (Chuck Berry) Dualtone Music Group.

Index

A

Acadia (National Park) 4, 23, 36, 50, 56, 147, 148, 153, 156, 157, 158, 159, 161, 170, 189

Air and Space Museum 212, 225

Airstream Trailers 5, 49, 142, 160, 212, 213, 217, 225, 244

Alamo Mission National Historical Landmark 81

Albright, Horace 41

Alaska 22, 43, 44, 55, 70, 84, 234, 287

Americana 1, 2, 4, 5, 6, 7, 8, 23, 29, 32, 35, 36, 38, 39, 46, 47, 49, 52, 64, 66, 68, 70, 71, 72, 76, 77, 78, 80, 88, 90, 96, 97, 98, 100, 110, 112, 114, 115, 116, 117, 121, 122, 124, 126, 132, 138, 139, 140, 142, 154, 155, 156, 160, 162, 164, 166, 167, 172, 179, 180, 182, 183, 184, 194, 196, 198, 199, 203, 212, 213, 215, 217, 218, 219, 221, 225, 226, 228, 231, 232, 236, 237, 244, 246, 247, 249, 251, 255, 261, 262, 264, 267, 268, 269, 271, 272, 280, 286, 287, 290

American Samoa (National Park) 22, 56

American South 5, 118, 229

Adams, Ansel 42

Antiquities Act 42, 250

Appalachian 119, 124, 161, 174, 203, 206, 209, 211, 224, 226, 292

Appalachian Trail 161, 174, 203, 209, 211, 292

Arches (National Park) 23, 55, 76, 125, 131, 134, 135, 136

Austin 95, 98

B

Badlands (National Park) 17, 56, 101, 111, 112, 121, 298

Bakersfield 60, 61, 65

Battle of Little Big Horn National Monument 101

Baudrillard, Jean 37, 195, 219, 280

Berkeley 103, 123, 175, 176, 198

Berry, Chuck 5, 229, 246, 268, 269, 271, 292, 298, 299, 300, 301, 302, 303, 304

Big Basin Redwoods State Park 173, 179, 180

Big Bend (National Park) 22, 56, 81, 82, 83, 84, 86, 87, 93, 100, 164

Biscayne (National Park) 55, 257, 277

Black Canyon of the Gunnison (National Park) 55, 125, 142, 143

Black Hills of South Dakota 26, 27, 109, 110

Blue Ridge Parkway 201, 202, 205, 208, 211, 221, 226

Boston 148, 153, 157, 162, 163, 169

Boulder 128, 253

Bretton Woods 160, 161

Bridges of Madison County 89, 101, 294, 296

Bryce Canyon (National Park) 55, 229, 241, 242, 243, 254

Burns, Ken 33, 90

Buffalo Soldiers 37, 91, 137

Burma Shave Signs 4, 138, 139, 140, 246

Byam, Wally 212, 213

C

Canyonlands (National Park) 55, 76, 125, 131, 135, 137, 145

Capitol Reef (National Park) 55, 145, 229, 243, 244, 254

Carlsbad Caverns (National Park) 22, 23, 56, 81, 82, 93, 94

Carter, Jimmy 43

Car rental 14, 15, 16, 50, 60, 102, 230

Channel Islands (National Park) 55, 59, 60, 78

Cherokee Indian Reservation 208

Chicago 17, 19, 99, 117, 121, 123, 124, 126, 144, 167, 230, 246, 247, 253, 262, 268, 292

Chisos Mountains 84, 86

Civil Rights 96, 97, 176, 267, 270, 271

Clinton, Bill 270

Colorado National Monument 42, 43, 125, 131

Colorado River 130, 136, 244, 249

Cody, William (Buffalo Bill) 127

Crater Lake (National Park) 24, 40, 41, 56, 173, 174, 189, 190, 191, 194

Craters of the Moon National Monument 101, 105

Crazy Horse 26, 27, 46, 101, 108, 110, 111, 112

Crazy Horse Memorial 101, 110, 111

D

Daytona 273, 282

Duncan, Dayton 33

Death Valley (National Park) 2, 23, 55, 124, 229, 234, 238

Denver 126, 128, 132, 144, 145, 201, 204, 301, 303

Detroit 99, 157, 169

Disneyland 37, 40, 219, 279, 280, 281

Disney World 258, 277, 278, 279, 280, 281, 282, 283

Dorr, George 157

Dry Tortugas (National Park) 56, 257, 277

Durango 142

E

Electronic System for Travel Authorization 27

Everglades (National Park) 25, 56, 164, 257, 258, 273, 275, 276, 277, 282, 283

F

Fairfax 196, 199

Flagstaff 13, 246, 247, 248, 249, 250, 251, 252

Florida Keys 274, 277, 278, 283

Fort Davis National Historic Site 81

Fresno 65

G

Gateway Arch (National Park) 43, 44, 56, 101, 116, 117, 124, 247

Getty, John Paul 79

Grinnell, George Bird 41

Glacier (National Park) 41, 55, 56, 61, 71, 101, 107, 108, 121, 189, 190, 287

Golden Gate Bridge 71, 104, 178, 193, 199

Grand Canyon (National Park) 5, 12, 43, 45, 50, 55, 76, 106, 107, 124, 209, 229, 243, 245, 247, 248, 249, 250, 251

Grand Teton (National Park) 36, 56, 101, 107, 108, 121, 287

Great Basin (National Park) 56, 229, 241

Great Sand Dunes (National Park) 55, 125, 144, 145

Great Smoky Mountains (National Park) 21, 36, 50, 56, 119, 164, 201, 202, 205, 207, 208, 209, 210, 211, 218, 219, 220, 221, 225

Griffith Observatory 233, 256

Guadalupe Mountains (National Park) 22, 56, 81, 82, 90, 100

Guthrie, Woody 4, 31, 36, 38, 39, 80, 246, 299, 301, 303

H

Harley Davidson Motorcycles 4, 49, 112, 114

Hawaii 22, 56

Highway 1 59, 73, 74, 78, 153, 156, 174, 179, 180, 181, 196, 199, 230, 273, 274, 275, 277

Highway 61 5, 24, 116, 257, 258, 260, 261, 262, 263, 264, 267, 283, 300, 305

Highway 101 73, 74, 174, 178, 179, 180, 181, 184, 190, 196, 232

Hitchcock, Alfred 72, 180, 295, 296, 297

Hitchcock Movies 5, 72, 110, 180, 182

Hire car 13, 15, 16, 17, 50, 62, 82, 95, 99, 128, 149, 159, 177, 196, 198, 199, 227, 228, 255, 256, 261, 262, 285

Home of Franklin D. Roosevelt National Historic Site 147

Hollywood Sign 232, 236, 256

Hot Springs (National Park) 56, 257, 267, 270

Humboldt Redwoods State Park 173, 181

J

JFK Airport 149, 169

Joshua Tree (National Park) 23, 55, 124, 229, 252, 253

Johnson, Lyndon Baines (LBJ) 95, 96, 184, 228

Johnson, Lady Bird 96, 97, 184, 228

K

Key Largo 274, 295

Kennedy, John Fitzgerald (JFK) 96

Kerouac, Jack 126, 132, 133, 162, 286, 294, 299

Key West 274, 278

Kings Canyon (National Park) 40, 55, 59, 60, 61, 62, 63, 65, 68, 80, 174

Kroc, Ray 154

L

Lake Tahoe 104, 105, 123

Lassen Volcanic (National Park) 55, 173, 174, 193, 197

Las Vegas 2, 235, 238, 239, 240, 241

Laurel Canyon 5, 231, 232, 236, 237, 255, 272, 295

LAX Airport 60, 61, 74, 174, 230, 253, 254

Lincoln Highway 4, 114, 121, 122, 123, 124, 262

Logan Airport 148, 169

London Bridge 247, 252

Los Angeles 5, 18, 51, 53, 60, 74, 77, 78, 79, 124, 174, 175, 178, 181, 186, 230, 232, 233, 234, 236, 246, 247, 249, 255, 256, 279

Lyndon B Johnson National Historical Park 81, 95

M

Mammoth Cave (National Park) 56, 201, 223

Mather, Stephen 41

Murie, Margaret 43

McQueen, Steve 4, 76, 77, 78, 114, 199

McDonald Observatory 91

McDonald's 4, 154, 155, 156

Memphis 258, 259, 260, 262, 263, 264, 265, 266, 267, 268, 270, 272, 300, 303

Mesa Verde (National Park) 20, 34, 40, 41, 55, 125, 137, 140, 141, 142

Mexican 66, 83, 84, 87, 99, 118, 174, 186, 187, 205, 225, 239, 244, 245, 248

Mexico 23, 43, 56, 82, 83, 84, 85, 86, 90, 93, 94, 118, 133, 167, 247, 259, 262

Miami Beach 273

Mills, Enos 41, 71

Mississippi River 116, 117, 129, 202, 260, 261, 262

Moab 131, 135, 137

Montgomery 270, 271, 302

Monument Valley 42, 229, 243, 244, 245, 248, 251

Mount Rainier (National Park) 40, 41, 56, 173, 187, 188, 189, 190, 191

Mount Rushmore Memorial 101

Mount Washington State Park 147, 160

Muir Woods National Monument 173

Muir, John 4, 31, 32, 35, 40, 41, 49, 61, 62, 64, 66, 67, 68, 69, 70, 71, 80, 100, 179, 187, 196, 199, 211, 251, 286, 287, 289, 292

N

Nashville 202, 218, 221, 222, 223, 224, 226, 261, 292

National Park Service 8, 22, 48, 54, 91, 95, 131, 157, 227, 250

New England 47, 148, 152, 153, 156, 160, 170

New Orleans 258, 259, 260, 262, 263

New River Gorge (National Park) 43, 57, 201, 224

New York City 4, 44, 120, 121, 122, 123, 133, 148, 149, 150, 151, 152, 153, 163, 164, 169, 170, 171, 185, 227, 280

Niagara Falls State Park 147, 168

North Cascades (National Park) 56, 173, 174, 189, 190, 197

O

Obama, Barack 39

Olympic (National Park) 56, 167, 173, 189, 197

On the Road (novel) 4, 126, 132, 133, 162, 172, 198, 257, 293, 295, 301

Oregon Coast Highway 5, 173, 174, 185, 186, 197

Orlando 258, 267, 272, 279, 280

P

Pacific Coast Highway 24, 59, 60, 74, 78, 80, 174, 256, 305

Parton, Dolly 5, 23, 201, 215, 218, 219, 221, 293, 298, 300, 303

Pacific Crest Trail 174, 294

Petrified Forest (National Park) 55, 100, 124, 229, 247, 251, 254

Pinchot, Gifford 33, 71

Pick-Up Trucks 4, 49, 88

Pinnacles (National Park) 55, 59, 60, 69, 72

Pirsig, Robert 194

Portland 185, 186, 187

R

Red Rocks 125, 128

Redwood (National Park) 55, 71, 97, 173, 177, 179, 180, 181, 184, 185, 197, 199

Redwoods 64, 71, 173, 179, 180, 181, 184, 196

Rio Grande 84, 85, 86

Rockefeller Jr, J.D. 36, 210

Roosevelt, Franklin Delano (FDR) 163

Roosevelt, Theodore (Teddy) 42

Rocky Mountain (National Park) 4, 41, 55, 71, 125, 128, 129, 301, 302

Reagan, Ronald 75, 160

Route 66 5, 13, 24, 100, 114, 117, 122, 124, 139, 155, 229, 230, 231, 246, 247, 248, 249, 251, 252, 262, 299, 305

S

San Antonio 82, 83, 98, 99

Stegner, Wallace 285

Student Radicalism 175

San Francisco Airport 60, 177, 178, 180, 196

San Francisco 5, 44, 53, 60, 68, 69, 71, 72, 74, 76, 77, 80, 102, 103, 104, 105, 106, 121, 123, 132, 133, 174, 175, 176, 177, 178, 179, 180, 181, 182, 186, 189, 193, 194, 195, 196, 197, 198, 199, 289, 302

Santa Barbara 74, 75, 78

Santa Monica 79, 230, 231, 247, 255, 256

Seattle 174, 186, 188, 189, 190, 197

Selma 270, 271, 296

Sequoia (National Park) 40, 41, 55, 59, 60, 61, 62, 63, 64, 65, 66, 67, 68, 71, 80, 174, 179

Sequoias 40, 62, 64, 71, 179

Shasta, Mt 173

Shenandoah (National Park) 56, 101, 119, 121, 148, 164, 201, 202, 203, 204, 205, 211, 226

Sierra Nevada 4, 42, 59, 60, 61, 62, 70, 71, 80, 124, 179

Skyline Drive 204, 205, 206, 226

Slices of Americana Pie 4, 29

St Helens, Mt 173

Sun Studio 263, 266, 267

T

Tamalpais, Mt 173, 192, 196, 199, 303

Texas White House 4, 96, 97, 98, 184, 228, 271

Trump, Donald 85

Turner, Fredrick 88

U

Upstate New York 4, 147, 148, 152, 163, 164, 166, 169, 170, 236

US Virgin Islands (National Park) 22

V

Venice Beach 79, 231, 255

VW Camper Vans 4, 49, 52, 156

W

Washington DC 5, 39, 41, 44, 202, 203, 212, 226, 227, 228

White Sands 43, 56, 81, 94

Wilderness 294

Wind Cave (National Park) 40, 41, 56, 101, 111, 112, 121

Woodstock 4, 147, 164, 166, 167, 236, 292, 296, 297, 303

Y

Yellowstone (National Park) 4, 6, 18, 21, 23, 33, 34, 35, 40, 41, 44, 56, 70, 71, 101, 102, 103, 105, 106, 107, 108, 118, 121, 127, 165, 194, 209, 234, 283, 287

Yosemite (National Park) 6, 18, 21, 23, 31, 32, 33, 34, 40, 41, 42, 55, 59, 60, 62, 65, 66, 67, 68, 69, 70, 71, 72, 80, 101, 104, 105, 121, 165, 174, 209, 240

Z

Zen and the art of Motorcycle Maintenance (novel) 5, 194, 293

Zion (National Park) 55, 145, 229, 240, 241, 242

About the Author

John was born in London and spent most of his youth in urban environments, but after winning a scholarship to study in California he increasingly came under the spell of the American great outdoors. He has criss-crossed the United States on many occasions, including driving on the Pacific Coast Highway, Route 66, and Highway 61. He has taught American Studies in a British university, and escorted British undergraduates on study trips to many American cities. He has written several books on the themes of higher education and American cultural studies.